The Future of Multicultural Britain

The Future of Multicultural Britain

Confronting the Progressive Dilemma

Pathik Pathak

Edinburgh University Press

© Pathik Pathak, 2008

Edinburgh University Press Ltd
22 George Square, Edinburgh

Typeset in 11/13pt Linotype Sabon by
Iolaire Typesetting, Newtonmore, and
printed and bound in Great Britain by
CPI Antony Rowe, Chippenham, Wilts

A CIP record for this book is available
from the British Library

ISBN 978 0 7486 3544 3 (hardback)
ISBN 978 0 7486 3545 0 (paperback)

Contents

Acknowledgements

Firstly, much gratitude to David Dabydeen for his guidance and comments during the completion of my Ph.D. thesis, and also to Neil Lazarus for his direction and assistance. Many thanks to my wonderful examiners, Stephen Chan and the *choti* boss Rashmi Varma, whose comments and suggestions led to this publication.

We only formed during the last two years of my Ph.D. but the camaraderie of my cronies Jim Graham, Mike Nibblet, Sharae Deckard, Kerstin Oloff and Jane Poyner was invaluable. Thanks to Pranav Jani and Thomas Keenan for their help in enriching my knowledge of previously unexplored disciplines. That extends to the Birmingham Postcolonial Reading Group too.

Kavita Bhanot's contributions have been empathy and a remarkable ability to take thrashings at badminton with good humour but bad language. I salute Ivi Kazantzi, Theo Valkanou, Bibip 'BJ' Susanti, Giovanni Callegari, Letisha Morgan, Celine Tan and especially Nazneen Ahmed for helping to stave off intellectual alienation.

Aisha Gill has been as supportive and enthusiastic as any colleague could be, and the time and space I've been given to finish this book are a consequence of CRUCIBLE's generosity. I'd also like to thank my students at Southampton and Roehampton.

Lois 'Bambi' Muraguri, take a bow. Without your constant support, patience and encouragement over the past three years none of this would have possible at all. Heartfelt appreciation goes to my Ma for steering me through the most crucial passage of my Ph.D., and to Dad for abusing his printing privileges time and again for my sake. I owe my brother Manthan a debt of gratitude for his efforts at reading through my work.

This book is dedicated to the thousands of victims of the Gujarati pogroms in 2002 and my adorable nieces Hema and Ciara, whom I pray grow up in more secular and equal times.

Journal acknowledgement

Chapter 1, 'The Trouble with David Goodhart's Britain', has appeared as a journal article in *Political Quarterly*, 78: 2 (2007).

Glossary of Indian Terms

adivasi Indigenous minorities in India, populous in the states of
Orissa, Madhya Pradesh, Chattisgarh, Rajasthan, Gujarat, Maharashtra, Andhra Pradesh, Bihar, Jharkhand and West Bengal.

Babri Masjid Otherwise known as the Babri Mosque or Babur's
Mosque, it was constructed by the Mughal Emperor Babur in
the city of Ayodhya, on the alleged site of a Rama temple that
consecrated the deity's birthplace.

Bajrang Dal Literally, the 'Army of Hanuman'. The youth wing of
the Vishwa Hindu Parishad (VHP).

Bharatiya Janata Party (BJP) Literally, the 'Indian People's Party'.
A right-wing nationalist political party, formed in 1980. It is
unified with other organisations affiliated to the Sangh Parivar
through the ideology of Hindutva.

dalit The name given to those who fall outside the Indian caste
system, who are also referred to as untouchables.

dharma In Indian morality and ethics, a term that refers to the
underlying natural order, and the laws that support it.

fatwa Historically, a ruling on Islamic law, issued by an Islamic
scholar. In the contemporary world it has been appropriated by
Islamic extremists to refer to an edict concerning a perceived
contravention of Islamic law.

Ganchi   A Gujarati minority, native to Godhra, the site of the petrol-bombing of the Sabarmati Express.

Hindutva   Literally, 'Hindu-ness'. The unifying ideology of the Sangh Parivar, espousing Hindu nationalism.

Janata Party (JP)   A political party that contested and won the 1977 *Lok Sabha* (general elections), defeating the Indian National Congress for the first time in India's democratic history. It was a rainbow coalition whose constituent members included the Bharatiya Jana Sangh ('Indian People's Alliance'), which was closely associated with the Rashtriya Swayamsevak Sangh.

kar sevak   A volunteer for a religious cause, commonly associated with Hindutva.

Lok Sabha   Literally, the 'People's House'. India's lower parliamentary house.

madrassa   Islamic seminaries.

mandir   The Hindi term for a temple.

masjid   The Arabic term for a mosque.

pracharak   Full-time worker of the Rashtriya Swayamsevak Sangh.

Ramjanmabhoomi   The supposed site of the birthplace of Lord Rama. It also refers to the movement to demolish the Babri Masjid, which was alleged to have been constructed on the site, demolishing an existing Hindu temple in the process.

rashtra   Used in the term 'Hindu *rashtra*', to denote a Hindu polity.

rath yatra   In its purest form, a chariot procession.

Sangh Parivar   Literally, the 'Family of Associations'. The conglomerate of organisations ideologically united by Hindutva.

sarva dharma sambhava   Denotes the validity of all religions, and is used as the grounds for religious freedoms in the Indian constitution.

shakha   Cell, commonly used to refer to the branches of the Rashtriya Swayamsevak Sangh, which number over 50,000 in India.

Shiv Sena   Literally, 'Army of Shiva', a Hindu and Marathi chauvinist political party, founded by Bal Thackeray.

swadeshi   Literally, 'self-sufficiency', a campaign popularised during the Gandhi-led independence movement

Swaraj **movement**   The movement for self-rule in colonial India.

trishul   Indian trident, often mounted on a stick.

United Progressive Alliance (UPA) The name of the Indian government's presently ruling coalition, formed soon after the 2004 general elections.

Vishwa Hindu Parishad (VHP) Literally, the 'World Hindu Council', an offshoot of the RSS, the 'socio-cultural' arm of Sangh Parivar, and with influential branches in the UK, North America and East Africa.

Introduction

Scene 1: Oldham, Bradford and Burnley, summer 2001

At the dawn of New Labour's second term, when they were returned to power with a daunting parliamentary majority, a cascade of civil unrest in England's northern towns stunned Britain. Even before the cataclysmic events of 11 September that year, multiculturalism had been battered and British tolerance towards minorities had stiffened. Though the 'race riots' have been eclipsed by the sensationalising implications of the so-called war on terror and receded from historical centre stage, they provided political capital for an assimilationist revival that has been unambiguously attributed to the threat of Islamic fundamentalism.

Britain was alerted to the latent violence in Oldham on 23 April 2001. Walter Chamberlain, a 76-year-old World War Two veteran, was hospitalised after a savage beating at the hands of three Asian youths. He had been walking home after watching a local amateur rugby league match and was alleged to have breached the rules of Oldham's racialised cartography by entering a 'no-go' area for whites. He was set upon by the youths for an unauthorised incursion onto Asian territory.

The attack viscerally confirmed the emergence of a new social problem: minority racism. The rise to power of Asian racists, in particular, preoccupied the local media. Oldham's racial problems were stated to have been 'inspired' and 'perpetrated' by Asians who were said to 'be behind most racial violence'. Statistics were wheeled out to prove this disturbing fact: Oldham police logged 600 racist incidents in 2000, and in 60 per cent of them, the victims were white. Of these 600, 180 were described as violent with the vast majority inflicted by Asian gangs of anywhere between 'six and twenty' on 'lone white males'.[1]

The attack on Chamberlain galvanised the National Front which held abortive attempts to march on three consecutive Saturdays. On 21 May, violence erupted between Asian youth and police in the Glodwick area. Though the police diverted the rioters away from the town centre, there was serious collateral damage to business, cars and residential property. Pubs were firebombed and windows smashed; there were even allegations of an assault on an elderly Asian woman.

What happened in Oldham was repeated in Burnley and Bradford. Both Asian- and white-owned pubs were torched in Burnley, with many burnt out. BBC plans to interview British National Party (BNP) leader Nick Griffin in Burnley were dropped amidst the violence. Like *Oldham Chronicle* editor Jim Williams, Griffin was still afforded a BBC platform, in a telephone interview on Radio 4's *Today* programme, to blame the violence on 'Asian thugs' for 'winding this up' by 'attacking innocent white people'. This contradicted the findings of an official report into the violence, which found that some of Burnley's white population had been 'influenced' by the BNP, and that Asian rioting took place in retaliation for an attack on an Asian taxi driver the preceding night. The report, entitled *Burnley Speaks, Who Listens?*, concluded that three nights of rioting was the result of machinations to elicit competition between rival criminal gangs into racial confrontation.

Bradford was the next town to fall, stung by violence over three nights in early July. Two people were stabbed, 36 arrested and 120 police officers injured during the first two nights, which mainly occurred in the predominantly Asian area of Manningham. On the third it subsided into a stand-off between Asian youths and police.

No one in Bradford can complain about being unprepared, though. The far-Right National Front and paramilitary Combat 18 had stalked the city for weeks preceding the general election, agitating in proxy for the BNP. And they had devised techniques to ratchet up the tension, honed in Oldham. While police were tied up with a rally composed of the main body of members, splinter groups would scamper to wreak havoc in Asian areas. The intention was to provoke Asian youth into retaliatory violence. If Oldham had become an 'open city', ripe for a bloody 'race war', Bradford was next in line. By the time the tension combusted into rioting, Asian youth had been worked into a frenzy and they craved the opportunity for retribution. Stores of petrol bombs were collected and gangs coalesced. One such gang named itself Combat 786 – the numerical representation of Allah.

A report by Lord Herman Ousley, former head of the Commission for Racial Equality (written several weeks before the violence in Burnley or Bradford), criticised Bradford's leaders for failing to confront racial segregation, particularly in schools, which, as in Oldham, were either 99 per cent white or 99 per cent Muslim. He warned that the consequence of the authorities' inaction was a city in 'the grip of fear'.

A separate independent report into the Oldham disturbances accused the council of failing to act on 'deep seated' issues of segregation. It also blamed racial tension on insensitive and inadequate policing and an administrative power structure that failed to represent Asian communities. Only 2.6 per cent of Oldham's council (the town's largest employer) was staffed by ethnic minorities. At a press conference announcing the report, its chair considered ethnic minority under-representation to be 'a form of institutional racism', evidence of an unwillingness to face realities.[2]

The riots fomented hostilities which broke new electoral ground for the far Right. The BNP capitalised on crisis in the north-west, saving five deposits and picking up over 10 per cent of the vote in three constituencies across Oldham. Its biggest success was delivered to its leader Nick Griffin, who gained over 16 per cent of the vote in one seat. In another the BNP took over 11 per cent of the poll off the back of an election campaign which encouraged voters to 'boycott Asian business'.

Scene 2: Gujarat, spring 2002

What happened in the western Indian state of Gujarat almost twelve months later was both more calculated and of a radically more barbaric order. In the words of Arundhati Roy, Gujarat was no less than the 'petri dish in which Hindu fascism has been fomenting an elaborate political experiment'.[3]

Gujarat's communalisation began in earnest when the the the Sangh Parivar's political wing, the Bharatiya Janata Party (BJP), assumed state power in 1998.[4] In its first year in power, in coordination with its extra parliamentary militia, the Vishwa Hindu Parishad (VHP) and the Bajrang Dal, the BJP began to poison relations between the majority Hindus and Gujarat's religious minorities. In the first half of 1998 alone, there were over forty recorded incidents of assaults on prayers halls, churches and Christian assemblies as a systematic attempt to terrorise Gujarat's Christian community was mounted. Baseless claims of Christianisation and the trafficking of Hindu girls to Asia's Islamic bloc were propagated by the agencies of the Sangh Parivar with the connivance of the Gujarati press.[5]

In January 2000 the BJP's paranoia was given legislative expression. A bill against religious conversion was proposed to the Gujarat state assembly, even though it directly contravened an article of the Indian constitution. Gujarat was the apogee of decimated secularism and feverish majoritarianism whipped up by an extremist state government. The hostility between Gujarat's increasingly vulnerable Muslims and its ideologically frenzied Hindus combusted on the Sabarmati Express at the religiously segregated town of Godhra on the morning of 27 February 2002.

On board the train were no less than 1,700 *kar sevak*s or 'holy workers' returning from the proposed site of a Rama temple at Ayodhya – the spark for nationwide rioting ten years earlier. The area immediately beneath the railway station was populated by 'Ganchis', largely uneducated and poor Muslims who were notorious participants in previous bouts of communal violence.

Alleged provocation from the *kar sevak*s (abuse of Ganchi vendors, the molestation and attempted abduction of a Muslim girl) resulted in a fracas on the platform between Ganchis and *sevak*s. But when the train pulled away fifteen to twenty minutes later, it was immediately halted when the emergency chain was pulled. A mob of 2,000 Ganchis had been hastily gathered from the immediate vicinity. They began pelting coaches S5 and S6 (speculation is that the offending *kar sevak*s were concentrated in those coaches) with firebombs and stones. S6 suffered the brunt of the missile attack: it was burnt out leaving the carcasses of 58 passengers, including 26 women and 12 children. Most of the able-bodied *kar sevak*s are believed to have escaped either to adjacent coaches or out of the train altogether. Godhra's incendiary precedent set the genocidal tone for several days of calculated pogroms.

Sixteen of Gujarat's twenty-four districts were stricken by organised mob attacks between 28 February and 2 March, during which the genocide was concentrated.[6] They varied in size from between five and ten thousand, armed with swords, *trishul*s (Hindu tridents) and agricultural instruments. While official government estimates of the dead speculated at 700 deaths, unofficial figures start at 2,000 and keep rising.[7] Incited by a communalised media and government which branded Muslims as terrorists, Hindus embarked on a four-day retaliatory massacre. Muslim homes, businesses and mosques were destroyed. Hundreds of Muslim women and girls were gang-raped and sexually mutilated before being burnt alive. The stomachs of pregnant women were scythed open and foetuses ripped out before them. When a six-year-old boy pleaded for water, he was made to forcibly ingest petrol instead. His mouth was prized open again to throw a lit match down his throat.

After consideration of all the available evidence at the time, an Independent Fact Finding Mission concluded that the mass provision of scarce resources (such as gas cylinders to explode Muslim property and trucks to transport them) indicated 'prior planning of some weeks'. In the context of that revelation, the Godhra incident was merely an excuse for an anti-Muslim pogrom conceived well in advance. The pattern of arson, mutilation and death by hacking was described by one report as 'chillingly similar' and suggestive of pre-meditated attack.[8] Dozens of eyewitnesses corroborate this theory, since many of the attacks followed an identical design. Truckloads of Hindu nationalists arrived clad in saffron uniforms, guided by computer-generated lists of Muslim targets which allowed them to ransack, loot and pillage with precision even in Hindu-dominated areas.[9] The sheer speed of the genocide indicts Narendra Modi's BJP government. Without extensive state sanction (of which partisan policing has proven to be the thin edge) the violence could have been contained within the three days that Modi disingenuously claimed it had. In many cases, police were witnessed actually leading charges, providing covering fire for the rampaging mobs they were escorting.[10]

It is also undeniable that Modi's and the BJP's reaction contributed to a climate of retribution. When asked about the retaliatory violence, Modi inanely echoed Rajiv Gandhi eighteen years earlier, quoting Newton's third law that 'every action has an equal and opposite reaction'.[11] He even commended Hindu Gujaratis on their restraint on 28 February – when the killing was at its most prolific and the rampage at its most devastating. Given Gujarat's anger at the events of Godhra he believed 'much worse was expected'. He later likened Muslim relief camps to 'baby making factories', promising to teach 'a lesson' to those 'who keep multiplying the population'.[12]

The pogrom drove over a hundred thousand Muslims into squalid makeshift refugee camps. Many of these were on the sites of Muslim graveyards, where the living slept side by side with the dead. The internally displaced were deprived of adequate and timely humanitarian assistance: sanitation, medical and food aid were in short supply in the supposed 'relief' camps. Non-governmental organisations, moreover, were denied access to redress the shortfalls of essential provisions. The systematic decimation of the Muslim community's economic basis was compounded by the emaciation of its surviving population.

The institutional failure to protect Muslim life did not end there. Despite immediate government boasts of thousands of arrests, many of those detained were subsequently released on bail, pending outstanding trials, acquitted or simply let go.[13] Human Rights Watch (2003) research suggests that very few of those culpable for the genocide are in custody: the vast majority of those behind prison bars are either Dalits (untouchables), Muslims or *adivasi*s (tribals). Modi retains ministerial control of Gujarat.

Muslims, on the other hand, have borne the brunt of the rule of law. Over a hundred Muslims implicated in the attack on the Sabarmati Express have been detained under the controversial Prevention of Terrorism Act (POTA), India's equivalent of Britain's new terror laws.

Of communities and citizens

Weeks after the Gujarat massacre, at the Bangalore session of its annual convention, the Rashtriya Swayamsevak Sangh (RSS) – the ideological father of the BJP and the 'moral and cultural guild' of its top brass – passed a resolution that unless minorities 'earn the goodwill of the majority community', their safety could not be guaranteed.[14] Notwithstanding the fact that they were the overwhelming victims of the carnage, or that it was they who were left intimidated, vulnerable and unprotected in its aftermath, the RSS believed that the burden of reconciliation and security should fall on Muslim shoulders.

In Britain, the political post-mortem was equally swift and equally skewed. Within months of the disturbances, newly appointed home secretary David Blunkett had categorically attributed the retaliations of British-born, second-generation Asian youth (actually to neo-fascist provocation) to the consequence of a poor facility with English and a failure to adopt British 'norms of acceptability'.[15] It was culturally inassimilable minorities who had 'failed' British society. Minority responsibilities assumed rhetorical centre stage in both instances.

By juxtaposing these incongruous episodes I am not trying to draw facile similarities between civil unrest and orchestrated genocide. Comparisons are grotesque given the disproportion between the incidents at Bradford, Burnley and Oldham and those at Ahmedabad, Vadodara and Surat.[16] It is not the similarity of the two incidents, or the two nations that was compelling. Instead, it was the shifting social attitudes towards minorities and the fact of cultural diversity that made such a comparison fascinating.

What both incidents indicated, across their disparate spaces, was a novel reflex of the (liberal and non-liberal) nation-state to demonise minorities as inassimilable communities and a disinclination to recognise them as citizens. The distinctions being drawn were between communities as illegitimate collective actors and citizens as individuals acting in the interests of the national good. Both cases, though through radically different degrees and dynamics, were expressions of actual or latent majoritarianism. And, most crucially, they were occurring in societies with a historical commitment to multiculturalist policies. What was intriguing was the correspondence between a declining multiculturalism and an ascendant majoritarianism. How were the two related?

They were particularly complex distinctions to be drawn at a time when community was being politicised in very different ways in Britain and India. In both cases, protection for minorities has been displaced by the aggrandisement of the majority community, circumscribed by conspicuously cultural parameters. The state's patronage of plural cultural communities has given way to the mandate for a single communitarian order: the seeds of majoritarianism. The double focus of this latent majoritarianism balances the coercive imperative for minorities to disaggregate as individuals with the enactment of government strategies to heighten the boundaries of an imagined national *common culture*. As New Labour's White Paper *Secure Borders: Safe Haven* (2002) makes plain, citizens should only tolerate newcomers if their own identities are 'secure'.[17] *Political* rights and responsibilities therefore correspond to individuals' positions either inside or outside these boundaries.

While Blairism has been premised on the bedrock of neighbourly communitarianism it had become increasingly anxious about the contradictions between secular and religious communities for social cohesion. Rather than address the causes of segregation in diverse conurbations like Bradford, Birmingham and Leicester, Britain's political centre has grown increasingly strident in its displeasure at the failure of some minority groups to 'integrate'. A commonplace expression of this exasperation has been the description of non-integrated minorities as 'communities', a description that has been politically contorted from celebration (under multiculturalism) to condemnation (the new assimilationism).

By figuring ethnic minorities as communities the British centre and Right have consciously avoided recognising individuals 'inside' these formations as citizens; on the contrary they have designated ethnic minorities as 'trainee Brits' at an earlier evolutionary stage of citizenship. Closeted within culturally impermeable communities, minority individuals are precluded from identification with the 'common good', a realisation of their identities as national citizens and their active participation in the aspirations of the nation.

The divestment of individuality from minorities has accentuated their *responsibilities* to the nation (even as their rights have been attenuated). Settled ethnic minorities have been placed under new obligations and expectations to be 'active citizens' to build on 'shared aims across ethnic groups', to avoid extremism and respect national values. The prevalence of the minority community has become the excuse under which citizenship has become more prescriptive and demanding than ever.

For the Sangh Parivar's ideological movement, the distinction between the inassimilable community and the patriotic citizen has been strategically central. Hindutva rests on the assumption that India is a Hindu nation (more precisely a Hindu land with a view to becoming a Hindu nation) whose citizens are those who cherish it as their fatherland and their holy land.[18] As believers in the 'Hindu-ness' (as Hindutva translates into English) of the Indian nation its citizens form an 'integral' community on that basis.

Despite differences between its limbs and organs, the body politic and social are all oriented towards the well-being of the whole. Members of religious minorities who refuse to accept India's Hindu genius cannot therefore be citizens; they are identified as communities external to the nation.

The Bharatiya Janata Party has long argued that the 'pseudo-secularism' of successive Congress 'comprador' governments has baited the Hindu majority by repeatedly pandering to religious-minority communities. It has pointed to political opportunism that has created 'vote-banks' among religious minorities to be manipulated according to electoral calculations. But as much as governments have been condemned for exploitative politicking, the greater accusation is that Muslim communities have been able to act collectively – through block voting – to unfairly influence the democratic process, gain political advantage and optimise their communal power.

Muslim communities have also been harangued by the RSS and its executive organs for exercising patriarchal communitarianism: suppressing individual choices and forcing women to be veiled and housebound. By refusing contraception and failing to control family sizes they have been accused of draining India's resources with excessive population growth. Secularism's failures can also be explained by their intransigence and intolerance. Anti-modern and culturally backward, Indian Muslims are constructed 'as the source and the dislocation of the Indian nation', 'stunting the economic growth and dynamism of the country'.[19]

The riots in the north of England and the Gujarati pogroms were ugly eruptions, stoked in the hothouses of British neo-assimilationism and Hindu nationalism. Though the latter took place at the height of Hindutva's powers while multiculturalism's reversal of fortune was only just beginning, they were both visceral symptoms of a declining confidence in existing regimes of minority governance, and the accompanying attenuation of national identity. But this doesn't merely take the form of a popular backlash against minority appeasement; as I've shown, it's an attitude that is sustained and even promoted by state agencies and the media. I call it the majoritarian reflex.

The majoritarian reflex

This reflex draws its strength from the isolation of so-called minority blocs from mainstream society by expressing exasperation at the reluctance of those communities to 'integrate'. Majoritarianism exploits popular anxieties, which are inflated into a mandate for the rightward shift of the political centre. The principal casualty of this shift is a weakened commitment – and in some circumstances an outright refusal – to recognise the cultural and religious rights of minorities. 'Multiculturalism' is pilloried as anathema to secular culture and the values of liberal democracy. The fact of cultural diversity itself is (sometimes spuriously) indicted for a host of social problems, from crime and disorder to the fragility of the welfare state (as we'll see in the discussion of the work of David Goodhart). This is often, but not always, compounded by a licence to rearticulate democratic rights in accordance with new political imperatives. In its most extreme forms, minorities are incriminated not only for sheltering illiberal values and practices and failing to act as citizens in the interests of the national good, but also in their social presence as communities for unravelling the very fabric of secular culture.

What I am careful to emphasise is the range of the majoritarian repertoire; it will not always beget pogroms. But it always seeks to bring cultural diversity into disrepute, and always seeks to privilege majority interests over those of the minority. The extent to which this mutates the terms of democratic debate, legal protection and social tolerance will vary from nation to nation. My argument is that it is a growing threat that succeeds where progressive politics fails to engage in a coherent way with ideas of community and culture.

The progressive dilemma

The second strand to this book addresses what, for the sake of convenience, I refer to as the progressive dilemma. Many intellectuals have claimed to voice this dilemma. In recent debates in Britain it has been used to denote the trade-off between diversity and solidarity. I use it in a different sense here. While majoritarian ideologies and imaginaries are a proliferating threat to democratic society, the extent of their credibility will depend on how effectively a progressive answer to cultural diversity emerges from what remains of the Left, as both an intellectual and a political formation.

To this end the questions that followed Gujarat and Bradford, Burnley and Oldham were not solely about state responses but equally about the reaction from secular and anti-racist politicians, intellectuals, activists and organisations. In which language, and by what means, would they assert the rights of the violated? How would they speak in the defence of the victims, and how would they seek to mobilise public opinion?

These are the questions that preoccupy this book, described in short as facing up to the 'progressive dilemma'. I have defined this as an ethical question for those who oppose the majoritarian reflex: what role, if any, should progressive voices play in pre-emptively addressing popular anxiety on issues usually reserved for conservatives, racists or bigots? This, in turn, is framed by other questions, such as how far should the Left move towards the orthodox territory of the Right before it becomes culpable for nurturing majoritarian instincts? How can we judge the efficacy of progressive interventions at all? This is how I evaluate the likely fortunes of cultural diversity; not as a predestined casualty of expanding majoritarianism, but as a contingent outcome of the inclination of progressive politics. I therefore invest considerable optimism in the ability of oppositional politics to renew itself, and the constitutive role of political agency at an individual level in shaping large-scale social attitudes.

To prepare for my treatment of the progressive dilemma I will now introduce the configurations of majoritarianism that currently (or threaten to) prevail in Britain and India respectively.

British majoritarianism

Britain's regression from liberal multiculturalism to liberal assimilationism has, like India's degradation of secularism, been incremental and propelled by a crisis of the Left. The British establishment's initial reluctance to allow Commonwealth immigration, despite the acute post-war shortages in the public sector, governed official and public attitudes to race relations until Roy Jenkins salutary (if over-determined) intervention in 1967. Until then racism was understood as a peculiar form of xenophobia, the result of the archetypal dark-skinned stranger disorientating the startled Anglo-Saxon population. The working assumption, as Jenny Bourne put it, was that 'familiarity would breed content'.[20]

It was not until Jenkins interjected with his vision of 'equal opportunity accompanied by cultural diversity in an atmosphere of mutual tolerance' that the face of race relations acquired liberal characteristics. Equal opportunity was treated with the soporifics of the Race Relations Acts of 1965 and 1968 that gravitated towards conciliation rather than prosecution. Racism was given renewed respectability with the 1968 Kenyan Asians Act, which barred the free entry to Britain of its citizens on the simple grounds that they were Asian. Exceptions were those with a parent or grandparent 'born, naturalised or adopted in the UK' – as presumably would be the case if they were born in geographically 'familial' places like Australia or New Zealand. Racism was further institutionalised in the state with the Immigration Act of 1971 when all primary non-white immigration was stopped dead. The right to abode was restricted to Commonwealth citizens of demonstrable Anglo-Saxon stock, known as 'patrials'.

Given the impotence of the race relations legislation and the respectability afforded to racist discrimination with the new immigration acts, Jenkins' multiculturalist vision was eventually distilled to the common sense that coloured people were likely to be just as disorientated by emigration as whites by immigration. The solution was to satisfy these ostensibly psychological needs by granting immigrants their own cultural spaces and institutions where they could cocoon themselves, away from the alienating swirl of mainstream society.

If the state was willing to tolerate cultural diversity (however ambivalently that tolerance might be manifested) it was complacently hoped that this would drip-feed through society. The public recognition of difference, rather than a hard line on racism, was the state's concession to liberals and immigrants.

Racism was concluded to be a matter of personal prejudice: a character trait to be weaned away by cultivating cultural respect. The logic of mainstream anti-racism was given full expression in the judicial inquiry into the Brixton riots of 1981, headed by Lord Scarman. Scarman rejected out of hand (and against the weight of evidence) accusations that institutional racism was prevalent in the Metropolitan police force. Though Scarman broke the news that racial 'discrimination' and 'disadvantage' continued to plague Britain's minorities, he offered no novel wisdom to challenge them.

His prescription was higher doses of political correctness and broader strategies towards moral anti-racism. Racial awareness training (RAT) was intensively and enthusiastically undertaken throughout local authorities to weed out personal prejudice.

Scarman's recommendations were the furthest the Thatcherite establishment was willing to move in anti-racist directions during its three terms in power. Thatcher's diminution and inflation of state and personal responsibility was indicative of her policy towards racism and racial justice. Racism was not deemed to be a social problem, redressed by social action, but a matter of personal prejudice and perception to be resolved individually.

When New Labour ascended to power in 1997 it articulated an uneasy compromise between the rhetoric of individual responsibility appropriated from Thatcherism (via the *New Times* project) and a longer-standing Labour tradition of endorsing multiculturalism. What has become apparent over New Labour's two terms in power is that the cultural *laissez faire* of the multiculturalist regime is incommensurable with its other objectives. Though the empowering of communities sits very comfortably with New Labour's programme to devolve authority, the strengthening of communal segregation militates against its promise of social cohesion, considered to be the lynchpin of a sustainable welfare society and of law and order.[21] It has withdrawn from its early support for faith communities to take a more prescriptive view of the kinds of community it wants to see, especially in Britain's most ethnically diverse cities. Though communitarianism was an early New Labour watchword it has now taken a more circumspect view of the role of faith and ethnic communities in promoting the kind of values it wants to promote as British values. The solution has been to sacrifice cultural diversity for integration. Race equality comes in a distant third behind those two 'Labour' priorities.

The shroud of assimilationism fell over Britain after the Cantle Report into riots in Oldham, Burnley and Bradford. It has become the government's gospel on what is euphemistically spun as 'community' relations. The new watchword is not 'equal opportunity' or even 'cultural diversity', but 'community cohesion'. Its influence is telling in *Secure Borders: Safe Haven*. Though affirming the commitment to accommodate immigrant identities, it hedges diversity 'with integration'. The term multiculturalism was dropped altogether from the government's proposals.

The recession of multiculturalism from liberal and conservative imaginaries has been superceded by the growth of a nationalist communitarianism. The culturalist door has been shown to swing both ways and its justification has now been reversed. While once Roy Jenkins' priority was to expose the white majority to minority cultures, David Blunkett's imperative was to school the Other into English civility. Immigrants and racialised others are patronisingly considered to be 'trainee Brits' at various stages of evolution to fully formed citizenship.[22]

The result has been the politicisation of citizenship and the disturbing revival of a correlation between race and immigration (at least in public discourse: it has been ever present in immigration law since 1962). Interventions such as David Goodhart's 'Too Diverse?' (2004) have set a new baseline for public debate, just as Enoch Powell's did in the 1960s. But Goodhart's position as a liberal, on the supposedly fairer side of the political divide, has given his comments something approaching common sense and heralded a point of political no return. It has afforded greater latitude to those to his right (politically) and restricted the latitude of those on his left, making his critics appear more radical than they actually might be.

Symptoms of the new assimilationism pervade British society. The daily tabloid tirades against refugees relentlessly dominate public attitudes. Domestic policy on asylum has played its part too. As Jenny Bourne adroitly observes, the dispersal system has marginalised refugees, while vouchers schemes have stigmatised them.[23] The Conservative Party's cynical attempts to make the last General Election a referendum on immigration are a barometer of the national mood.

'Managed migration' has brought in its wake new policing strategies which don't address but exacerbate anxiety about Britain's Muslims. The criminalisation of Pakistanis and Bangladeshis, supposedly made permissible by the 2001 urban violence, has included racial profiling as part of anti-terrorist operations. Stop and search among young Asians is at record levels. Slight reforms to the criminal justice system have dramatically emaciated the legal safeguards available to ethnic minorities. The proposal to abolish the right of defendants to elect to be tried by jury for 'minor offences' – for which Asians and Afro-Caribbeans are disproportionately charged with thanks to higher incidences of stop and search – will have more of an adverse effect on ethnic minorities than on white Britain. Being subjected to summary trial before magistrates, who are widely perceived to work in the interests of the police, will further shake an already frail confidence in the criminal system's ability (and will) to deliver real justice to Britain's ethnic minorities.[24]

Economically, disadvantages persistently race along racial and religious divisions. The palpable unease at the dilation of cultural enclaves throughout the country masks the uglier realities of urban ghettoes stalked by economic inactivity and social immobility

(Home Office figures estimate that almost 52 per cent of Muslims are economically inactive). Residential segregation is as much about social exclusion as it is about cultural separation. The spectre of terrorism and the ambivalence of the government towards diversity have furnished racism with a new respectability, made real in the explosion of racially and religiously motivated attacks on mosques, gurdwaras and Asian-owned businesses.[25]

Indian majoritarianism

Indian majoritarianism is more complex than that of Britain, rooted as it is in historically entrenched prejudice and social inequality. It is also the consequence of political opportunism. But what it does share with less explicit forms of majoritarianism is a tendency to exploit – and exalt – popular anxieties to justify discrimination, and consequently to attribute the material disadvantage of minorities to cultural factors.

Modern India's birth at Partition was founded on the tenets of the Nehruvian consensus – the principles of socialism, secularism, non-alignment, and the developmental state. Given the brutal ravages of Partition and the vulnerability of India's remaining Muslim population, secularism was crucial in safeguarding the citizenship rights of India's numerous minorities. Constitutional secularism was the backbone of an official state discourse which recognised India's diversity through linguistic rights, cultural rights for minorities, the funding of minority educational institutions and legal pluralism.

As many observers have argued though, the Nehruvian administration is culpable for failing to properly secularise public culture. While avowedly secular it made only faint-hearted efforts to curtail 'obscurantist practices' which continue in the public sphere, 'often with the open participation of public officials elected to uphold secular values'.[26] In practice, secularism has really existed only as the indigenised, profoundly Gandhian inflection *sarva dharma sambhava*. Under the regime of this variant secularism, the state is not mandated to abstain or disassociate entirely from religion, but to maintain an even-handed approach to all.

This unique take on secularism has, despite Rajeev Bhargava's protestations otherwise, progressively debilitated the credibility of the Indian state.[27] This became especially obvious in the post-Nehruvian vacuum, when Indira Gandhi's flirtations with communalism compounded her flirtations with authoritarianism in her desperation to retain power. Communalist electioneering was also a recurrent feature of her filial successor Rajiv Gandhi's tenure and he, like her, in his assassination in 1991, reaped the same sectarian harvest she had sown.

In 2002, Gurcharan Das' *India Unbound* and Meera Nanda's *Breaking the Spell of Dharma* pronounced the death of the Nehruvian consensus, and threw up a cluster of new images with which to identify twenty-first century India. While Nanda hits out at the demise of scientific secularism, the intellectual hallmark of Nehru's India, Das hails the achievements of middle-class India, projecting millions to cross the poverty line in the next forty years. What's intriguing is the absent correspondence between the two narratives since neither work makes reference to the other's account of modern India. To my mind, it is imperative to read these two histories side by side because they unfurl the schizophrenia of India's contemporary character. The spirituality and poverty which India has projected around the world for so long are more complex and political than is commonly understood in the West, and there is a tight fit between them in the process of national reinvention which has taken place since the early 1990s.

As Jaffrelot (*Hindu Nationalist Movement and Indian Politics*, 1996), Blom Hansen (*The Saffron Wave*, 1999) and Rajagopal (*Politics after Television*, 1999) have all commented, the salience of Hindutva coincided with the restructuring of the Indian economy in the image of the New Economic Policy (NEP), instituted by Narasimha Rao and Manmohan Singh under the watchful instruction of the International Money Fund (IMF) and World Bank. Their 'rescue package' for India's debt-ridden economy was a succession of privatisations and deregulations that brought India into belated alignment with globalised neo-liberalism.

The net effect of the reforms has been a perceptible renunciation of welfare as a state concern – a clear abandonment of the premise of Nehru's developmental state – and the consolidation of elite and middle-class power. The mushrooming presence of the 'new middle classes', the primary beneficiaries of the NEP, has compounded the Indian state's plunging disregard for poverty. The dissolution of 'the licence Raj' and the ascendancy of market freedom precipitated a boom in Indian consumerism which effectively defines the character of India's bold new demographic.[28] Das, the self-appointed spokesman for 'Middle India', has this to say about the new middle classes:

Thus we start off the twenty-first century with a dynamic and rapidly growing middle class which is pushing the politicians to liberalise and globalise. Its primary preoccupation is with a rising standard of living, with social mobility, and it is enthusiastically embracing consumerist values and lifestyles. Many in the new middle class also embrace ethnicity and religious revival, a few even fundamentalism. It has been the main support of the Bharatiya Janata Party and has helped make it the largest political party in India. The majority, however, are too busy thinking of money and are not unduly exercised by politics or Hindu nationalism. Their young are aggressively taking to the world of knowledge. They instinctively understand that technology is working in our favour. Computers are daily reducing the cost of words, numbers, sights, and sounds. They are taking to software, media and entertainment as fish to water. Daler Mehndi and A. R. Rahman are their new music heroes, who have helped create a global fusion music which resonates with middle-class Indians on all the continents.[29]

The new middle classes have been suckled to maturity in a uniquely Hindu idiom which has saturated their experiences of consumerist modernity. The weekly screenings of the Hindu epics *The Ramayana* and *Mahabharata* in the 1990s on Doordarshan, India's state-run television channel (widely believed to be a result of intense lobbying by the Vishwa Hindu Parishad) completed an unlikely circuit of consumerism, communications technology, religion and nationalism. The unprecedented national dimensions of their popularity awakened long-dormant stirrings of Hindu nationalism.[30]

The triumvirate wings of the Sangh Parivar which comprise the agencies of the Hindutva project capitalised on the bleeding of religiosity from private to public consciousness. The proto-fascist Rashtriya Swayamsevak Sangh was established in the 1920s. Under the leadership of the Maharashtrian Keshav Baliram Hedgewar it eschewed political visibility in favour of underground status with a purpose to roll out Hindu India's leaders. It modelled itself on military training camps, and the achievement of martial prowess among its members was a key objective. Parallels to Mussolini's National Socialist drill centres have not gone unnoticed.[31] To this day, it is comprised of individual cells, known as *shakha*s, which are run on obsessively strict lines, enforcing discipline and adherence to a common code. The RSS recruits predominantly from the urban lower middle classes, from the shopkeeper classes, whose upward mobility is frustrated by societal bottlenecks, minority reservations in salaried positions and limited political influence.

After RSS ideologue Nathuram Godse's assassination of Mahatma Gandhi in 1948, the organisation was banned by Nehru's Congress government, despite Godse's protestation that he had no connection to it.[32] The RSS is insistent on its apolitical nature, and describes itself as a character-building, cultural institution. As a recent report shows, it does not have charity status either, and procures funds through its affiliation to charities which deny affiliation to the Sangh Combine, despite documentary evidence to the contrary.[33]

It was the VHP who led the movement to 'liberate' the supposed *Ramjanmabhoomi* (birthplace of Rama) site in Ayodhya through the 1980s, L. K. Advani's *rath yathra* from Somnath to Ayodhya in 1990, which culminated in the destruction of the Babri Masjid by Hindutva's *kar sevak*s in 1992, and the spiral of violence that convulsed India for six months afterwards. Subsequent to the razing of the *masjid*, Narasimha Rao's Congress government banned the VHP for two years, and this was re-imposed once the period elapsed (in 1995). The ban was barely enforced out of fear of driving the organisation to greater prestige underground, and VHP operations ran as visibly as before.

The VHP was set up in 1964 to promote Hindutva in a more open, modern and ultimately more aggressive way than could be achieved through the quasi-underground mechanisms of the RSS. Its earliest mission statement was 'in this age of competition and conflict, to think of, and organise the Hindu world, to save itself from the evil eyes of all three [the doctrines of Islam, Christianity and Communism]'.[34] Its rise has been instrumental in the renaissance of Hindu nationalism and its recovery from near obscurity in the 1960s and 1970s. Like the RSS it has set up mirror bodies abroad, with operations of the VHP in the UK and US. It also possesses a paramilitary wing (Bajrang Dal or Lord Hanuman's Troopers) recruited from discontented urban youth. The VHP remains arguably the most influential arm of the Sangh Parivar and continues to exert a civil influence which should counsel caution in premature obituaries for Hindutva as a hegemonic project on the basis of the BJP's recent electoral demise.

The *Ramjanmabhoomi* movement catapulted the Bharatiya Janata Party (the VHP's sister organisation and the political façade of the Hindutva project) into government, briefly in 1998 and then for a lasting tenure from 1999 to 2004, as the majority member of the rickety National Democratic Alliance (NDA). The BJP was the first Hindu nationalist party to govern India, elected through a coalition of the NDA. It was the most powerful of the NDA members in terms of parliamentary strength and the party's former leaders, Atal Bihari Vajpayee and Lal Krishna Advani, were prime minister and deputy prime minister respectively. Both also rose through the cadres of the RSS, rendering transparent its role as a feeder to the BJP and the gelatinous relationship between the two organs of the Sangh Combine. Because of the nationwide rioting incited by the Sangh's agitation for the *Ramjanmabhoomi* movement, the Indian Supreme Court has circumscribed the ideological content of its election campaigns under the threat of disqualification of its candidates, though this has barely led to a moderation of its agenda.

The *Ramjanmabhoomi* movement aside, the BJP's accession to power emboldened the Sangh to pursue other means to 'Hinduise' the nation. Nanda narrates how the most sophisticated technological advances have been credited to the expression of Hindu *dharma* and the glory of the Hindu *rashtra* (nation). In *Breaking the Spell of Dharma* she documents some of the attempts by the VHP to 'Hinduise' the nuclear test at Pokharan in 1998:

> There is plenty of evidence for a distinctively Hindu packaging of the bomb [. . .] Shortly after the explosion, VHP ideologues inside and outside the government vowed to build a temple dedicated to Shakti (the goddess of energy) and Vigyan (science) at the site of the explosion. The temple was to celebrate the Vigyan of the Vedas, which, supposedly, contain all the science of nuclear fission and all the know-how for making bombs and much more [. . .] Plans were made to take the 'consecrated soil' from the explosion site around the country for mass prayers and celebrations [. . .] the Hinduization of the bomb has continued in many ways: there are reports that in festivals around the country, the idols of Ganesh were made with the atomic orbits in place of a halo around his elephant-head. The 'atomic Ganeshas' apparently brought in good business. Other gods were cast as gun-toting soldiers.[35]

A disturbing example is the appearance of Vedic science in the educational curricula. In this case, another government agency, the University Grants Commission, has been promoting Vedic science as the equivalent of natural science. All this has led to a boom in the popularity of Vedic knowledge, to the extent of warranting the staging of the first ever International Vedic Conference (held in Kerala in April 2002). At the conference university professors from around the country called for 'the teaching of Vedas to all'.[36] An article in the BJP's *Organiser* reported the following:

> New courses in 'mind sciences' such as 'meditation, telepathy, rebirth and mind control' are being planned. *Archarya* [holy teacher] Narendra Bhoosan, the Chairman of the organising committee and an authority in the Vedas and Sanskrit, delivering his presidential address said that the Vedas contained knowledge on many subjects like science, medicine, defence, democracy, etc, much before they were discovered in the West. He said that due to Western influence, India waited for the West to discover the wisdom she had with her for thousands of years. 'The conference [. . .] through a resolution [. . .] called for an establishment of Vedic departments in universities'.[37]

Bhoosan's pronouncements typify the consensus on the epistemological status of the Vedas in pro-Hindutva circles. The Vedas has become as singularly authoritative for Hindu chauvinists as the Bible and Qu'ran have been to Christians and Muslims. This is consistent with the 'semiticisation' of Hinduism where one avatar (Ram) and one dogma (the Vedas) have been elevated above all others.

Other attempts have been made to rewrite Indian history textbooks, to encourage Hindu prayer in school and to plant Hindutva stooges in influential regulatory positions. The 'Hinduisation of the bomb' and the equivalence of natural science with Vedic science are more than isolated instances of Hindutva's influence in the public sphere.[38] They are symptomatic of the growth of what Nanda terms a 'reactionary modernism' – which has gripped the very middle classes Das takes so much pride in extolling as the future of India society:

> These mobs are only the visible signs of a large ideological counter-revolution that has been going on behind the scenes in schools, universities, research institutions, temples and yes, even in

supposedly 'progressive' new social movements, organising to protect the environment or defend the cultural rights of traditional communities against the presumed onslaught of Western cultural imperialism.[39]

All in all, it has been no-holds-barred, frontal assault on secularism: the communalisation of India. So deep have been the incursions, impressions and influences of the Sangh both on India's polity and society over the past fifteen years that despite Congress's recapture of power at the centre, much conviction and innovation will be needed to reverse the 'saffronisation' of India's individuals and institutions. Hindutva's insemination of India has been interrupted, not arrested. Secularism is as much in crisis now as it was at the apex of BJP power.

It is critical to understand the disarticulation and disenfranchisement of minority citizens, not only through transparent acts of discrimination but also as a function of the reciprocity between cultural nationalism and neo-liberalism. While the NEP has been credited with the explosion of middle-class growth it is also culpable for the hardening of poverty and the entrenchment of ghettos. There is a nexus between neo-liberalism and majoritarianism in the process of national reinvention which has taken place since the early 1990s, which will be explored further in Chapter 2.

I will also argue that the NEP, by accentuating inequalities between structurally advantaged and disadvantaged religious and ethnic groups, has led to deteriorations in secular intersections between them. Ashutosh Varshney has suggested that even religiously diverse societies have proven to be 'riot-proof' because of high incidences of interdependence in working, political and recreational lives. The concentration of economic opportunities to culturally dominant groups has exacerbated the segregation between communities and deepened their isolation from each other. Communal identities have congealed where alternative, worldly identities have not been able to germinate in secular institutions of the school, the trade union or even through everyday contact.

Multiculturalism and anti-secularism

Multiculturalism
If there are obvious incongruities between the prevailing forms of discrimination against minorities in Britain and India, there are

equally obvious convergences between political and intellectual approaches to redressing discrimination by managing diversity.

Anti-racist opinion on multiculturalism is roughly reducible to two perspectives: those who perceive it to be a form of appeasement and those who see it as a form of struggle. Though multiculturalism is a highly contested concept, it has become heavily associated in academia with communitarian advocates such as Bhikhu Parekh, and politically with state-administered multiculturalist policies, even if there are sharp divergences between the two.

Champions of multiculturalism would make capital from the distinction I've made above between its academic or theoretical imagining and the corruptions of its political realisation. Multi-culturalists such as Parekh have a grand sense of multiculturalism as a human sensibility (what he calls the 'spirit of multiculturality') which cannot be politically compartmentalised as an anti-racist strategy but which is intended to suffuse the broad spectrum of political decision-making.

Parekh's multiculturalism refuses to be reduced to an anti-racist strategy even though it is ethnic minorities who are perceived to be the beneficiaries of multiculturalist policy. Parekh considers multi-culturalism to have a global constituency because cultural diversity is 'a collective asset'.[40] He makes a case for the acceptance of cultural diversity as a legitimating, democratising energy for civil society and the polity.

His understanding of multiculturalism steers a moderating course between the excesses of liberal universalism on the one hand and those of cultural relativism on the other. Multiculturalism reflects his understanding that we are 'similar enough' to be 'intelligible' but different enough to be 'puzzling' and make 'dialogue neces-sary'.[41] The conclusions he reaches for conflicts in diverse society issue from this dialectic image of human nature since they demand non-'liberal' political virtues such as sensitivity, understanding, compromise and patience, virtues which can only be forged through intercultural dialogue.

Parekh therefore makes a reluctant anti-racist and it's revealing that there is no sustained engagement with racism in his monograph *Rethinking Multiculturalism* (2000) (in fact it is only fleetingly referred to in the context of communal libel). Even though he is more concerned with the overall reconciliation of justice with diversity, his recommendations concerning the political structures of multicultural societies, free speech and religion all err on the side of cultural and religious minorities. The coincidence between multi-culturalism's theoretical prejudice towards minorities and the obvious minority bias of anti-racism goes a long way, I think, to explaining the conflation between two radically different if not incommensurable discourses.

Of course, practitioners of multiculturalist *policies* would insist that ethnic minorities are their predominant beneficiaries. To vindicate this claim they might cite benefits brought for the analysis of educational attainment, socio-economic status and health statistics by the debunking of catch-all ethnic categories. They would also (presumably) draw attention to the numerous cultural rights won for minorities: from headwear and cultural dress in workplaces to the proliferation of mosques, mandirs and gurdwaras and the establishment of religious-minority schools. The commonplace appearances of minority culture in the national media and recognised taboos on racist language are further evidence of multiculturalism's transformation of British attitudes to race and cultural difference.

The problem is that multiculturalism as anti-racist praxis is bereft of an adequate critique of *state* racism. It acknowledges that racism plagues society but cannot accept that it is endemic to liberal societies or a compulsion of the capitalist system. It believes that cultural diversity has confounded the liberal order but also that this is a relatively novel situation and multicultural societies are on a steep learning curve. Multiculturalist polities are not born fully formed but through greater intercultural knowledge can reform and evolve to reflect and serve more fairly multicultural societies. Since racism arises through cultural absolutism it can be cured with cultural dialogue; racists have misconceived ideas about and attitudes to the Other which can only be unlearned by engaging with them on the basis of discursive equality and dignity. On the basis of its modest ambitions, it is fair to surmise that multiculturalism can never really go 'beyond liberalism' because it is premised on existing liberal culture and practices. Multiculturalism and liberalism are deeply implicated in each other, despite their superficial and constructed differences.

So even though multiculturalism has spectacularly fallen from favour at the political centre it is crucial not to overplay the ideological incompatibility between the two in practice. After all, liberal and multiculturalist policies have co-existed for the past thirty years and Parekh for one is too savvy to pretend that liberalism can be dispensed with entirely or that multiculturalism is an autonomous political doctrine. Parekh readily admits that the operations of multiculturalism, at least in the British context, are reliant on a liberal infrastructure.

Anti-secularism

Indian expressions of multiculturalism have been more hostile towards liberalism because of Indian society's general discomfiture with the principles of secularism that underwrite liberal ideas about justice and equality. The liberal accommodation of multiculturalism doesn't interfere with secularism because it refuses to accept that religion and culture can be conflated. It makes a firm and intractable distinction between religion and societal culture.

India has never been able to work with the version of secularism found in Western constitutional models. Curiously for a nation renowned for its constitution, secularism was not incorporated into the Indian constitution until the mid-1970s (and then under the instructions of Indira Gandhi, who has probably done more than anyone to bring it notoriety). The variant of secularism she constitutionalised, and which has prevailed through most of India's national history, has been that of *sarva dharma sambhava*, which approximates to the understanding that the state has to keep a principled distance from all public or private religious institutions so that the values of peace, dignity, liberty and equality are not compromised. The Indian model acknowledges the religiosity of India's societal culture in its very articulation of secularism.

There are those (notably liberals, Marxists and rationalists) who would argue that Indian secularism has always been compromised by its concession to societal religiosity. Chetan Bhatt makes the point that a state that consorts with religious groups is a state that invites accusations of bias, favouritism and corruption.[42] Others would go further to describe it as a constitutional loophole through which Hindu nationalism has been able to inseminate the political centre.

Others, like Rajeev Bhargava, would counter that *sarva dharma sambhava* is really only an application of multiculturalist ethics to the 'somewhat encrusted' formula of secularism.[43] Parekh's conception of human beings as fundamentally similar yet simultaneously culturally embedded dictates that colour and culture-blind justice fail to take into account the culturally mediated differences between people. Neutrality may work in a homogenous society but fails in a diverse one. In other words, multiculturalists favour cultural particularism above abstraction. India's 'multiculturalist' secularism is governed by the same logic.

Firstly, recognition of the multiplicity of India's religions (and religious cultures) inheres in this model. The public character of religions is also affirmed even if the state declines to associate itself with any particular one. It also has a commitment to multiple values of liberty and equality existing in plural religious traditions to supplement more basic values for security and tolerance between 'communities'.[44] Indian secularism also practically approximates to Indian multiculturalism.

So, in principle at least, the Indian model seems capable of conciliating justice and (religious) diversity by recourse to multi-culturalist ethics. It admits the difficulty of distinguishing between religion and culture and the political structure of multireligious India seeks to take religious differences into account.

Despite Bhargava's confidence, this hasn't persuaded more hostile critics of secularism who challenge the ability of secular polities to allow the full expression of religiosity and traditional values. Their critiques incline further towards cultural relativism than Parekh's multiculturalism and are fundamentally epistemological rather than ontological doctrines. Having said that, they also rest on premises which are familiar to multiculturalism, particularly visible through their communitarian leanings.

'Anti-secularism' is by no means as coherent a political pro-gramme or doctrine as multiculturalism but it has attained formid-able resonance as the name of an intellectual impulse on issues of minority equality, statehood and as a credible voice against reli-gious nationalism and communal violence. Since it is so nebulous, contested and diffuse, I will only sketch its most salient character-istics to help explain why it cannot be reductively described as multiculturalism's derivative distant cousin.

Anti-secularists commonly argue that the homogenisations of the nation-state have trampled on India's native cultural re-sources for managing religious diversity. Despite their manifold differences they share the conviction that India's traditional cultures should be foregrounded, not ignored, and consequently that the rationalities of secular liberalism cannot speak to the religious inspiration of public ethics. Strains of anti-secularism therefore regard the abstractions of liberalism, the nation-state and the foundational concept of secularism as intellectual beachheads of British colonialism, a persistent form of cultural imperialism. Merryl Wyn Davies and Ziauddin Sardar have described a war on secularism as 'a matter of cultural identity and survival for non-western societies'.[45]

Anti-secularists believe that Indian society bears the imprimatur of its religiosity in historically formed community formations. The interdependencies which sustain these traditional communities have been corroded by the rationalisations of the postcolonial state. The requirements of the 'masculinised modern state' have disfigured the Indian social landscape, atomising communities through remote government.

Like multiculturalists, anti-secularists also take exception to what they perceive to be a liberal bias against these traditionally occurring communities and collectives. They argue that certain forms of community – predominantly cultural or religious – are not reducible to the individuals who comprise them but have distinct social personalities. Anti-secularists want the state to re-cognise communities as political actors in the same way that it recognises individuals.

Anti-secularists also believe that the erosion of indigenous social relations has catalysed communal tension. Ashis Nandy, for ex-ample, writing in a special issue of *Seminar* after the Gujarati pogroms, speculated on whether the spatial proximity of urbanised Gujarat could not be held accountable for the pogroms.[46] It is not only the bypassing of India's indigenous communities that anti-secularists are aggrieved by but also the declining socio-cultural currency of responsibilities and its usurpation by 'a language of unitary rights' which fails to cope with the 'respect for cultural diversity' and 'other ways of life'.[47]

It is this characteristic privileging of responsibility over rights, the valuing of the common good above individual sovereignty, that prompts Achin Vanaik to label anti-secularists as 'religious com-munitarians':

Anti-secularists are religious communitarians who (like commun-alists and fundamentalists) see the relationship between individual and society as primarily based not on rights but on 'moral responsibility' and 'consensus' Though they are generally less hostile to issues of individual rights, both are programmatically unspecific about how personal freedom will be organised in their respective social utopias.[48]

Marxists like Sumit Sarkar (2000) likewise criticise anti-secularists for misguided resolutions to the questions of minority equality and anti-fundamentalism. Sarkar accuses anti-secularists of sharing discursive 'spaces' with Hindu fundamentalism and in so doing granting them intellectual legitimacy and respectability. The romanticised anti-secular whitewashing of traditional community echoes Hindutva's own hierarchical authoritarianism, while claims for India's exceptionalism rehearse Hindu nationalism's derogation from universal human rights.

Multiculturalism and the progressive dilemma

This book identifies two urgent, interrelated themes. The first is that contemporary global politics has rendered many of the world's democracies susceptible to the rhetoric and policy of majoritarianism. The second is that majoritarianism plays on popular anxieties that invariably gravitate towards cultural identity. The Left, historically reticent on such issues, has to ask important questions about how oppositional political solidarities might be ordered through 'culture' when the principles of multiculturalism are in crisis.

The book moves beyond a critique of majoritarianism to assess the role of the conglomerate of political actors and intellectuals opposed to it. I argue two things here. Firstly, I examine how intellectual and organisational support for identity politics has impacted on the mobilisation of coherent resistance to majoritarianism, both in Britain and India. I argue that the experience of both nations, in different but not incommensurable ways, warns that investing political faith in inherited communities abets the growth of majoritarianism. By explicitly supporting ethno-religious 'monoliths' nurtured by policies of state patronage, they foreclose on the possibility of individuals rearticulating existing communitarian ties to interrogate discriminatory institutions. When it is only community interlocutors whose voices are heard, voices that are uniformly conservative and extreme, national debates on race and faith become polarised. Tensions are ratcheted up, and majoritarianism becomes further entrenched.

But secondly (and uniquely) I challenge the conflation between state and philosophical multiculturalism and explain why the latter's attentiveness to identity and belonging is invaluable if we are to arrive at a nuanced and fully democratised anti-majoritarian politics.

I argue that the sclerosis of the Indian resistance to Hindutva, like the current inertia of the British Left, is indicative of a global oversight in oppositional politics. I suggest the growth of majoritarian politics can be partially explained by the Left's inarticulacy on cultural identity. While the established Left has failed to join its battle for secular principles on the terrain of culture, recuperating old utopias that merely alienate those it would seek to represent, the new Left has made recourse to an identity politics that is conservatively communitarian, intrinsically undemocratic and vulnerable to appropriation by cultural fundamentalists.

The recovery of secular solidarity – and with it the prospect for joined-up resistance – is as unlikely to be realised with those who only recognise inherited culture as it is with those who disavow culture altogether. Whether one position is taken or the other, genuine political agency remains corralled by historical elites or traditional hierarchies, but denied to the silent majorities they undemocratically represent.

The book suggests that the challenge for those who might speak in opposition to majoritarianism lies firstly in enabling individuals from historically marginalised communities to realise some kind of political autonomy, and secondly in dismantling hierarchies of inherited and experienced culture. It offers the hope that such a move will ameliorate the majoritarian reflex by diminishing the impulse for enclavism among national minorities. It is only from this political ground zero that a more progressive agenda for citizenship and culture can be tabled.

How this book is organised

The following chapters alternate between Britain and India, situating the progressive dilemma in three contexts: contemporary Britain, Britain in 'new times' and contemporary India.

This begins with Britain, where I look at the muddled majoritarian response to the unrest in England's northern towns, concerns about Asian self-segregation, and the flow of asylum-seekers. I argue that these are not intermittent anxieties, but manifestations of a discernible turn to majoritarian thinking exemplified by *Prospect* editor David Goodhart's proposal for a 'progressive nationalism' that fundamentally questions the merits of cultural diversity and the twenty-first-century mandate for liberal politics.

Chapter 2 relocates to India, and the complementary rise of Hindutva and neo-liberalism since the early 1990s. It reflects on the

Left's struggles to categorise the threat posed by the Sangh Parivar, and why some commentators insisted on representing Hindutva as India's fascism. By relating Hindu nationalism's ascendancy with the growth of 'Middle India' it concludes that it is more usefully described by the politics of majoritarianism.

Chapter 3 returns to Britain to retread the debates that splintered the Left and thereby compromised a robust, progressive answer to majoritarianism. It takes a revisionist approach to the struggles of the old Left to renew itself and looks at how this was rendered into a stark ideological choice between collectivism and individualism, with far-reaching limitations for secular coalition in the twenty-first century.

Chapter 4 examines how India's Left assigned blame for the rise of Hindu nationalism to its rival factions. In particular, it scrutinises the common accusation that anti-secularism is complicit with Hindu nationalism and questions whether other voices on the Left have been able to answer meaningfully to Hindutva by way of alternative.

The final chapter obituarises multiculturalism, as both a theory and a political practice. I argue that the conflation between state and philosophical multiculturalism is misguided and has condemned the latter without sufficient attention to its nuance. Rounding out the book's appraisal of the progressive challenge to majoritarianism, I argue that the task for the Left is not to repudiate multiculturalism altogether, but to go beyond it, and dismantle constructed hierarchies between inheritance and experience.

I conclude by teasing out the global lessons from the three instances of the progressive dilemma examined in it: the contest over 'new times', the right response to Hindutva, and Britain's post-multiculturalist future. I will assess whether majoritarian pressure for the political centre to drift rightwards is being resisted by the emerging generation of political actors, whom I call 'multiculturalism's children', and what the Left as a whole can do to support their struggles.

Notes

1. David Ward, 'Ignorance, Misunderstanding and Fear', *The Guardian*, Special Report: Race in Britain, December 2001.

2. Ibid.

3. Arundhati Roy, *The Algebra of Infinite Justice* (New Delhi: Penguin, 2002), p. 267.

4. It remains the only major Indian state to be controlled by the BJP.

5. 'Dateline Gujarat', *Communalism Combat*, March/April 2002, http://www.sabrang.com/cc/archive/2002/marapril/dateline.htm.

6. 'Mapping the Violence', *Communalism Combat*, March/April 2002, http://www.sabrang.com/cc/archive/2002/marapril/dateline.htm.

7. S. P. Shukla, Kamal Mitra Chenoy, K. S. Subramanian and Achin Vanaik, 'Gujarat Carnage 2002: A Report to the Nation by an Independent Fact Finding Mission', 2002, http://www.outlookindia.com/special featurem.asp?fodname=20020411&fname=chenoy&sid=1.

8. Human Rights Watch, 'Compounding Injustice: The Government's Failure to Redress Massacres in Gujarat', December 2003, http://www.hrw.org/reports/2003/india0703/India0703full.pdf.

9. Ibid.

10. Ibid.

11. At the time of the Amritsar massacre, Gandhi declared that 'when a tree falls, the earth shakes'. *Times of India*, 3 March 2002.

12. Modi was speaking at a press conference in Ahmedadbad, Gujarat's capital, on 28 February 2002.

13. Human Rights Watch, 'Compounding Injustice'.

14. Narendra Modi, Lal Krishna Advani (the current leader of the BJP) and Atal Bihari Vajpayee (the former leader) were all reared by the RSS. Quoted in Arundhati Roy, 'The Modern Rationalist', April 2002, http://www.themronline.com/200204m2.html.

15. 'We have norms of acceptability and those who come into our home – for that is what it is – should accept those norms just as we would have to do if we went elsewhere.' David Blunkett, quoted in BBC News Online, 'Blair backs Blunkett on race', 10 December 2001, http://www.news.bbc. co.uk/1/hi/uk_politics/1700370.

16. To spell out the obvious, there were no deaths reported in the summer riots of 2001; over two thousand are reliably estimated to have died in Gujarat. In England's race riots economic disadvantage is widely believed to have been a decisive factor, in Gujarat many of the perpetrators are well known to have been of middle-class stock. Thirdly, there is compelling evidence that state authorities colluded with Hindu fundamentalist yobs in Gujarat; despite accusations of the police's failure to protect Asian communities, they stood off the rioters in Bradford, Burnley and Oldham. And of course the tens of thousands of refugees left destitute and homeless in Gujarat were in no way foreshadowed in Britain.

17. The Home Office, *Secure Borders, Safe Haven: Integration with Diversity in Modern Britain* (London: The Stationery Office, 2002).

18. V. D. Savarkar, *Hindutva: Who is a Hindu?* (Bombay: V. D. Savarkar Prakashan, 1969), p. 2.

19. T. B. Hansen, 'Globalisation and Nationalist Imaginations:

Hindutva's Promise of Equality through Difference', *Economic and Political Weekly*, 9 March 1996, p. 6113.

20. Jenny Bourne, 'The Life and Times of Institutional Racism', *Race & Class*, 43.2, 2001.

21. See Chapter 1 on David Goodhart's 'The Discomfort of Strangers' for the former, and David Blunkett's White Paper *Secure Borders: Safe Haven* for the latter.

22. Yasmin Alibahi Brown, quoted in David Faulkner, *Civil Renewal, Diversity and Social Capital in a Multi-ethnic Britain* (London: Runny-mede Trust, 2004), p. 10.

23. Bourne, 'The Life and Times', p. 14.

24. A. Sivanandan, 'Poverty is the New Black', *Race & Class*, 43.2, 2001, p. 4.

25. See the Institute of Race Relations' News Network for a catalogue of racist violence since the London bombings of July 2005, http://www.irr.org.uk/2005/september/ha000016.html.

26. Meera Nanda, *Breaking the Spell of Dharma: A Case for Indian Enlightenment* (New Delhi: ThreeEssaysPress, 2002).

27. Rajeev Bhargava, 'India's Model: Faith, Secularism and Democracy', *openDemocracy*, 3 November 2004, http://www.opendemocracy.-net/content/articles/PDF/2204.pdf.

28. It is indicative of this that the India's National Council of Applied Economic Research (NCEAR) has substituted the term 'middle class' for the 'consuming class'.

29. Gurcharan Das, *India Unbound: From Independence to the Global Information Age* (London: Profile, 2002), p. 287.

30. Rajiv Gandhi's relaxation of import duties on televisions during the 1980s, to celebrate India's hosting of the 1982 Commonwealth Games, was instrumental in the massive boom in television ownership during that decade, particularly since large numbers were remitted by Non Resident Indians (NRIs) resident in Dubai and the Middle East.

31. Sabrang and South Asia Citizens Web, 'The Foreign Exchange of Hate: IDRF and the American Funding of Hindutva', 2002, http://www.stopfundinghate.org/sacw.

32. This has recently been disproved through testimony from Godse's brother in 1948.

33. Sabrang and SACW, 'The Foreign Exchange of Hate'.

34. *Organiser*, Deepavali Special, October 1964.

35. Nanda, *Breaking the Spell*, p. 7.

36. S. Chandrasekar, 'Teaching of the Vedas to All', *Organiser*, 15–21 April 2002, p. 225.

37. Ibid.

38. Such as Prasar Bharti (responsible for broadcasting).

39. Chandrasekar, 'Teaching of the Vedas', p. 5.

40. Bhikhu Parekh, *Rethinking Multiculturalism* (Basingstoke: Palgrave, 2000), p. 196.

41. Ibid., p. 124.

42. Chetan Bhatt, 'Democracy and Hindu Nationalism', *Democratization*, 11.4, August 2004, pp. 145, 149.

43. Bhargava, 'India's Model'.

44. Ibid.

45. Ziauddin Sardar and Merryl Wyn Davies, *Distorted Imagination: Lessons from the Rushdie Affair* (London: Grey Seal, 1990), p. 32.

46. Ashis Nandy, 'Obituary of a Culture', *Seminar*, 417, 2002.

47. Partha Chatterjee, 'Secularism and Toleration', *Economic and Political Weekly*, 29.28, 1994, p. 1227.

48. Achin Vanaik, *The Furies of Indian Communalism* (London: Verso, 1997), p. 179.

Chapter 1

The Trouble with David Goodhart's Britain: Liberalism's Slide towards Majoritarianism

Western Europe will implode by 2018. A terrifying whirlwind of insecurity, political disloyalty and new-wave piracy will dismember our societies within eleven years. Waves of mass immigration from Third World disaster zones will surge over Britain's borders, reducing it to a hollow shell sacked by 'reverse colonisation'. 'Indigenous' Britons will soon become minorities in a land overrun by a multitude of diaspora groups.

Future immigration will be characterised by little allegiance to host countries; the idea of assimilation will become 'redundant'. People will reside in Britain out of convenience, expediency and necessity as regional economic crashes, natural disaster and failed city-states propel a mass exodus from the Third World to Europe. As Europe's leading destination for immigrants, Britain will be in the most perilous position.

Such is the belief of Rear Admiral Chris Parry, head of the Development, Concepts and Doctrine Centre (DCDC) at the Ministry of Defence. He already believes that is almost impossible to 'integrate' new immigrant groups. In a briefing speech he warned that 'globalisation makes assimilation seem redundant and old-fashioned ... [the process] acts as a sort of reverse colonisation, where groups of people are self-contained, going back and forth between their countries, exploiting sophisticated networks and using instant communication on phones and the internet'.[1] In a speech designed to outline the challenges that will shape Britain's security policies in the coming decades, Parry was unequivocal that the diaspora issue is 'one of my biggest current concerns'.[2]

Parry's bleak prophecies make an interesting accompaniment to the imperatives of David Goodhart's controversial 'liberal realism'. Parry extrapolates the consequences of today's insecurities, highlighted by Goodhart, into tomorrow's nightmare. It's a projection you can imagine Goodhart being sympathetic to: a vindication of his warning about the dire consequences of a society devoid of common culture and obligations.

It is not my intention in this chapter to comment on the accuracy of Parry's predictions, but to ask how our liberal spokesmen contributed to the propensity for the majoritarian reflex. I argue that the political reaction to the riots in England's northern towns has become consolidated in the shape of a new 'liberal realism' that unites conservative elements of Left and Right. This is a realism that is neither liberal nor sympathetic to the normative fact of Britain's multiculture. The ideas of *Prospect* editor David Goodhart will be used to exemplify a so-called 'progressive nationalism' that is unapologetically prostrate before the anxieties of a demographic majority. I will show how Goodhart's liberal realism paradoxically appropriates the communitarian ethics of Bhikhu Parekh's multiculturalism while violating the latter's imperatives for cultural diversity.

Goodhart on diversity and solidarity

Goodhart's body of writing on the push and pull of diversity and solidarity spans two years and, principally, three pieces: two *Prospect* articles, 'Too Diverse?' (2004), 'National Anxieties' (2006); and *Progressive Nationalism* (2006), commissioned by Demos. While there are appreciable differences between 'Too Diverse?' and his most recent publications, all are founded on the same premise and speak with one voice on immigration, multiculturalism and citizenship.

A summary of his ideas would look something like this: diversity (of which ethnic diversity is the most threatening) destabilises liberal society by weakening the common culture, which informs the reciprocities that such a society depends on to sustain its projects for social justice (such as a welfare state and the health service). At the same time, white working-class communities become isolated as this common culture fragments, and increasingly envious of ethnic-minority communities which enjoy the neighbourly support they used to share. Extremists from the Right woo the abandoned white poor by peddling xenophobic nationalist politics that exacerbate the segregation of minorities from the ethnic majority. Salvation arrives in the shape of 'liberal realism'. Though the Left has historically been reluctant to engage with questions of national identity and has retired to the sanctuary of cosmopolitanism, it is now vital that it claims these issues as its own. A liberal nationalism born of this realism can shore up withered solidarities with a renewed commitment to the idea of a national community and in turn restore the viability of liberal projects for justice and redistribution.

The focal point of Goodhart's recommendations is the reinvigoration of citizenship. He is in agreement with Hall and Held that citizenship can only be decisive for the Left if it is actively integrated with a set of related political ideas.[3] A culture of citizenship can both heighten the collective belief in a 'stakeholder society' and cohere diverse Britain around a set of agreed values. Whereas blood-and-soil national identities may be anachronistic for a globalised nation, citizenship is invested, by virtue of its legal origins, with greater inclusivity:

> The modern idea of citizenship goes some way to accommodating the tension between solidarity and diversity. Citizenship is not an ethnic, blood-and-soil concept, but a more abstract political idea – implying equal legal, political and social rights (and duties) for people inhabiting a given national space.[4]

Citizenship is capable not only of transcending the narrow exclusivities of ethnic loyalty, but also of expressing legal equality. It should not only convey abstract political status, but also membership of a community that is not assumed but bestowed. Citizenship also presupposes an acceptance of 'moral values, however fuzzy', and contractual obligations between the state and individual.

Existing measures to popularise the virtues of citizenship (such as in curricular education) should be augmented by playing up its 'symbolic aspects'. He proposes, for example, a 'British national holiday' or a 'British state of the union address' to reinforce the tacit understandings that (apparently) can no longer be taken for granted in society. He also makes a case for ID cards on the same logistical grounds as those already mooted by the home secretary (national security) but also as 'a badge of citizenship', presumably to be worn at all times with national pride.[5]

In another endorsement of New Labour proposals, he advocates substantial investment to facilitate cultural integration. To help achieve a 'British version of the old US melting pot', he wants schemes such as citizenship ceremonies, language lessons and the mentoring of new citizens. Newcomers are also encouraged to adopt British history with the intention of making the transition from 'immigrant "them" to citizen "us"'.[6]

But while Goodhart offers the benign solidarity of citizenship, he doesn't exactly abandon national culture either. Because while citizenship appears to promise reconciliation between diversity and solidarity, he says that a bland and abstract citizenship culture will make little headway in creating a sustainable shared culture. While citizenship creates a peer group of equals, unalloyed it doesn't get very far as an adhesive for national community. He predicts it to be very unlikely to inspire the kind of mutual obligations required to support a redistributive, equitable society. The political task facing the Left (or the progressive centre, which-ever he might prefer to identify himself with) is to inscribe the contours of Britain's unique history and geography into the sterile language of citizenship:

> The anxieties triggered by the asylum-seeker inflow into Britain now seem to be fading. But they are not just a media invention; a sharp economic downturn or a big inflow of east European workers after EU enlargement might easily call them up again. The progressive centre needs to think more clearly about these issues to avoid being engulfed by them. And to that end it must try to develop a new language in which to address the anxieties, one that transcends the thin and abstract language of universal rights on the one hand, and the defensive, nativist language of group identity on the other. Too often the language of liberal univers-alism that dominates public debate ignores the real affinities of place and people. These affinities are not obstacles to be overcome

on the road to the good society; they are one of its foundation stones.[7]

It has to be said that there's nothing genuinely racist about what Goodhart is proposing. Neal Ascherson is justified in pitying him for being put up in media cockfights as a spokesman for the anti-immigration brigade. Goodhart has an honest liberal conscience and his programme for the renewal of citizenship reflects this. Who could genuinely take exception to 'accepting the rule of law', to 'play by the economic and welfare rules', the 'broad legal and political equality of women' and speaking 'the language well enough to take part in social and economic life'? None of these are particularly controversial; they actually place remarkably mundane and mediocre demands on us as citizens.

Those who denounce him for politicising immigration or refuse to enter into debate are also irresponsible and short-sighted. Goodhart is right that it is incumbent on the Left to make a stand on issues of identity and security. They loom large and foreboding in the public conscience now more than ever.

His position is striking not for its controversial stance on multiculturalism and immigration, but for how unerringly it confirms the trajectory of liberal opinion and the xenophobic assumptions underlying it. Most of his policy prescriptions – citizenship initiatives above all – have already been proposed or enacted by the government.

It could be argued that Goodhart is only exaggerating Brian Barry's critique of multiculturalism in *Culture and Equality* (2001), to be discussed in Chapter 5. Like Barry, who warns that 'a politics of multiculturalism undermines a politics of redistribution', Goodhart worries that a public favouring of diversity over solidarity challenges the basis of the welfare state.[8] The difference is that Barry does not discuss the merits of a multicultural society, but the dangers of a multiculturalist *polity*. His concern is not whether multicultural societies undermine redistributive goals, but the incapacity of multiculturalist policy to redress the material inequalities that disadvantage poor black, white and Asian communities alike.[9] But while Barry refrains from explicitly connecting cultural diversity to immigration, Goodhart shows no fear in making such a claim. This telling difference between Barry's and Goodhart's liberalism is directly attributable to a watershed in political attitudes to immigration and race relations which I propose to have taken place in 2001.

While Barry might be classified as an anti-multiculturalist liberal, I will suggest that Goodhart is more perceptively understood as a child of the times: he is a *post-multiculturalist*. He is the figurehead for a strain of avowedly progressive politics that has been given wings by a political climate born of the transatlantic war on terror and growing anxiety over inassimilable Muslims (especially in the northern towns). Their perspective has been shaped more by external events than internal reforms on the Left. Goodhart therefore depicts his quandary over the competition between solidarity and diversity as a 'progressive' rather than a personal dilemma, on whose axis the Left is expected to spin.

The real problem with Goodhart and his political vision is not that it is racist but that it is imprisoned in the stagnant realms of a liberal imagination atrophied through a chronically smug aversion to issues of identity and culture. Goodhart's liberal realism also has to be rejected not because it is racist but because it is founded on insecurities and neuroses rather than aspiration or principle. It propounds the politics of envy, anxiety and mediocrity rather than offering a credible route out of the wreckage of multiculturalist policy.

Illiberal community

For one, Goodhart imagines community in a peculiarly illiberal way. To be more precise, he sanctions a sovereign form of community – nationalism – and stigmatises all others. The community he wants for Britain bears no resemblance to that he imputes to its so-called 'ethnic minorities'.

Four years ago, Claire Alexander reflected that Asians were condemned for having too much culture.[10] Nowadays, they are rounded on for having too much *community*. While on the one hand this agitates middle-class liberals who worry that this will lead to social and cultural reclusion and the rejection of reciprocal obligations, on the other it stokes resentment in the white poor who, bereft of the ideological coordinates of class, 'look on enviously' at ethnic cousins who enjoy solidarities they have lost.

'Too Diverse?' expressly sympathised with 'poor whites' who are virtually atomised relative to the 'mutual support and sense of community' that characterises ethnic-minority social life.

What was 'once a feature of British working-class life' is now almost exclusively associated with immigrants (Asians in particular). All that's left for many people in Britain is to look back nostalgically on a time of more 'tightly knit and supportive communities'.[11]

Community has become the covert slur for people who self-segregate. It is no longer a neutral reference to a group of people unified by a common defining characteristic, but to a politically distinctive way of *behaving*. It baldly evokes the way in which Hindu nationalists condemn Indian Muslims for block-voting to optimise communal power, for being anti-modern, for being culturally backward and for stunting the economic growth of the nation. Community is something that happens outside society. In today's liberal rhetoric, when you're identified as belonging to a community, you cease to be a citizen.

Perhaps it's not too bizarre, then, that Goodhart takes pride in British antipathy to other Britons. Though the demise of working-class neighbourliness may be a recent phenomenon, the rest of our society has historically been less inclined to 'national solidarity and culture' than our European brethren. While old Europe has, at best, only grudgingly accepted immigrants as 'guest workers' or coerced them into uniform patterns of national behaviour, Britain's dwindling 'mutuality' has dovetailed happily with successive waves of immigration. Our apathy for nationalism is a boon because, as his formula goes, 'the degree of antagonism between groups is proportional to the degree of co-operation within groups'. Perhaps revealing more than he wants to, Goodhart attributes Britain's resistance to extremist politics to 'that weakness of national solidarity' that finds most conspicuous expression in the 'stand-offishness' of suburban England: 'We are more tolerant than, say, France because we don't care enough about each other to resent the arrival of the other'.[12]

It is therefore surprising, and a little alarming, that what he considers to have been a 'bulwark' against extremism should suddenly (under the right conditions) transform itself into the salvation of centre-Left ambition. That a tradition that has so staunchly attended to the rights of the individual against community trespass should relocate its political emphasis to a community most hostile to the individual – the nation – is a startling U-turn for liberal principles.

What becomes evident is that Goodhart's resort to national

solidarity stems unashamedly not from liberal commitments but from a dismal brew of anxiety and envy. Goodhart, like many of our liberal middle classes, sees community everywhere but at home: they see it in an America unified by common fear and obstinance; they see it in old European neighbours retrenching into chauvinistic bunkers; they see it in terrorist groups bonded in vengeful brotherhood; they even see it in their own inner cities, where so-called 'ethnic' minorities abound in pockets of terraced solidarity.

Liberal England peers at extended families, neighbourly concern and the semblance of street life that stream in footage of areas such as Forest Gate as remnants of a lost age. Though Goodhart claims to be empathising with the working classes, he is really displacing liberal envy on to them; his liberal nationalism is a covert lament for irreversible sociological changes from Middle England.

From multiculturalism to community cohesion

Politically, these liberal complaints have dovetailed with a fore-boding attack on multiculturalism which has masqueraded under the moniker of liberalism's 'progressive dilemma'. Goodhart, and those of his persuasion, have been given covering fire by a discernible reversal of the government's position on cultural diversity. In the Campaign against Racism and Fundamentalism's (2002) review of the government's position post-2001, they discerned an acknowledgement that the preservation of separate, parallel cultural blocs is no longer considered a 'viable option':

> Whereas before, black youths were assumed to be rioting because of a lack of culture (what was referred to as an 'ethnic disadvantage'), now youths were rioting because of an excess of culture – they were too Muslim, too traditional. For the state, the laissez-faire allowances of before had to be ended and cultural difference held on a tighter rein. The 'parallel cultural bloc' was now seen as part of the problem, not the solution.[13]

As Back et al. (2004) suggest, the civil unrest during the summer of 2001 in Bradford, Burnley and Oldham has been an important factor in the drift away from a celebration of multicultural diversity.[14]

What Goodhart's strain of majoritarianism exemplifies is a 'blame the victim' response that has afflicted public attitudes to minorities ever since the so-called war on terror (especially towards Muslims in the wake of the civil unrest during the summer of 2001). Rather than identify the cause as one of deprivation (racialised or otherwise) it has been misdiagnosed as one of 'too much culture', as opposed to 'too little culture', which was perceived to have caused the Tottenham and Brixton riots of 1981, and which precipitated the adoption of multiculturalism as its sovereign remedy.

Cultural diversity has been emphatically indicted as the problem. The Cantle report was the official response to the 2001 riots and has become the definitive word on race-relations management. In the words of Kundnani, 'the new strategy is "community cohesion" and the Cantle report is the blueprint'.[15] He concludes that 'according to the Cantle report, it is not so much institutions as attitudes that are the focus of change'. Like its conceptual cousin, 'social exclusion', 'community cohesion' is about networks, identity and discourse, rather than poverty, inequality and power.[16] In the report's opinion (by implication the government's), multiculturalism has erected cultural barriers to the desired goal of 'community cohesion'. Redressing that necessitates the socialisation of immigrant groups (not just recent arrivals but also older troublesome ones, like the Yorkshire Pakistanis) in British civility.

Rolling back the cultural latitude afforded to south-Asian communities over the decades (and in particular by Labour governments), the former home secretary David Blunkett publicly denounced 'forced marriages' and 'female circumcision', making further stipulations that arranged marriages should only take place between men and women resident in the UK. In the preface to his 2002 White Paper *Secure Borders, Safe Haven: Integration and Diversity in Modern Britain,* he explicitly relegates diversity to the interests of integration:

> To enable integration to take place and to value the diversity it brings, we need to be secure within our sense of belonging and identity and therefore to be able to embrace those who come to the UK [. . .] Having a clear, workable and robust nationality and asylum system is the pre-requisite to building the security and trust that is needed. Without it, we cannot defeat those who would seek to stir up hate, intolerance and prejudice.[17]

Central to this new position is a dialectic that operates through two Manichean figures: that of the stigmatised immigrant and that of the righteous native society. This is reflected in the discourse of liberal nationalism, with its rediscovered taste for the intrinsic virtuosity of majority British values. This is evident not in Goodhart's fears for the erosion of the British way of life, or even in the assumption that it is worth protecting, but in the insinuation that incoming cultural elements are polluting but not enriching. It is the kind of stealth 'racelessness' that David Goldberg describes with such economy in *The Racial State*: '[Racelessness] is achieved only by the presumptive elevation of whiteness silently as the desirable standards, the teleological norms of civilised social life even as it seeks to erase the traces of exclusion necessary to its achievement along the way.'[18]

Multiculturalist policy, as mainstream anti-racism, fertilises this ventriloquised racelessness. While outwardly striving towards the evolution of 'cultural mosaic' through liberal *laissez faire*, the failure of minorities to assimilate to the society proper elicits exasperation from the white majority.[19] It is immigrants who frustrate the pursuit of social cohesion, and who feed the far and New Right by perpetuating their 'identification as the problem'.

The threat of ethnic diversity

It is against this backdrop that champions of so-called liberal majorities, like Goodhart, have had licence to assault cultural diversity for unravelling social or community 'cohesion'. But he can go one step further: unlike the government, he specifies ethnic difference as the form of diversity most difficult to integrate into a culture of shared values:

> The visibility of ethnic difference means that it often overshadows other forms of diversity. Changes in the ethnic composition of a city or neighbourhood can come to stand for the wider changes of modern life. [. . .] If welfare states demand that we pay into a common fund on which we can all draw at times of need, it is important that we feel that most people have made the same effort to be self-supporting and will not take advantage.[20]

The inference is that ethnically different newcomers (raising suspicions because of their 'different appearance') may not possess the same values of reciprocity as the settled population, who are presumably well socialised in such virtues. In turn, their perceived lack of mutual obligations induces faithlessness among the majority of the welfare state's capability to redistribute fairly. If newcomers are not believed to be 'self-supporting' (but reliant on others to support them) then this also ruins the climate for a culture of individual responsibility as instances of state dependency grow. To be reassured that 'strangers, especially those from older countries' believe in the same ideas as 'we do', their divergent views have to be flattened into agreement with a common culture. Only then can cultural barriers to cohesion be overcome and the twin aspirations of mutual obligation and individual responsibility flourish.

Goodhart's communitarianism

So it is with one eye on Middle England and another on ethnic minorities that Goodhart insists 'security and identity issues should mainly be seen as questions about *community*'.[21] It is unsurprising (but no less ironic) that Goodhart turns not to his liberal peers to justify his communitarian proclivities, but to the grandmaster of multiculturalism, Bhikhu Parekh.

Goodhart legitimates the progressive dilemma through an argument for solidarity that echoes that made in Parekh's 'Cosmopolitanism and Global Citizenship' (2003). Like Parekh, Goodhart rejects the cosmopolitan (or 'liberal universalist') aspiration for obligation to all human beings by discrediting the implications of its application, and subsequently naturalising assertions of group identity.

As he sees it, the logical conclusions of liberal universalism are that 'we should spend as much on development aid as on the NHS', 'or that Britain should have no immigration controls at all'.[22] He believes, on the contrary, that the calculus of affinity obtains in all our social choices and human behaviour in general. Parekh likewise defends group obligations on utilitarian grounds, as special duties, a necessary division of labour through which the sum total of general duties could be 'discharged more efficiently'.[23] He also sees a moral hollowness in cosmopolitanism, since it neglects people's attachments to their communities and is too abstract to galvanise 'emotional and moral' commitment.

Goodhart conversely finds in-group identification harmless. Though he states conclusively that 'most of us prefer our own kind' (it is difficult to discern his point of view from his representation of the Burkean perspective), he qualifies this in manifold ways. The bottom line remains obvious, though: the instinct to favour our own is both natural and defensible, corroborated by evolutionary psychology:

> The category 'own kind', or in-group, will set alarm bells ringing in the minds of many readers. So it is worth stressing what preferring our own kind does not mean, even for a Burkean. It does not mean that we are necessarily hostile to other kinds or that we cannot empathise with outsiders. (There are those who do dislike other kinds, but in Britain they seem to be quite a small minority.) In complex societies, most of us belong simultaneously to many in-groups – family, profession, class, hobby, locality, nation – and an ability to move with ease between groups is a sign of maturity. An in-group is not, except in the case of families, a natural or biological category and the people who are deemed to belong to it can change quickly.[24]

The nominal difference between Goodhart and Parekh is that while the former espouses a conformist form of communitarianism, the latter's model is pluralist. In the first model, community is formed by normative values that all included under the compass of the community are expected to respect. Individuals have obligations to the community which they have to perform or face punitive measures, such as stigmatisation, loss or rights, status, or even expulsion. The focus is on the 'common good' and individual freedom is often sacrificed for the higher objective of commonality. Goodhart's communitarianism corresponds most closely with this ideal-type.

Under the second it is only commonality that is important; it is geared instead to the recognition of diverse communities in which difference can flourish. The desired outcomes are therefore plurality and heterogeneity. It doesn't presume the absence of a framework under which pluralist communitarianism can exist, since this is often essential (multiculturalism is such a framework).[25] This model best describes Parekh's multiculturalism. The trouble is that our most prominent articulations of pluralist communitarianism do not address the enforcement of conformity that takes place *within* plural communities (something I will also look at later in the book). The conformist bent of Parekh's multiculturalism, in particular, leaves it vulnerable to appropriation by majoritarian-leaning arguments like Goodhart's.

So while from some aspects Parekh's vision of a British 'community of communities' might outwardly appear incongruous to Goodhart's common culture, the differences are only superficial. This is because despite his objections to the homogenous construction of British nationality, Parekh also concedes necessary respect for Britain's 'operative public values', to which all immigrant communities are expected to defer. He describes this deference as important to counter the 'resentment their [immigrants'] presence generally provokes among some sections of society'.[26]

The two do not repel each other from opposing sides of the political spectrum, but are undeniably conservative in similar ways. Parekh's multiculturalism, with its emphasis on inherited rather than chosen identities, sinks into what Amartya Sen has condemned as 'plural monoculturalism'.[27] Rather than allowing us to open out onto diverse ways of thinking and understanding the world, we become culturally asphyxiated by the inner world of our differences. It does not propel cultural exchange, but territorialises it in impermeable communities with segregated identities.

The only difference between Parekh and Goodhart is that while the former advocates plural monoculturalism, the latter champions singular monoculturalism. Ultimately, Goodhart, like Parekh, is trying to bring communitarian notions of identity to social policy, except that he wants a single communitarian order in Britain: a renewed appreciation of national community held in place by a publicly recognised culture of mutual obligation. It's telling that Goodhart and Parekh have collaborated on a *Prospect* article explaining the innocence of in-group preferences in retaliation to overly defensive definitions of racism.[28]

What I'm arguing is that the recession of multiculturalism in liberal and conservative imaginaries has been offset by the growing appeal of a communitarianism that is nationalist rather than minority in expression. Kundnani's (2002) indictment of Blairist multiculturalism's compatibility with 'anti-immigrant populism' is thus explained by the collapse of pluralist into conformist communitarianism at the 'progressive' centre, a consequence of the majoritarian reflex.

In other words, the culturalist door has swung the other way. Liberal (that is, mainstream) anti-racism is still resolutely culturalist, only the justification has been reversed. While the old orthodoxy sought to change majority attitudes to minority cultures, the new regime dictates that minorities must change their attitudes to show deference to the majority culture.

The politics of anxiety

While some of the impetus of Goodhart's communitarian 'liberal-ism' derives from popular envy and longing, it is also a hostage to popular anxieties. It aims to do what New Labour patently hasn't done enough of – 'responding to widely held beliefs' and reflecting 'changes in public mood'. There is, he claims, 'nothing politically dishonourable' about that.[29] As an unashamed characteristic of the 'realism' he believes liberal policies are bereft of, Goodhart wants a centre-Left manifesto on identity and security dictated by popular attitudes.

Though he acknowledges research into the dynamic between diversity and welfare policy (by Parekh, Kymlicka and Rattansi), he discounts it in favour of polls and surveys of mainstream British *opinion*. In fact, it is the only qualitative analysis on Britain that he draws on in 'Too Diverse?' Here is a typical insight into current British psychology:

> Thanks to the race riots in northern English towns in 2001, the fear of radical Islam after 9/11, and anxieties about the rise in asylum-led immigration from the mid-1990s (exacerbated by the popular press), immigration has shot up the list of voter concerns, and according to MORI 56% of people (including 90% of poor whites and even a large minority of immigrants) now believe there are too many immigrants in Britain. This is thanks partly to the overburdened asylum system, which forces refugees onto welfare and prevents them from working legally for at least two years – a system calculated to provoke maximum hostility from ordinary Britons with their acute sensitivity to free riding.[30]

It is obvious from this roll-call of fears, sensitivities and anxieties that it is general unease among the British population that endangers solidarity most of all, rather than fiscal burden on the welfare state from immigrant claims. His principal argument, inspired by the Conservative MP David Willlets, is that 'value' diversity imperils the legitimacy of a risk-pooling welfare state. 'People ask: "Why should I pay for them when they are doing things that I wouldn't do?".'[31]

The problem is that Goodhart's entire argument is bent towards mollifying Middle England rather than shoring up the legitimacy of the welfare state. Even the qualifications he himself makes are sufficient to undermine the logical basis of his argument. He admits that 'attitudes have, for many people, become more instrumental: I pay so much in, the state gives me this in return'. Prosperity has rendered 'generosity' more abstract and 'compulsory' to the point at which it is a matter of 'enlightened self-interest rather than mutual obligation'. Moreover, he concedes that 'welfare is less redistributive than most people imagine', since 'most of the tax paid out by citizens comes back to them in one form or another so the amount of the average person's income going to someone they might consider undeserving is small'.[32]

If this is the case, then surely a better-informed public – the bedrock of any worthwhile democratic society – would unravel the progressive dilemma? If we reassure citizens (through hard facts and numbers) that they will be the overwhelming recipients of their hard-earned pay and that their tax pounds don't line the pockets of bogus asylum seekers, wouldn't that relieve their anxieties?

This reveals the hazard of being accountable to anxieties: they rarely have any basis in fact. Goodhart himself admits that the 'beliefs' he claims to be responding to have been fanned by the tabloid press. Why should liberals join in the rabid rush to panic over diversity? Goodhart is more concerned that New Labour has '*seemed* confused and defensive' than whether it actually has been. The government's failure to devise a 'coherent liberal realist narrative' to reassure the 'anxious and the liberal' is the greatest indication of its crisis of legitimacy.[33]

Whom does liberal nationalism serve?

What is curious is that Goodhart believes that Labour's constituencies are restricted to the 'anxious and the liberal' (they've obviously done enough for everyone else). Just who are the anxious and how are they different from the liberal? Even if we accept this distinction, it excises huge swathes of Britain who could safely be discounted from being either 'liberal' or 'anxious'. The large majority of immigrants for one, as the same MORI poll he refers to reveals. Many settled minorities would fall outside of these categories too, together with the huge 43 per cent poll minority who don't think that the British way of life is threatened by immigration.

Liberal realism's great flaw is that it speaks only – and exclusively

– to the concerns of a constructed majority. It is therefore wholly unreceptive to the interests of Britain's minorities (whether or not they are racially, culturally or religiously defined) and their real or imagined grievances.

It also means that it is difficult to meaningfully distinguish from neo-assimilationism. Goodhart's views on the accommodations that immigrants and host societies should respectively make are, by themselves, innocent enough.

Goodhart wants public policies that 'tend to favour solidarity' to arrest the perceived degradation of cohesion. The 'idea' of a common culture should inform public policy as an 'underlying assumption'.[34] This preference should be expressed in three key areas: immigration and asylum, which need to be tightened and made more discriminating; welfare policy, where new immigrants would be subjected to the lower rung of a two-tier system with limited access to the welfare state; and culture, where immigrants are encouraged to 'become part of the British "we"'.

In the Demos proposal he goes further, chiding the Left for traditionally espousing an 'equality of adaptation' perspective, where Britain must 'radically adapt its way of life or reach out to meet newcomers halfway'. He sees this as an upshot of the Left's discomfort with the concept of national solidarity and its 'recent focus on minority grievance'. Again conceding that 'equality of adaptation' is a fallacy that survives only in the anxieties of 'middle Britain', he nonetheless goes on to emphasise that 'most' of the adaptation should fall on the shoulders of newcomers who have chosen to live in an already existing society with established norms and traditions.[35]

These are all reasonably benign, if banal, observations. But such is their banality – and their inevitability, as he himself acknowledges – that it begs the question of why these should represent policy. More troublesome, especially from a liberal perspective, is that the accommodations immigrants are expected to make in cultural terms are compounded by penalties they incur simply by virtue of being newcomers: 'we should consider establishing a more formal two-tier citizenship' extended to 'purely economic migrants or certain kinds of refugees' who would be 'allowed temporary residence and the right to work (but not to vote) and be given access to only limited parts of the welfare state'.[36] Goodhart would want these second-class citizens to enjoy 'fewer rights and duties' than their top-tier compatriots.

Liberal nationalism and the diminution of human rights

This supposedly 'just' discrimination is also, arguably, the thin edge of the wedge. National anxieties have moved on from undesirable immigrants to undesirable British-born Muslims since 'Too Diverse?' came out, but Goodhart's communitarian compromises extend far enough to address these too.

Last year, Goodhart admonished the Human Rights Act and its advocates for an 'anachronistic' dislike of the nation-state and endorsed the moral right of the government to revoke the claim of non-citizens to residence if there is 'enough information about someone to be convinced they are a threat but not enough to prosecute'.[37]

Debates about revoking the democratic rights of those who might threaten the nation are relatively embryonic here, but they resonate with a more mature discussion about the 'divisibility' of democracy and human rights in India. The recent paramilitary activities of the Hindu chauvinist RSS have even prompted intellectuals with impeccable anti-fascist credentials to declare that fascists do not deserve democracy. Sumanta Bannerjee, back in 1993, had argued that the majoritarian Sangh Parivar does not respect democracy and that its growth will corrode India's constitutional values, such as secularism. Weighed against the preservation of democracy and the protection of innocent lives, upholding the human rights of fascists appeared to him as a negligible sacrifice.[38]

It is easy to trace Bannerjee's logic in Goodhart's argument – but for fascists read *jihadists* and for 'democratic space' read 'judicial rights'. Both ask the question of why those who violate constitutional (or, in the absence of a constitution, 'national') interests should be democratically tolerated. Both present cases for the decision to suspend the rights of national and constitutional threats to be made by government, who should be allowed to overrule the judiciary. They tell us that we have to be undemocratic and violate the human rights of some to preserve our hard-won democracies and constitutions.

The proposition of cracking a few undemocratic eggs to make a democratic omelette, however reasoned, remains deeply flawed. When the state draws the line between terrorists and citizens, how objective can that line be? When states that have been perceived to be complicit in the institutionalisation of racist and religious prejudice are liberated from the burden of proof and allowed to waive human rights on the basis of suspicion, those who deserve democracy will most likely not be the ones who get it.

Conditional communitarianism

The reintroduction of stop and search saw over 35,800 accosted by the police during 2004 – with a yield of just 455 arrests. It is inevitably being perceived as a tool of harassment; even senior police officers describe it as another stick with which to beat ethnic minorities. In this context, David Blunkett's pronouncement that 'a rights and responsibilities culture really is our goal' deserves to be unscrambled; it does not describe equal empowerment, but the reservation of rights for Britain's chosen citizens, and responsibilities for everyone else.[39]

It speaks of a conditional communitarianism, which is consonant with Goodhart's own recommendations for two-tier or earned citizenship, with newcomers entering on the lowest rung of the ladder. In conditional communitarianism, emphasis is characteristically placed on the obligations we accrue for our entitlements. Out of reciprocity for the rights that are bestowed upon us by the community, we are bound by reciprocal duties. In other words, those responsibilities only arise as a consequence of our enjoyment of rights.

In Goodhart's, and New Labour's, current communitarianism, this conditionality applies to some British residents, but not all. For those who are not yet citizens, and arguably for groups identified as degrading social cohesion (such as Muslims, young black men or Eastern Europeans) the rules do not apply. Even if it may not occur through deliberate policy measures, permission to discriminate by front-line state agencies (and society in general) together with rhetorical implication for the well-being of the nation results in a inequitable ratio of rights to responsibilities. It is acceptable for these groups to be obligated to the national community and, in practice, to enjoy fewer rights in return.

The impact of this discriminatory conditionality is the reason that Goodhart's 'liberal nationalism' would spectacularly backfire. Policies that ride roughshod over human rights in the interests of the common good will only fan perceptions of persecution that already agitate Muslim communities. As Mick Hume wrote in 2006, Muslim community leaders, well drilled in the art of playing the victim after decades of inter-ethnic competition, 'are now ready to elevate any slight into evidence of a wave of Islamophobia'.[40] Although critics such as Munira Mirza are understandably discomfited by Muslim leaders' readiness to brandish the victim card, it is not simply about the psychology of persecution. It is about the impact of repeated liberal exceptionalism on the collective Muslim sense of belonging.

We cannot, on the one hand, trumpet democratic values and individual rights as the cornerstones of a common culture if, on the other, we are prepared to selectively negate those values and rights when they are claimed by citizens who are imagined outside the magic circle of national virtue. We cannot build a common culture of shared citizenship if some citizens are more equal than others; if some have more rights and some have more duties; and if we discriminate against the very citizens we want to bring into the common fold. Don't be surprised if cohesion politics, abetted by discriminatory policies, alienates the very elements of society that excite our anxieties. This is because belonging is reciprocal: no one can belong to anything that rejects them, abuses them or incessantly questions their commitment. And that's something Goodhart chooses to ignore.

For these reasons, his arguments for liberal nationalism have to be firmly rejected. In Goodhart's manifesto for the Left's appropriation of the nationalist ground he only succeeds in dusting off tired traditions. None of what the centre Left really claims to be priority policy issues, such as winning the 'hearts and minds' of young Muslims, creating genuine participatory democracy or renewing the institution of citizenship, will ever be achieved by the vapid conjugation of two of Britain's most redundant ways of thinking.

Both liberalism and nationalism are musty, familiar and quintessentially English – ideological analogies to warm beer and village cricket. And only people who have an appetite for those anachronisms would willingly embrace liberal nationalism. If Goodhart is coaxing young immigrants and those of immigrant descent into the British compact – the benefit claimants and taxpayers of the coming years – he will have to do a lot better than to offer them the bizarre incentives of 'informal ceremonies' at birth registrations or ID cards.[41]

Corrupting liberalism's legacy

The trouble is that Goodhart has betrayed the decent aspects of liberalism – its easy-going attitude to cultural diversity, its rejection of nationalism, its supreme regard for individual rights – and persisted with its most unappealing aspects. After Goodhart's 'realist' facelift, the liberal tradition that he puts under the knife looks noticeably mutilated. Liberalism's abiding legacy is, arguably, the innovation of citizenship as an institution of equal individual enfranchisement, but this is precisely what Goodhart mortgages to mollify Middle England. When a political tradition that has spent its life championing the sanctity of individual rights abandons fundamental process such as *habeus corpus* in the name of 'the common good', it brings its entire mandate into disrepute. A liberalism that defines the relationship between individual and state (or national community) not on the basis of rights but on consensus is so gratuitously communitarian that it cannot rightfully claim the name.

As little more than a corrupted affirmation of past traditions, liberal nationalism will only crown existing political vocabularies as sovereign in the public sphere, stigmatising all others and exacerbating the alienation that can only drive segregation even further.

We cannot build a common culture of citizenship around birth ceremonies, citizenship tests or compulsory voting. Like Conservative Party leader David Cameron, Goodhart protests that we're not the kind of society that is 'comfortable planting flags on our front lawns'.[42] The problem is that his programme for fostering national solidarity isn't a great deal more sophisticated than that. His roll-call of citizen acts is singularly uninspiring and patchy, mainly extensions of existing Labour policies. They barely add up to a programme for renewing citizenship.

In his comparison of citizenship initiatives, Will Kymlicka is critical of the unevenness of the British approach. In Northern American contexts citizenship has been relatively less controversial because it has been publicly (and consistently) distinguished from policy on immigration and multiculturalism even though they are acknowledged to be related. In Britain, by contrast, the configuration is politically electrified by a refusal to separate each aspect either in public discourse or legislation. Kymlicka figures immigration, citizenship and multiculturalism as a three-legged stool whose overall stability is contingent on each leg. Suspicions about the soundness of one leg imperil the other two: confidence in one can conversely reinforce the others. This is his metaphorical assessment of British reforms: 'Britain has adopted the citizenship leg of the stool, but not the other two legs [immigration and multicultural-ism], and the resulting package may be less stable, or at least more controversial.'[43] In other words, revaluing citizenship will inevita-bly benefit from a public commitment to genuine cultural diversity, and this cuts both ways. New Labour may succeed in pre-emptively containing the far Right by pandering to Middle Britain's illiberal opinions to these issues, but its current rhetoric on citizenship is unlikely to enlighten public attitudes on immigration and multi-culturalism, let alone instigate the cultural understanding to take on racism in either its institutional or street faces.

Neither do Goodhart's (or New Labour's) proposals go very far towards empowering citizens who, as Mick Hume has advocated, would be concerned with 'sorting out the kind of society we want to live in together that others might aspire to integrate into'.[44] Com-piling a profile of Goodhart's ideal citizen is like writing out a shopping list of mediocrity: relinquishing 'their native culture to make accommodations for British values', unquestionably accept-ing 'the rule of law and the "legitimate authority" of the state and its institutions' and accepting 'national norms on such things as the role of religion and free speech'.

By any stretch of the imagination, this minimalist citizen would hardly trailblaze towards a better, more just nation. So much of what he expects the British citizen to do involves concession, acquiescence and obedience that we lose every sense of the citizen as a proactive political actor. But, more worryingly, it demonises those virtues on which all democratic societies thrive. Did Doreen Lawrence 'accept the legitimate authority of the state and its institutions' when she rightly hounded the Metropolitan Police for failing to bring the killers of her son to justice? Does that make her any less of a citizen?

The neurotic citizen

Goodhart's interventions resonate at a perfect pitch with Engin Isin's concept of governing through neurosis. There are several compelling reasons to describe his progressive nationalism more appropriately as an exemplary articulation of 'neuro' liberalism.

To briefly gloss Isin's hypothesis, recent history in so-called 'state societies' (by which he means the Anglophone Northern nations) has been marked by the arrival of a new object for government analysis; what he terms the 'neurotic citizen'. Unlike the 'bionic citizen' who is asked to make decisions through rational deliberation and calculation of risk, the neurotic citizen is incited to adjust their behaviour irrationally with no other intention than to manage anxieties. Neurotic citizenship heralds neuropolitics and more specifically, neuroliberalism.[45]

Goodhart ascribes neurosis to a national majority, to Middle England (more of an ideological than demographic majority, of course). I have sought to expose the awkward truth that his policy prescriptions are not geared towards resolving the underlying causes of 'national anxieties' about immigration or identity, but towards managing them. Goodhart practically admits as much by self-consciously referring to them as anxieties, expressly pointing out that 'there's nothing politically dishonourable' about building a manifesto for policy change around 'changes in the public mood'.[46] He insists this to be the case even when 'deeply held beliefs' about the vulnerability of the welfare state do not rest on any evidence that increased immigration places undue fiscal stress on it. In Isin's parlance, it exemplifies a situation where the 'problem is not that there is inadequate knowledge but that knowledge has lost its rational subject.'[47] This describes the movement from the 'bionic' to the neurotic subject: from a subject who calculates risks based on evidential knowledge to a neurotic subject who is habituated to a disposition that bears no relation to knowledge of the 'threat' it is responding to. What Goodhart does throughout his body of work is announce the arrival of this neurotic subject, making a case for the validity of its neurotic claims, and heralding it as the *sovereign* constituency for neo-liberal governance in Britain.

If there is an intriguing ambiguity in the priority of the subject to governmentality in Isin's framework (is the neurotic subject produced by neuroliberal governance or does the latter simply respond to it?), Goodhart is far less reflexive about the role of the state in reproducing anxieties by governing through neurosis.

Isin's neurotic citizen is not an exact match for Goodhart's, however. Because while Isin's neurotic subject is called into citizenship by being asked to adjust its conduct on the basis of its anxieties and insecurities (shared with its neurological species), Goodhart's neurotic subjects are *naturalised* as citizens; there is no expectation on them to calibrate their own conduct to guarantee the 'wealth, health and happiness' of the 'species-body' in question. The burden of expectation, of adjustment and citizenly duty, falls squarely on the shoulders of newcomers to British society. If they do not calibrate their conduct accordingly – by integrating as they are expected to – they become guilty of ratcheting up the neurosis of the subject. In other words, to become citizens newcomers have to govern themselves in response to the anxieties of national majorities.

As Isin says of the neurotic citizen, it develops an acutely sensitised conviction about its entitlements that enables it to make neurotic claims with seeming impunity. It therefore 'shifts responsibility to objects outside of itself with hostility' – as precise a description of the collective neurotic claims of Goodhart's Middle England as you will find.[48]

What Isin doesn't consider (or only briefly in his consideration of 'the border' as the inspiration for his investigation into neurotic citizenship) are those situations where anxieties are not self-manageable, but sedated only by the conduct of others. 'The neurotic citizen' doesn't address whose anxieties, insecurities and fears are responded to by neuropolitics.

While we may all be neurotic (and for different reasons) when it comes to immigration and identity, the anxieties of some can be calmed but others will be inflamed. How are the anxieties of Muslims soothed by ill-timed sniping about the destabilising effects of women wearing the veil? How are the insecurities of all British minorities pacified when they hear that they're not doing enough to integrate?

Neurotic citizenship; illiberal community

Again, this begs the question of what kind of national community Goodhart invokes when its identity is parasitic on the exclusion of others, and when it's cohering cultural values are nothing more than anxieties and insecurities. His is a trembling community constituting itself through fear rather than a confident one assured of its place in the world, and certainly not one that many would aspire to join or proudly serve.

For all the flaws with Goodhart's national imaginary, it does alert us to one irrefutable truth: we cannot begin to develop a normative position on citizenship until we have a normative position on community. Citizenship is not reducible to entitlement, to residence, or to nationality. It is all of these things but one above all – a sense of belonging. This is, as I have shown, reciprocal. It cannot be engineered or prefabricated. It cannot be expected to be 'earned' if the burden of 'earning' falls entirely on one side of the relationship. What might a more inclusive understanding of the relationship between community and belonging look like?

A starting point would be to enable an imagination of community where the individual is written a more important role in its definition. This could be achieved simply by presenting the community as an evolving idea rather than a lost treasure.

Too much writing on Britain addresses it as such a historical artefact, perfected sometime in the early twentieth century and in irreversible disrepair ever since. It's no wonder that citizenship tests worldwide fixate on a combination of pop-cultural and historical trivia. Such an approach, directed towards futures, might also avoid the postcolonial melancholia and neurotic inability to mourn imperial ghosts that nationalist talk inevitably inspires.[49]

Presenting the community as fully formed also suggests that lines of inclusion and exclusion have already been drawn. It therefore *impels* talk of integration. Integration, as Goodhart suggests, is predicated on two subjects: 'immigrant-them' and 'citizen-us'. But while 'citizen-us'[50] are somehow ontologically coterminous with the existence of the community, 'immigrant-them' are not; they are continuously labouring to achieve a form of belonging that 'citizen-us' take for granted. They are constantly under scrutiny, and their often 'visible differences' compromise their acceptance into the predefined community as they fail to map perfectly onto the image of its first citizens. Integration therefore constructs two orders of belonging that cannot be considered equal.

To compound this division, the presentation of a fully formed community denudes membership – read citizenship for national community – of its substantive dimensions. It denies (or at best compromises) the individual a stakeholding in the community because it says that the stakes have already been settled. In other words, the purpose of the community, its character and aspirations, have all been agreed upon. It is up to the individual to work towards the achievement of those purposes and aspirations in the manner deemed fitting for the community; it is not for the individual to question or dissent from those principles. It should be obvious that this kind of membership carries with it a limited sense of stakeholding and, unsurprisingly, is unable to inspire great commitment (or the elusive virtues of solidarity).

Ash Amin has suggested that the twin problems of asymmetric belonging and stakeholding can be resolved through recourse to the principle of 'mutuality' where no groups have claim on being a (political) community's first citizens, but that it develops through 'active engagement with, and negotiation of, difference'. The emphasis is not on being, but becoming: a collaborative project where prior claims are relinquished in the establishment of a new commons 'based on values and principles' to unite the diverse without stigmatising diversity.[51]

If this imagination of community seems hopelessly abstract and unrealisable, it's worth remembering that such solidarities are 'alive and well' in a multitude of locations that escape liberal cartographies of community; it thrives in local pressure groups, in voluntary organisations and in online lobby networks.[52] Many of these communities are informed by a globalised awareness of human rights concerns (the possible basis for a new commons) but they are also voluntary, fluid, and empowering.[53] It's instructive to map this profile of inclusive community onto Hugh Starkey's characterisation of a politically literate citizen. Starkey writes that:

> A politically literate citizen will require knowledge and understanding of human rights, opportunities to develop confident and multiple identities; experience of democratic participation; and skills for social inclusion, for participation and to effect change.[54]

Although such prescriptions for 'active' or 'politically literate' citizens are disturbingly programmatic, the disjuncture between their ideal qualities and the community that Goodhart projects onto Middle England is striking. It is difficult to see how such a citizen could express herself in Goodhart's community, or why she would want to be part of it. People get the communities they deserve; citizens get the nations they deserve too. Those who are receptive to difference, committed to creating new social relations and eliminating social, political or economic exclusion could never form the communities of anxiety that Goodhart sees in contemporary Britain.

Conclusion

To foster genuine citizens, we need to take the bold step of refusing the demands of the 'public mood' in the name of public interest. This involves acknowledging existing anxieties among all sections of society, but not making them the axis around which our long-term aspirations revolve. It involves sending out the clear message that cohesion and national solidarity will not 'inform public policy as an underlying assumption', but that they will evolve as a consequence of policies that promote social, economic and political inclusion.

By retreating into some lazy hybrid of what makes Middle England feel on safe ground, we're missing the opportunity to strive for the real political devolution that many are crying out for. We need to recognise this moment for what it is: not a time to reassure majorities by shrinking into familiar, comfortable positions that relieve the burden of responsibility, but to pose the question of whom liberals and the Left claim to speak for, and how best to serve their interests.

This question becomes important when Goodhart (triumphantly) cites 'the discomfort of settled minorities' caused by incoming strangers who have replaced them as national scapegoats. It tells us that Asians and Afro-Caribbeans are as illiberal as the rest of Britain. But this is not news. Unless xenophobia is the new barometer of integration, such knowledge serves no purpose to a purportedly liberal agenda. Bringing neurotic but ethnically different citizens into the fold of Britishness on the basis of their shared neuroses should not be trumpeted as vindication of liberal tolerance.

It is true enough that all immigrants who remain for long enough become as jealous guardians of their little corner of Britain as those who have been in Britain longer, and become just as bitter when they think that newcomers are stealing their parking spaces, making them queue a little longer or crowding them out of buses. Periodically the centre Right and its more extreme cousins will inflate these issues into headlines for easy – and usually slim – electoral advantage. The question is whether this should compel liberals and the Left to change their colours so cheaply.

Notes

1. Peter Almond, 'Our World Will Crumble by 2018', *Sunday Times*, 11 June 2006, pp. 1, 3, 4.

2. Ibid., p. 1.

3. Stuart Hall and David Held, 'Citizens and Citizenship', in Martin Jacques and Stuart Hall (eds), *New Times: The Changing Face of Politics in the 1990s* (London: Lawrence and Wishart, 1990), p. 175.

4. David Goodhart, 'Too Diverse?', *Prospect*, 95, February 2004, http://www.prospect-magazine.co.uk/article_details.php?id=5835.

5. Ibid.

6. Ibid.

7. Ibid.

8. Brian Barry, *Culture and Equality: An Egalitarian Critique of Multiculturalism* (Cambridge: Polity, 2001), p. 8.

9. Barry's critique of multiculturalism shares features with its anti-racist critique. In common with the latter, Barry complains that it does nothing to change the structure of unequal opportunities, that it perpetuates these inequalities by miring those in the lower reaches of the distribution system in internecine warfare, and that it diverts energies from more substantive issues of poverty and material deprivation. He of course diverges from anti-racist perspectives by refusing to recognise the racial weighting of these inequalities, referring to them only as 'shared disadvantages'. His anti-racist politics would not bear too much dissimilarity to a politics of redistribution: the former would reliably result from the latter. Barry would therefore reject outright the contentions of Balibar (1991) and Goldberg (2002) that racism inheres in the democratic state.

10. Claire Alexander in *Connections*, the quarterly magazine of the Commission for Racial Equality, Autumn 2002, p. 15.

11. David Goodhart, *Progressive Nationalism* (London: Demos, 2006), p. 22.

12. David Goodhart, 'National Anxieties', *Prospect*, 123, June 2006, http://www.prospect-magazine.co.uk/article_details.php?id=7478.

13. Arun Kundnani, 'Death of Multiculturalism', IRR News, 1 April 2002, http://www.irr.org.uk/2002/april/ak000001.html.

14. Les Back, Michael Keith, Azra Kahn, Kalbir Shukra and John Solomos, 'The Return of Assimilationism: Race, Multiculturalism and New Labour', *Sociology Research Online*, 7.2, 2004.

15. Kundnani, 'Death of Multiculturalism'.

16. Kundnani, 'Death of Multiculturalism'.

17. David Blunkett, cited in Back et al., 2.2.

18. David Theo Goldberg, *The Racial State* (Oxford: Blackwell, 2002), p. 206.

19. Alana Lentin, 'Racial States, Anti-Racist Responses', *European Journal of Social Theory*, 7.4, 2004, p. 432.

20. Goodhart, 'Too Diverse?'

21. Goodhart, *Progressive Nationalism*, p. 17.

22. Goodhart, 'National Anxieties'.

23. Bhikhu Parekh, 'Cosmopolitanism and Global Citizenship', *Review of International Studies*, 29.2, 2003, p. 6.

24. Goodhart, 'National Anxieties'.

25. Steven Driver and Luke Martell, 'New Labour's Communitarianisms', *Critical Social Policy*, 52, 1997, p. 30.

26. Bhikhu Parekh, *Rethinking Multiculturalism* (Basingstoke: Palgrave, 2000), p. 273.

27. Amartya Sen, *Identity and Violence: The Illusion of Destiny* (London: Allen Lane, 2006).

28. See Bhikhu Parekh and David Goodhart, 'Not Black and White', *Prospect*, 110, May 2005.

29. Goodhart, *Progressive Nationalism*, pp. 9, 12.

30. Goodhart, 'Too Diverse?'

31. Ibid.

32. Ibid.

33. Goodhart, 'National Anxieties'.

34. Ibid.

35. Goodhart, *Progressive Nationalism*, p. 32.

36. Goodhart, 'Too Diverse?' and 'National Anxieties'.

37. David Goodhart, 'Liberals Should Beware of Giving Rights to People who Hate Us', *Sunday Times*, 28 August 2005, p. 8.

38. Sumanta Bannerjee, 'Sangh Parivar and Democratic Rights', *Economic and Political Weekly*, 21 August 1993, p. 265.

39. An argument made by Britain's highest-ranking Asian police officer, Metropolitan Police Assistant Commissioner Tarique Ghaffur, during the National Black Police Association Conference, Manchester 2006. David Blunkett, 'New Challenges for Race Equality and Community Cohesion in the Twenty-first Century', speech to the Institute of Public Policy Research, 7 July 2004.

40. Mick Hume, 'Latest Drama from the War on Terror: All Quiet on the Walthamstan Front', *The Times*, 18 August 2006, p. 19.

41. Goodhart, 'National Anxieties'.

42. Ibid.

43. Will Kymlicka, 'Immigration, Citizenship, Multiculturalism: Exploring the Links', *Political Quarterly*, 74 (s1), p. 204.

44. Hume, 'All Quiet on the Walthamstan Front'.

45. Engin Isin, 'The Neurotic Citizen', *Citizenship Studies*, 8.3, September 2004, p. 223.

46. Goodhart, 'Too Diverse?'

47. Isin, 'Neurotic Citizen', p. 229.

48. Ibid., p. 233.

49. Paul Gilroy, 'Joined Up Politics and Post-Colonial Melancholia', London Institute of Contemporary Arts Diversity Lecture, 1999.

50. Goodhart, 'Too Diverse?'

51. Ash Amin, 'Multiethnicity and the Idea of Europe', *Theory, Culture & Society*, 21.2, 2004, p. 4.

52. Phillip Legrain, 'Reponses', *Progressive Nationalism*, p. 73.

53. We should remember that there is also a multitude of commonplace communities whose solidarities do not rest upon shared conceptions of the good: think about workplaces, schools, universities and sports clubs. They don't collapse simply because some of their participants have moral disagreements.

54. Hugh Starkey, 'Citizenship, Human Rights and Cultural Diversity', in Audrey Ousler (ed.), *Citizenship and Democracy in Schools: Diversity, Identity, Equality* (Stoke-on-Trent: Trentham, 2000), p. 14.

Chapter 2

Saffron Semantics: The Struggle to Define Hindu Nationalism

No nation can prosper if its more well-to-do citizens actually think that the best way to counter the unspeakable squalor and poverty and disease and illiteracy of the vast majority is to take as little notice of them as possible.*

'India's underachievement in the social and economic spheres has been especially glaring in the view of the rapid growth achieved by many developing countries in the world. Our poor developmental indicators have predictably had an adverse impact on India's global image and influence.†

At the apex of Hindutva's pre-eminence in Indian polity and society, the Left was collectively scratching its head. It was racked by hermeneutic anxiety: was it witnessing homespun fascism, or was this merely the new face of national conservatism?

Outside of lecture halls, away from radical newspapers and removed from diasporic pressure groups, this might appear to be

---

* Pavan Varma, *The Great Indian Middle Class* (London: Penguin, 1998), p. 273
† Bharatiya Janata Party, 'The Chennai Declaration', December 1999.

an overwrought tussle over semantics. But it preoccupied India's Left and its satellites around global academia for several good reasons.

As intellectuals, major and minor, arranged themselves on either side of the debate, the battle lines were carefully drawn. What was at stake went far beyond academic allegiances; the ensuing arguments would not only consecrate new hierarchies of intellectual prestige but also, far more importantly, set the compass for organised resistance to the dominant ideology in the world's largest democracy.

Advocates of fascism – so to speak – were not restricted to those who aligned themselves to Marxism, whether dyed-in-the-wool Hegelians or avowed materialists. It's true that for those on the leftward extremity of this formation, Hindutva's ascent to the peak of the Indian polity symbolised the grandstand confrontation of revolution and anti-revolution, of fascism with freedom. Hindutva was simply the emperor's newest clothes; bourgeois power in saffron skin. The collusion between market liberalisation and religious authoritarianism was far from schizophrenic but simply the latest opium to distract the attention of the masses.

For others still, Hindutva was, ultimately, to be conceived of through an economic frame. While they were sceptical that it mapped perfectly onto past avatars of fascism, that description retained considerable appeal for them. It served to underline the depth of Hindutva's reserves of socio-economic muscle and the severity of its challenge to India's widening democratisation. It was handy as political shorthand for the authoritarian personality that animated the political Right. Hindutva might not be National Socialism, but given the lip service it paid to Aryan fantasies, and what it potentially implied for religious minorities, how better to alert the world to what the Sangh Parivar was capable of?

But it would be wrong to conclude that all of a common ideological hue were comfortable labelling Hindutva as Indian fascism. Because while this debate would offer itself as a forum for the confirmation of ideological allegiances, a space where the Left could regroup, in practice it proved to be more fractious. Those expected to be seen lining up shoulder to shoulder emerged in profound disagreement. It was possible to be an avowed Marxist but argue – from within that heritage – that Hindutva was no more fascistic than Zionism (in fact, for many, that comparison is far more credible). An absence of the structural conditions that presaged the European fascist eras of the early twentieth century precluded historically conscious Marxists from clumsily bundling Hindutva with Mussolini and Hitler's counter-revolutions. By resorting to 'hyphenated' adjectival qualifiers out of 'pugnacious insistence', those on the Left who clung to the importance of a fascist name for Hindutva were moving further and further from arriving at a 'relevant theory of fascism', let alone coming to terms with the singularity of the Hindu nationalist project.[1]

There were other titles for twenty-first century India that implied that the spectre of fascism was looming large, even if it wasn't apparent in its full-blown Hitlerite guise. Meera Nanda's use of the term 'reactionary modernism' (in *Breaking the Spell of Dharma*, 2002, and *Prophets Facing Backword*, 2003) borrows from Geoffrey Herf's collective name for the intellectual culture of pre-1933 Germany, spearheaded by the figures of Oswald Spengler and Martin Junger. Herf describes an alliance between anti-modernist romanticism and technological fascination in their writing; contempt for reason, a selective borrowing of cultural tradition and a romantic commitment to the emancipation promised by technology. Nanda identifies these same characteristics in contemporary Indian cultural psychology: embracing technology but rejecting Enlightenment rationality. This is never more glaring than with the spectacular Hindu packaging of the bomb, which as a bemused Arundhati Roy remarked at the time, was accompanied by stupefying feats of erratic indigenisation by 'jeering, hooting mobs' who claimed nuclear weaponry as an ancient tradition while simultaneously emptying Coke and Pepsi into drains out of protest at foreign culture.[2]

This chapter probes the congruence between India's New Economic Policy (NEP) and the cultural nationalism of the Sangh Parivar. It contends that the dilation of India's middle classes, exponentially achieved through the NEP, has created the conditions under which majoritarianism flourishes. This is a majoritarianism that seeks to continually remake itself in the image of more recognisably 'western' nationalisms. I therefore suggest that Hindutva should not be caricatured as Indian fascism but as a complex and illustrative majoritarian riposte to the threat of widening democratisation posed by groups mobilised around caste and minority religion. I propose that Hindutva's strength is found not in the million-strong membership of the paramilitary

RSS, but in the middle-class backlash against the supposed 'mandalisation' of national politics, the consequent assertiveness of caste-based parties, and the so-called 'plebianisation' of democratic structures. Ultimately, Hindutva seeks to bring into existence an extrapolated idea of Indian citizenship from its fantasy of Hindu community, and this is what the 'Left' has to repel.

Indian fascism?

To begin with, I want to expand on the specific arguments mobilised in defence of understanding Hindutva as an Indian variant of fascism and those that take a contrary position. The commentators I will select as illustrative of either position are Achin Vanaik, a Left-leaning radical whose reflection on India's communalism was ground-breaking when published in 1997, and Aijaz Ahmad, a Marxist who made his name with polemics against the anti-materialism of Edward Said's Orientalism. These totems of Indian intellectualism make an interesting comparison not only because their interventions act magnetically (in the same way that those of Sivanandan and Hall did in Britain over 'new times') but also because their very different framing of Hindu nationalism has profound implications for how resistance should be organised. It illustrates, in microcosm, how the phenomenon of Hindu nationalism became a lightning conductor for fissures within the diffuse ranks of the Indian Left.

The relevance of fascism

I will start with Ahmad's advocacy for the retention of a fascist label for Hindutva in the first place. Even though it comes several years after Vanaik's rejection of that description, it conveys with some dramatic power how Hindutva's threat to Indian democracy had become imminent in the intervening years since Vanaik's *The Furies of Indian Communalism* (1997). Of course, Ahmad was writing at the time of the BJP's clamber to the Centre, after the Left's electoral miscalculations in the general elections, and, most significantly, long enough after the demolition of the Babri Masjid to feel its political aftershocks.

Ahmad makes a case for Hindutva's fascistic character in strong, unequivocal terms. He eschews alternative paradigms in favour of provocative parallels between Hindutva and classical fascisms, and an insistence (Vanaik might see it as 'pugnacious') that where rational nationalism fails, irrational nationalism succeeds.

Inevitably this cannot be divorced from the cyclical anomalies of imperialism, of which global capitalism is its latest face.

Firstly, Ahmad says that Hindutva is to be understood as fascism because that is how it articulates itself. Secondly, he describes fascism as a tendency that is preferentially adopted when others are weak. Thirdly, he identifies this tendency as a lurking danger in societies like India's, given its industrialised infancy and place in the global imperialist chain.

It was the razing of the Babri Masjid, an event that had been frenziedly anticipated for many years, preceded by 'many preparatory spectacles', that Ahmad identifies as the moment at which we were compelled to comprehend Hindutva as fascistic. It was the fascist spectacle the Sangh Parivar had been threatening since the early 1980s. And it was the fact that it was a carefully choreographed spectacle that distinguishes it from other random acts of communalism.[3] It was a premeditated act that had been conceived as a sinister statement of intent by the Sangh Parivar. Ahmad describes it not as the spontaneous combustion of inter-denominational conflict but, in characteristically suggestive terms, as nothing less than 'a fascist assault on the Indian Constitution'.[4]

As anyone with a passing knowledge of the VHP's patiently orchestrated agitation will know, what was staged as the release of pent-up collective Hindu frustration was nothing of the sort. But the Sangh's great achievement was the veneer of spontaneity it brought to a meticulously calculated intervention designed to elicit a divisive response:

> What was visually the most striking, however, was the immaculate methodical staging of mass hysteria and the orgiastic destruction; the spectacle had been most carefully prepared but then released with the force of a hurricane that left much of the country simply stunned.[5]

Like so much of the Sangh's ideological machinery it was designed for electronic consumption: video cassettes both of the destruction and subsequent acts of violence were made available throughout the country to be replayed in domestic comfort (and reportedly not only for the viewing pleasure of men indulging in violent voyeurism).

But what marks Ahmad's analysis as different to others is that he is prepared to look beyond the fascist spectacle itself to the conditions in which it is received. Because Ahmad describes fascism as an intermittent 'tendency' he is saying that it can only occur under favourable cultural conditions.

By this he means a tolerance towards the forms of violence that fascism (and authoritarianism in general) perpetrates. He talks about this as a licence for atrocity – like the pogrom in Gujarat – that is awarded on the back of a 'culture of cruelty'. This goes far beyond the institution of state terror. Fascism here is not recognisable by the militarisation of the state or even by acts of terror waged against citizenry. What brings fascism into being is anaemic resistance to those acts by citizens, built up gradually over years of casual acceptance, and by the enactment of routinised violence by society at large. Ahmad detects in the everyday operation of gender and caste violence the 'making of a fascist project'.[6] When tensions between caste fractions are resolved through arson, and dowry shortfalls are redressed through torture or death, then state pogroms assume the legitimacy of consent.

These tendencies and consents are born, he suggests, out of the insufficient penetration of secularism in Indian society. Without a 'revolutionary transformation of cultural life' the potential for 'fascist resolutions is particularly strong'.[7] India is destined to vacillate between fascism and secularism as a direct reflection of its democratic and industrial infancy. It is invariably so in 'semi-industrialized societies such as ours which have inherent powerful traditions of classicism, cultural conservatism, and authoritarian religiosity, and which have failed to undertake revolutionary trans-formations of cultural life and a radical redistribution of material resources.'[8] It's a suggestion that Meera Nanda would agree with; hence her calls for a belated Indian Enlightenment.

For Ahmad this leads to the conclusion that fascism is irreducible to an abstract paradigm: it is discernible only through examination of the 'basic structure, actions, and objectives' of the movements that arise out of such societies. No two fascisms can therefore be alike, and it is futile to analogise with 'the German experience' as the sovereign example. He reasons that every country gets the fascism it deserves. The historical form of the fascism always shifts according to the historical, economic, political, social, even religious and racial physiogomony of a given country, and it is useless always to seek an approximation with the German experience.[9]

In this sense Ahmad's use of fascism is descriptive rather than strictly bound by the conventions of Marxist approaches. He is not as concerned with producing an inventory of the fascist state as he is with the dynamics of Hindutva as a movement. Though he writes from a nominally Marxist position, the organisation of fascist power and its complicity with state operations is arguably sub-ordinate to his emphasis on Hindutva's ideological dimensions, its motifs and goals. This is exemplified by his elevation of Ayodhya as symptomatic of Hindutva's fascistic character: its articulations of youth (the presence of the Bajrang Dal), the militarisation of political behaviour, its emotional register, its glorification of violent masculinity.

But if this non-Marxist account of contemporary India as under siege by fascism may seem alarmist, it is perhaps only because it answers to alternative descriptions that were more relaxed about the possible incursions that Hindutva would make into the polity.

The irrelevance of fascism

Achin Vanaik (in *Furies*) was one of those who pre-emptively denied that Hindutva (or 'Hindu communalism', as he called it) could rightfully be known as fascism, either in the classical un-disputed sense attributed to interwar Germany, Italy and Spain or as a 'Third World' fascism.

As evidence Vanaik cites the popular qualification of fascism in contemporary descriptions. Since it is hardly ever used nakedly in reference to occurring or recent forms of authoritarianism he concludes that the (predominantly) Marxist perseverance with the term betrays 'unease and pugnacious insistence'. If judged purely on the basis of the names given to contemporary movements or states it would appear that fascism lives on only in political sociology's hall of mirrors; distorted and diluted as quasi-fascism, pseudo-fascism, proto-fascism, and neo-fascism. Very few commentators dare to ditch the prefix. So why persist with it? Vanaik suggests it is to lend credibility to the Marxist claim that fascism will inevitably recur as long as capitalism exists, as a resolution to the system's habitual and cyclical crises. The problem is that this credibility is stretched when:

> It has recurred in forms which leave one uncertain just how fascist it is or even whether it belongs to the genus. Such hyphenated fascisms are sometimes used simply to suggest that characteristics of some fascist entities of the past exist in its contemporary look-a-

likes. This usage has descriptive value but hardly offers much in the search for a contemporaneously relevant theory of fascism.[10]

So it's not so much that Vanaik fails to see how fascism is manifest in Hindu nationalist movements as how apprehending it in that way can be of service to the Left's response to Hindutva. Instead, he has grave reservations about fascism as a conceptual tool (even if it retains some use as a label for 'political phenomena' and as a 'descriptive term of abuse').[11]

To this end he disputes the need to contemporise theories of fascism in light of the behaviour of seemingly fascistic movements in favour of 'newer and better ways of understanding newer, even generic, phenomena thrown up by the late capitalism of our times'.[12]

Vanaik takes this further by seeking to locate Hindu nationalism in the context of India's democratic history rather than a pantheon of potentially fascistic movements.

He sees the conditions for Hindutva's pre-eminence not in the cyclical failures of bourgeois capitalism but in the collapse of the Nehruvian consensus that defined India since the nation-state's inception. Hindutva thrives in the ideological vacuum born out of the uncertainty that has followed Congress's progressive implosion (and communalisation). Consider the fact that India had six prime ministers between 1947 and 1989; between 1989 and 2008 it has had eight.

But at the same time it will not do to underestimate Hindu nationalism. It is not a transient movement, but one that has lain periodically dormant since independence (and very much alive since before then). Fascist theories simply cannot scale its depth or its reach, its ubiquity or its versatility, embodied by the diversity of organisations – from political parties to paramilitary groups to charities – who drape themselves in some shade of saffron. Vanaik is right to warn that 'in a sense that phenomenon [Hindutva] is more deep-rooted that fascism, more enduring and more difficult to completely or comprehensively destroy'.[13]

Not fascism, majoritarianism

In presenting an overview of these two noticeably incongruent ideas on the character of Hindu nationalism I have not sought to depict them as mutually exclusive, even if they disagree on the relevance of fascism as the prism through which to see it. In fact it's possible to be sympathetic to both Vanaik and Ahmad, as contradictory as that might seem.

Ahmad's impassioned perseverance with the fascist paradigm is not wholly unconvincing, especially when taken in the light of the Gujarati pogroms. It could well be argued that denying Hindutva's fascistic tendencies is delusional given the Gujarat state's connivance and reported complicity in the backlash to the burning of the Sabarmati Express. Though Hindutva hasn't arisen as a reaction to capitalist crisis (the Marxist paradigm) and doesn't revolve around the deification of a charismatic leader (non-Marxist), its origins and hardline tactics, its grass-roots operations, are unmistakably fascist or inspired by fascism.

That said, Hindutva doesn't manifest itself in these terms on an everyday basis. What it indisputably presents is an alternative to Nehru's vision of India that will shift India's political centre to the Right, slowly but deliberately. As Vanaik concludes, Hindutva's appeal is that it offers what no other movement in India can: a unifying project that can equip the nation to face the world on confident terms, 'culturally united through a clarification, recognition, acceptance and consolidation of its nationalist essence'.[14] There will be 'fascistic' excesses to this project, as Gujarat and Ayodhya tesify, but they will be presented as incidental to India's elevation to international prestige. What the Left has to do is approach Hindutva with that in mind; not as fascism but as a majoritarian vision of India's place in the world with authoritarian consequences. How it contests this vision, and on what terrain, will therefore be paramount to its success.

Hindu majoritarianism and the New Economic Policy

To illustrate why Hindutva is better apprehended as majoritarianism than fascism,

I will offer an overview of the BJP's ideological manipulation of market liberalisation (a process begun, ironically, by the current prime minister Manmohan Singh, then a finance minister in Narasimha Rao's short-lived coalition). While much has been written on how India's nuclear programme has been Hinduised by the Sangh, a more sustained (and therefore most insidious) attempt has been made to align economic reform with Hindu India's civilisational destiny. Imagining the economic nation is integral to imagining the nation as a whole, and in particular to its self-perception in the world order.[15]

Congress socialism and Indian servility

Out of power, the Sangh Combine were deft exploiters of that self-perception, which had suffered some heavyweight blows in the twenty years preceding the BJP's accession to power. While the brotherhood of Bandung crumbled and India lost its political leadership of the Third World, its economic sluggishness under the stifling rule of 'Licence Raj' (especially relative to South-East Asian neighbours) slid India further down the scale of international recognition.

This is duly reflected in a succession of Sangh Parivar pronouncements that attribute India's economic degradation to the socialist policies of Congress nationalism. They mobilise the nebulous semantics of *swadeshi* to denounce socialism as divisive and hence anti-national. In political opposition, the BJP correlated India's material underdevelopment with the surrender of its national sovereignty and concluded that paths towards socialism recuperate colonial dependencies.

The Sangh argued that by reducing itself to a debtor country, a servile satellite of the West, India had stagnated behind the colonial frontier. Although the economy had grown overall under the successive Nehru administrations, the state had been borrowing heavily from the IMF and World Bank (who forced Congress's hand into the economic reforms and NEP). This propagated the image of India as a lowly parasite among the community of nations, its economic dependence on multinational organisations leaving it languishing, in the eyes of the BJP, at 'the bottom of the international pile, an abject basket case that has to beg regularly for alms from international agencies which treat it with disdain'.[16] The BJP jeered India's leaders for mortgaging the nation's sovereign spirit (*swadeshi*) to donor agencies as the country had fallen further and further into dependency. The foreign ownership of Indian resources had, in turn, wounded national pride and degraded the national spirit. This theme of deprivation at external hands, invoked time and again to decry the evils of colonialism, has been recycled to describe India's failure to control its own modernity. The following excerpts from RSS and BJP propaganda index national indebtedness and underdevelopment to the erosion of sovereignty:

> While Independent Bharat started with a balance of Rs. 18,000 crores, the Bharat of 1992 is in debt to the tune of 400,000 crores.

The so-called 'Industrial Revolution', supposed to have led to the prosperity of the West, was made possible from the post-Plassey loot from Bharat. With no such plundered capital, Bharat obviously could not reach the heights of material progress scaled in the West. This externally induced impoverishment has been used by the West to make Bharat a debtor country [. . .] there is a need to recreate the self-confidence of the people of Bharat. Not so long ago, Bharat produced such superior yarn that Britain had to ban the sale of textiles from Bharat. Likewise, Bharat produced the best steel in the world [. . .] [T]hat the indigenous science and technology of Bharat were deliberately crushed by the West is undisputed. Curiously, the same colonialist intervention from the West continues even on the eve of the twenty-first century, now in the form of GATT, World Bank and IMF conditionalities.[17]

This narrative India finds itself 'lagging behind' and 'reduced to 'beggars'. India's 'externally induced impoverishment' had recapitulated its colonial bondage, and it now goes with 'begging bowls before the affluent nations and multinationals'.[18] This resonates with a popular perception among the provincial and urban lower middle classes who felt that 'betting on socialism' has been a major historical miscalculation that has left India stranded among the ruins of a fatigued and defeated ideological empire.

The BJP has been adept at nurturing contempt for socialism and turning that contempt to its advantage. While in opposition it assaulted the Congress as an anti-nationalist party, claiming it had staked and was bartering with India's very sovereignty by reducing it to a debtor country in the mismanaged gamble that it had advertised as socialist development. It rhetorically pointed to the pollution of national identity by foreign economic governance, seeking to leverage popular disillusion into a coherent nationalist revolt. As importantly, it spoke in sympathy with the people, consistently identifying itself with their plight with avuncular praise such as that it 'is proud of the patriotic dedication and daring of the people who are not enamoured of the structural adjustments in alien clutches and cosmetic changes on borrowed plumage'.[19]

Socialism as cultural imperialism

The Hindu nationalist denunciation of socialism took place in a culturalist idiom. Socialism was regarded not as an aspiration or alternative to a hegemonic world system but as the cultural beachhead of neo-colonialism. It was portrayed as having been imported by a Congress comprador class bent on subduing indigenous technologies and knowledge under the thumb of Enlightenment rationality. Nowhere in Sangh appraisals of social-ism is there a recognition of Nehru's understanding of it as the 'uplift of the poor' and, according to his own unique definition, of 'giving every Indian the fullest opportunity to develop himself according to [his or her] capacity'.[20]

Instead it was ideologically bundled with other tenets of the Nehruvian consensus responsible for shackling India to the ethno-centric master-narratives of the West. Instead of interrogating how global capitalism had fractured the nation along the vast fault lines of property and dispossession, the Sangh Parivar has articulated national disunity around the cultural identities of Indian against alien, indigenous versus Western intelligences.[21]

This was encapsulated by Hindu nationalism's repudiation of Third World solidarity by repeatedly insisting that any kind of outside influence was invidious to India's national spirit. It con-demned socialism as the voluntary perpetuation of foreign rule in India. Since it is not a 'Bharatiya idea', it is depicted as cancerously aggravating a series of debilitating reactions that has gradually induced the infirmity of the national soul. Not only did it stifle growth and roadblock entrepreneurship, but also its manner of sectioning pockets of society against each other is culpable for national disunity and dishonour. David Frawley's rallying mani-festo, *Awaken Bharata*, elaborates on these themes to denounce socialism because of its over-reliance on the state. Frawley articu-lates a reasoned neo-liberal rejoinder that echoes Gurcharan Das' argument that socialist policies discouraged entrepreneurship and that market liberalisation stimulates economic growth. He writes that it had reduced citizens to 'beggars', and 'wards of the state' clamouring for its patronage:

It [socialism] does not encourage independence and effort in the masses but turns them into children and wards of the state. Leftist political leaders in India, as elsewhere, found that they could easily control such uneducated masses, fashioning them into vote banks under the promise of government rewards, which encourages the government to keep the people backward [. . .] The result is that socialism stifles economic development and a large section of the country becomes dependant upon government favours, which

further creates corruption and bribery. This has happened to some
extent in all socialist states but India is among the worst. The
nation instead of raising all of its people together, has its different
classes trying to feed off one another and fighting with each other
for government patronage.[22]

From Frawley's critique it is easy to deduce why majoritarian
politics are so hostile to socialism. Firstly, poor minorities are often
perceived as being carried by the socialist state; in the particular
instance of India under Nehruvian socialism, these minorities were
often religious (such as Muslims). Hindu nationalism is thus
instinctively equated with secularism by the Hindutva ideologue
because both are deemed to put the (cultural) majority at a
disadvantage. Under alien regimes, the estrangement of the cultural
majority from the state is correspondingly projected as an inevitable
outcome of its undemocratic bias.

This virulent anti-socialism takes its precedence from Hindutva's
Spenglerian insistence on India's cultural exceptionalism. It follows
that Hindu culture has an innate temper which must govern all its
cultural products from mathematics to poetry and inform its
political philosophy in particular.[23] This 'strategically essentialist'
apprehension of the national culture therefore rejects socialism as a
supreme form of imperialism – as violence against this cultural
essence. Correspondingly, national liberation is conceptualised in
irreducibly culturalist terms. As Nanda observes, a brigade of
subalternist critics of modernity, led by Partha Chatterjee, Dipesh
Chakrabarty and Ashis Nandy, has risen in defence of this view of
Indian culture as ineffable and exceptional through their own
efforts to answer back to the epistemic violence of Eurocentrism.[24]

An excuse for neo-liberalism: *swadeshi* capitalism

This disavowal of socialism as culturally inimical and intellectually
alien to India, coterminous with a persistent anti-statism, has had
profound implications for the passage of neo-liberal ascendancy.
Through the deeply held reciprocity between political and intellectual formations, the return of capitalism to ideological centre stage
– in its latest and most baleful avatar – passed without observation
in significant quarters of the postcolonial academy.

So a consequence of amputating capitalism from the exchange
between metropole and periphery has been to allow capitalism itself
to re-emerge innocent of its operational role in the production of

racialised disadvantage. The failure of socialism to successfully enfranchise the poor Indian populace is expressly contrasted with the possibilities for national rejuvenation made available by economic liberalisation. Neo-liberalism is therefore deemed to be instrumental in the destiny of the Hindu *rashtra*.

Instrumentality

As the Third World imperative to create alternative social formations has subsided into a preoccupation with producing customised cultures of capitalism, capital itself has been rearticulated as expressive of a cultural essence. Ultimately this has meant suturing a rampant neo-liberalism with the nationalist conceit of a sovereign national culture. It has been seamlessly reworked into the nationalist 'cultures of capitalism', which, having been popularised in East Asia, have now become the official rhetorical stance of the Hindu nationalist BJP in India. Gurcharan Das' conclusion that despite being the original 'owners of the reform packages', the 'BJP behave as though wealth and poverty is a secondary issue' is a disingenuous alibi for the fraternal instrumentality between neo-liberalism and cultural nationalism.

A significant rhetorical move in the domestication of the latest capitalist offensives has been to depict the global economy as instrumental to the (Hindu) nation. It has sought to portray the global economy as an arena in which India can parade its national achievements. To this end, the information or knowledge industries have been to the BJP what the economic historian Andrew Wyatt calls a 'political boon'.[25] The now deposed prime minister Atal Bihari Vajpayee has used India's growth in these sectors to inflate India's global status, going as far as to declare India a 'software superpower'.[26]

Vajpayee's speech on Independence Day 2003 exemplified the centrality of the NEP to the identity of the Hindu *rashtra*. Once the opening speech establishes the unity of India around a set of conventionally popular figures (the martyrs of the independence struggle, the soldiers patrolling the Kashmir border, and the national flag itself) Vajpayee orientates the remainder of his speech towards the economy. He goes on to congratulate a spectrum of economic agents, from farmers and workers to businessmen and professionals. The software industry is singled out for special praise as a source of 'dynamism' that provides employment and boosts exports. The continued high growth of these areas assures the government's pledge that India will be a 'Developed Nation' by 2020.[27] The predilection for the 2020 benchmark, reiterated by Jaswant Singh among other ministers, is indicative of the critical importance of economic India's global prestige to the Hindutva project. Capitalism is instrumental to Hindu nationalism because 'development' is indispensable to the rising expectations of the middle classes and guarantees the support of its electoral heartland. It is also expressly set in opposition to Nehruvian socialism, which is characterised as perpetuating colonial captivity and the flow of wealth from India to the West.

Other senior ministers, including former deputy prime minister (home minister at the time) L. K. Advani, have argued that liberalisation is an inevitable and irreversible process to which India is fully committed:

> Neither its reality nor its irreversibility can be questioned. If anything, it is a development that bids fair to advance rapidly and in ways that cannot even be fully envisioned today. This being the truth, any position that opposes, and seeks to roll back globalisation *per se* is as futile as it is untenable.[28]

In the 2004 'Vision 2020' document, published to coincide with the ultimately unsuccessful re-election campaign, this substantive shift in economic policy was given equally concrete expression. Globalisation is openly embraced and geared to consolidating India's position in global corporate capitalist frameworks. The utopian idealism of Deendayal's Integral Humanism – together with its aspiration of Third-Worldist autonomy – has been dispensed with now that it is no longer politically expedient. Though it retains the vocabulary of *swadeshi*, it does so for emotive affect and cachet rather than any commitment to its original connotations of indigenous self-reliance. The BJP has redefined it to the generalised sense of 'a philosophy of India First'. More expressly, the document states that their concept of *swadeshi* (as distinct from earlier usages) can be apprehended as

> a strong, efficient and high-growth Indian economy, in which Indian products, services and entrepreneurs dominate the domestic and global markets. This can be achieved by making Indian products and services competitive on both cost and quality.

According to Praful Bidwai, this only codifies what the BJP has actively pursued since its accession to power at the centre.[29] The neo-liberal bent of economic policy is 'irreversible' and its opposition 'futile' because such a reversal would compromise the compact between national bourgeois interests and foreign capital. Due to their very nature, the bourgeois classes are incapable of being either autonomously national or globalised, but maintain their elite status through a perpetually negotiated dependence on both national and foreign capital.[30] Today, all sections of Indian industry seek to collaborate with outside capital. The more flexible, manageable associations with capital enabled by the growing sophistications of globalisation have been widely embraced by India's industrial elite.[31] If anything, globalisation and the race for advanced industrial technology are likely to exacerbate the developing world's structural dependence on foreign capital.[32]

Swadeshi

The second rhetorical strategy of this domestication of late capitalism is its customisation to Hindu culture. This move is more expressly ideological and resonant with the theme of Hinduism's messianic role in national and world society. Its place in repeated instances of the BJP's political language – including the 'Vision 2020' document – betrays an accommodation of RSS extremities in the BJP's manifesto.

The two discursive strategies – instrumentality and indigenisation – are mediated by the concept of *swadeshi,* central to both narratives. As the rhetorical locus of both, it metonymically stands in for Hindutva itself in the ideological triangulation between the politics of culturalism, neo-liberalism and cultural nationalism.

Swadeshi's appropriation into the logic of the Hindu culture of capitalism is advanced further in Advani's address to the Federation of Indian Chambers of Commerce and Industry in 1998, 'Globalisation on the Solid Foundations of *Swadeshi*'. Advani cites *swadeshi* as a compass with which to navigate globalisation, reiterating the imperative for India to serve 'as a light unto itself' and preserve its cultural sovereignty. What Advani excludes from *swadeshi*'s semantic compass is as revealing as what he includes; it does not denote antagonism to foreign capital's assault on India's sovereignty because capital itself is benign, posing little threat to security or sovereignty.[33] The nebulous threat of global capitalism is casually mentioned as something to be wary of, but is negligible in the context of the entire speech. Advani is unequivocal, however, on the issue of protectionism and chastises those who might seek to appropriate *swadeshi* as the basis of Indian 'isolationism'.[34] It is worth quoting from an extended section of the speech where Advani substitutes *swadeshi* for Indian sovereignty, as the expression of a cultural ethos and a messianic light not only for India but also for the world:

> By *swadeshi* I mean the belief that there can be no uniform solution to the problems of economic and social development in a world which is both inherently diverse and also unequally structured today because of historical factors. Nature abhors uniformity. That is why in the social sphere too we see an immense degree of diversity, all of which tied together by an underlying unity. Many of the economic and other problems in the 20th century have been created by the attempts to impose a uniform solution – be it the capitalist model or the socialist/communist model – on the whole world. [. . .] This is all the more true in the case of a continental country like India which is sustained by the world's oldest living civilisation. India cannot simply ape models and solutions worked out elsewhere. We must design our own path of economic development, confident in our ability to do so and proud of our many national achievements not only after we have become independent but also in our millennia-long history. Our achievements in culture, especially, are of great relevance to the world community facing an uncertain and worrying future. That is what I mean by *swadeshi*. It has a positive content and thrust.[35]

In the new economic imaginary, *swadeshi* is extolled as the spirit of national pride and power rather than an insular retreat from globalisation. It is abstracted from specific economic practice to refer to a commitment to Indian social values, which must be protected from the erosive effects of global integration.

Swadeshi here is not depicted in conflict with globalisation (as it is in the more archaic ideologies of early Hindutva practitioners) but re-imagined as a critical 'pre-requisite' to meeting the 'challenges of globalisation'; of preserving 'our identity without compromising our sovereignty and self respect'.[36] In the policy document *A Humanistic Approach to Economic Development* (1992) for example, the BJP proposes a '*swadeshi* of a self-confident hardworking modern nation that can deal with the world on terms of equality', with *swadeshi* defined as the 'self-confidence to be able to face challenges of a rapidly changing world which is arming itself all the time with new technologies . . . a confidence and capability in consonance with our cultural mores and ethos'.[37]

Hindu cultures of capitalism

This resonates very clearly with what Arif Dirlik (1997) writes of contemporary cultures of capitalism in the developing or Third World. The evolution of this breed of cultural nationalism follows the contours of a series of historical ruptures, including the anti-colonial movements, the geopolitical configuration of the cold and post-Cold War eras, and the influences of the Bretton Woods institutions. The new elites in these nations have found their efforts to integrate at economic, political and social levels hamstrung by the interventions of 'globalisation and internationalisation' on the national economy. Having compromised control and sovereignty at these fundamental levels, they have sought integration at a cultural level by expressing national cultural essences which are capable of moderating the 'disruptive forces of global capitalism':

> Neither should it be very surprising that, in many cases, these national essences are constructed to legitimise incorporation into Global Capitalism; in other words, to demonstrate that the national culture in essence in one that is consistent with, if not demanding of, participation in a capitalist economy.[38]

The 'incorporation' of 'national essences' into global capitalism rests upon a fundamentally culturalist apprehension of capitalism. In order for the national culture in essence to be 'consistent' with participation in a capitalist economy, capitalism itself needs to be conceptually described as singularly *cultural* rather than material. Such 'culturalised' readings of capitalism excuse it from the production and operation of discriminating disenfranchisement nationally and globally. This figurative act also brings to mind Jean Baudrillard's concept of seduction, where the visible (or material) is rendered invisible (or symbolic).

Its logic animates, in equal measure, the articulation of Hindu cultures of capitalism in the mainstream political language of the BJP and the more explicit cultural fascism of the RSS. It authorises ideologues such as David Frawley to proclaim that the Western capitalist culture's 'ability to truly represent freedom and the individual remains compromised unless it allies itself with a higher spiritual force', which is 'what the Hindu tradition can impart to it' and to declare that the 'the true global age will be one in which science and religion become reconciled'.[39]

This spiritually tempered materialism is aptly described by Frawley as an authentic *'Bharatiya vaishya dharma'* (roughly translated as an 'Indian business ethic') to guide India into the twenty-first century.[40] It articulates the hybridised inflection of both Hindu and business cultural 'essences' in the formation of a syncretic ethic. The 'Hindu ethic' is declared as a challenge to Western 'capitalist, socialist' and 'religious groups', together with their attendant 'destructive behaviour, moral corruption, propaganda distortions, and efforts at world domination'.[41] Its uniqueness, like all cultural nationalist claims, is blatantly overdetermined. The integration of an essentialised civilisational ethos with capitalist development places it, ideologically, with a cluster of religiocultural revivalisms which have coincided with intensifications of market liberalisation. It is this phenomenon that Dirlik refers to as to the creation of developing-world 'cultures of capitalism' but which can be located in the much broader rightward drift of both intellectual and political formations. In the conceptually incongruous juxtapositions between 'Hindu', 'business' and 'ethic' is a open revelation of Hindutva's commitment to sustaining national inequalities in the interests of the cultural elite in whose image it is made.

The economic reforms presaged monumental implications for India as a distinctive historical project. If we accept Crane's conviction that 'representations of the economy are part and parcel of specific definitions of a nation', then the fall-out of the great historical conjunctures of the early 1990s dismembered the soul of Nehru's India.[42] In the course of a few weeks, Manmohan Singh, with Narasimha Rao's endorsement, 'shifted the nation's centre of gravity'.[43] India could no longer be defined by state socialism but was now identified with advanced capitalism.[44]

The role of swadeshi *capitalism in majoritarian discrimination*

Though it is patently misleading to claim that the Sangh Parivar speaks with one voice on questions of economic nationalism or that the BJP's 'calibrated globalisation' follows edicts from RSS *pracharak*s, it is critical to apprehend that Hindutva's relationship to neo-liberalism is founded on fraternity not coercion.

A discriminatory state that actively sustains symbolic and material inequalities between rightful citizens and national Others is indispensable to the realisation of an exclusive Hindu *rashtra*. The NEP is consistent with these aspirations because it enhances the status and financial muscle of Hindutva's constituent communities relative to the progressive disenfranchisement of a racialised poor. These outcomes do not only discriminate in favour of the imagined Hindu *rashtra*, but also ideologically dovetail with the symbolic demonisation of overwhelmingly poor religious minorities.

The motivations of eschewing a class for a 'community' analysis are evident when the elite moorings of Hindutva's cultural nationalism are interrogated. Like all cultural nationalisms, Hindutva imagines the nation with the economically dominant identity within it, which is indisputably that of the predominantly upper-caste Hindu capitalist class. Threats to it from the disenfranchised and demonised minorities that often form the bulk of the working classes are managed by diverting class consciousness into the fantasies of a nationalist imagination, weaning them away from the 'progressive projects of socialism and anti-imperialist nationalisms'.[45] A universal feature of cultural nationalism, according to Desai, is to order its 'modernist core of revolution' around its dominant class position:

In this form, cultural nationalism does provide national ruling classes a sense of their own identity and purpose, as well as a form of legitimisation among the lower orders. [. . .] Cultural nationalism is, in every country, usually structured around the culture of the economically dominant classes, with higher or lower positions accorded to other groups within the nation relative to it. These positions correspond, on the whole, to their economic positions, and as such, it provides the dominant classes, and concentric circles of their allies, with a collective national identity.[46]

The social compulsion for Hindu nationalism – particularly over the last twenty-five years – has therefore been staged in correspondence with the growing prominence of the economically dominant classes in whose image Hindutva is made and whose interests it serves.[47]

The rise and rise of the middle classes

Global capitalism, domesticated by the BJP to become a cultural energy serving to invigorate the Hindu *rashtra,* has nurtured a massive internal bourgeoisie which has swelled year on year in the era of the New Economic Policy. India's elite has been the chief beneficiary of the NEP. Poverty, meanwhile, (in real terms) has been so inadequately managed that it has failed to decline in the thirteen years since the reforms were inaugurated.

The BJP has positioned itself at the heart of the neo-liberal consensus. Having depicted Congress socialism as anti-modernist as well as anti-nationalist, and in place of its crumbling economic vision, the BJP conjured the seductive prospect of a technologically progressive, consumer-friendly nation anchored by a vibrant and resolutely sovereign culture for the consuming middle classes. In a press statement they claimed to stand 'for a modern and progressive India, open to new ideas, new technology and fresh capital. A modern India to the BJP is not a westernized India; a pale copy of the Western economic models'.[48]

The neo-liberal turn took place against the evolving transparency between the economic interests of Hindutva's core constituencies – the petty bourgeois and middle classes – at the levels of both rhetoric and policy.[49] The growing vociferousness of the latter demographic, and its hunger for upwardly mobile consumption, meant they were the principal actors 'pushing the politicians to liberalise and globalise'.[50]

The Sangh Parivar was able to articulate these consumerist desires as part of the nationalist imaginary by virtue of a subtle narrative which sought to domesticate the public currency of the concepts of 'globalisation' and 'liberalisation'. I have argued that this was sought by expressing capitalism as an instrumental and 'culturalised' essence. Woven together, this has been the logic of what we might term a Hindu 'culture of capitalism', driven by a highly autonomous bourgeois bloc happy to surrender the ambition of an idealistic 'Third World' liberated from structural dependence.

The size, shape and character of this first-world formation are heavily contested by those who would either seek to fly the NEP flag or denounce it. Gurcharan Das, by way of obvious example, applauds the 'rise and rise of the middle class' as the democratisation of the Indian economy and the indices of India's unbound development. Through their 'dynamism', 'social mobility' and 'consumerism', the middle classes vivify the opportunities made possible once the dead hand of the 'Licence Raj' was lifted from an immiserated India. But Das' descriptions are problematic because he fails to distinguish between the bourgeoisie and the petty bourgeoisie, and because he aggregates them into a consumerist category rather than into distinguishable socio-economic classes. In fact, Das assigns middle-class status on the strength of consumption by following the example of the National Council of Applied Economic Research (NCAER) to benchmark a specific level and quality of consumer spending.[51]

Achin Vanaik and Praful Bidwai, who speak in conspicuous opposition to the NEP, insist that middle-class growth is more accurately understood as the dilation of the upper crust of Indian society.[52] The distinction is significant rather than merely semantic. While Das excitedly talks up India's economic miracle, they regard the NEP era with greater circumspection. For them it represents less a national revolution than an entrenched bifurcation between India's fortunate and unfortunate where the former are 'culturally, economically, and politically' 'closer to Northern elites and their own kin in North America and Europe' but alienated from the poorer, less educated and less globalised latter.[53] This alienation is the thin edge of an effectively racialised disparity which threatens to make the fracture of the dispossessed and proprietary unbridgeable.

Hindutva and the growing anti-poor bias

The alienation also has to be historicised in the context of majoritarian reprisals for supposed minority appeasement in the 1980s and 1990s. The 'mandalisation' of state policy, preceded by the 'plebianisation' of democratic structures, incited a growing middle-class resentment towards India's poor.

The supposed beneficiaries of Nehruvian socialism were regarded as recipients of state largesse and impediments to Middle India's aspiration to capitalist parity with the developed world. Increasing numbers of reservations of public-sector jobs and university places were viewed as unnecessary social engineering that undermined natural societal meritocracy. While Das celebrated the 1991 reforms as the unshackling of the Indian economic 'elephant', other social commentators look back on that moment (perhaps together with the Mandal report) as the dawn of an ideological backlash against the poor and the justification for the pursuit for individual wealth.

Middle-class alienation from Congress ideology reached its apotheosis with the acceptance of the Mandal report by V. P. Singh's Congress administration in 1991.[54] Perceptions of Congress pandering to religious minorities and backward castes – which coincidentally form the bulk of India's poor – had been inflamed by the concession to Muslim fundamentalists by Rajiv Gandhi in the Shah Bano case but truly reached a watershed in 1991.[55] On the recommendation of the Second Backward Classes Commission (the Mandal Commission), Singh announced a 27 per cent reservation of jobs in the central government services and public institutions for 'socially and educationally backward classes', aside and separate from the 22.5 per cent allocated to Scheduled Castes and Tribes. Implemented publicly in the service of 'social justice', the Mandal commission broke the back of middle-class patience with left-wing ideologies of any hue.

The anti-poor bias was therefore just one arm of a comprehensive assault on the Nehruvian consensus. The BJP in particular brought business classes with 'the people' as a whole together as victims of a misconceived political arrangement known as 'Nehruvianism'. In an interview with Thomas Blom Hansen in the early 1990s, a lower-middle-class Maharastrian family lamented on a perceived gamble on socialism which has only further impoverished India:

> While so many other countries in the world prosper India lags behind and is even forced to ask foreign companies to upgrade even basic elements in the technical and organisational infrastructure of Indian industrial production. Betting on socialism, planning and friendly relations with the Communist bloc has been a major historical miscalculation executed by a corrupt and incompetent political leadership. In the meantime, the global development has overtaken and bypassed India.[56]

Pavan Varma is one of those who see in the new middle classes 'a crippling ideological barrenness which threatens to convert India into a vastly unethical and insensitive aggregation of wants'. Varma's pessimistic assessment of the Indian middle classes draws on his perception of an absent ideological compass with which to guide social actions. Into this ideological vacuum, the overpowering drive for personal wealth and the rush for consumer goods have replaced what he terms the social consciousness bequeathed by the 'Gandhi–Nehru legacy' as the

engine of middle-class behaviour.[57] Varma contends that this
legacy imparted social sensitivity, and an 'unambiguous ethical
imperative as a powerful attempt to counter the fragmented and
individualistic vision of the educated Indian'.[58] Hansen histor-
icises this renunciation of socialist goals:

> This assertive and self-confident urban middle class discarded
> socialist rhetoric and Gandhian temperance and wanted India
> to fall in tune with global trends as fast as possible. The improved
> access to jobs and consumption, tax-relaxation and increased
> access to private ownership of stocks, made the urban middle
> classes feel that they had joined the global modernisation and were
> joining the modern world on increasingly equal terms and along
> increasingly similar cultural patterns of consumption.[59]

The policies of economic liberalisation have licensed an emerging
creed of social Darwinism which has seen the middle classes
attempt to ruthlessly sinew the poles between themselves and the
destitute even further. Varma argues that the NEP 'deadened even
further any remaining sense of concern in it for the disadvantaged'
and 'gave a flamboyant ideological justification for the creation of
two Indias, one aspiring to be globalised, and the other hopelessly,
despairingly marginalized'.[60]

But what Varma's mournful and occasionally moralistic lament
is blind to – pulling his account into sympathy with Gurcharan
Das' – is recognition of the fraternity between Hindutva and neo-
liberalism. For all their obvious differences, they ultimately find
themselves in agreement: while Das talks up the middle classes as
being 'non-ideological', 'pragmatic and result-orientated',[61] Varma
sees the polity as tragically 'devoid of an ideology that can inspire a
larger vision'.[62]

Both fail to register that the middle classes are saturated with the
imaginings of the Hindu *rashtra*, and that this larger vision is
perfectly amenable to their interests. Though decidedly a partial,
elitist vision of the nation that has 'never been equivalent to the
expression of national identity of India or Indians', its efforts have
been directed to 'make its parochial concerns grandly stand in for
the totality of Indian nationalism' and so 'the Sangh Parivar does
present a hegemonic project'.[63]

Jaffrelot likewise believes that the BJP were all the more successful because of their constructed vision of a modern India, and due to

the fact their politics were so deeply ideologically anchored.[64] They were 'the sole proponent of a political project – the building of a strong India'.[65] It is Hindutva which stokes the fires of the middle classes' majoritarianism, provides rationale for the bias against the poor, and manages dissent from below. Inheriting existing structures of hegemony, Hindutva frames the nation in the image of its dominant classes and attributes all social problems to demonised minorities as threats to 'the nation'. Because of its cultural definition of India, it organs have branded the socialist as 'unIndian' and slandered the dissident Left as 'resident non-Indians'.[66]

For all the ways in which socialists and socialism have been cast as national Others, this has remained symbolic rather than substantive. To draw on a distinction well made by Sivanandan, the 'rhetoric of demonisation' may be racist but the 'politics of exclusion', experienced by the poor, are economic.[67] These exclusions manifest themselves in the 'infra-citizenship' that Chetan Bhatt observes as characterising the relationship between federal and central states and the poor populace.[68]

As of 2005, India spent less per capita on health than it did half a century ago. Public health services are on the verge of collapse while private hospitals flourish. Primary education, where India lags behind sections of sub-Saharan Africa, is beyond one third of its children. Elsewhere, an enlarged military budget has drained state funding for schools.[69]

Will India continue to lurch to the Right?

There has been renewed hope that two of the Left's core aspirations for India, a secular future and the reduction of mass poverty, can be salvaged in light of the BJP's shock defeats in the 2004 national elections. It has certainly trimmed majoritarianism's sails for the time being but there is a danger in assuming that electoral fortunes are any barometer of India's likely inclination in the long run. It is certainly foolish to assume that a Congress-led alliance, having vaulted back into the saffronised seat of power, can reverse the majoritarian gains made by the BJP over a full term in power (the first ever completed by a non-Congress-led government).

As many Indian commentators have pointed out (and in spite of widespread misreporting in the international media) the elections did not represent a massive swing from the BJP to Congress. It was certainly not the referendum on India's pluralism that the Congress manifesto billed it to be (a contest between 'a party that saw India as a pluralist and modern nation' and another that stood for 'the forces of obscurantism and bigotry').

In fact, both parties saw their share of the vote slide by 1.8 per cent compared to 1999: the Congress down to 26.69 per cent and the BJP to 22.16 per cent (in states where Congress and BJP fought it out one-on-one, the BJP wiped the floor with Congress, picking up seventy-one seats to twenty-seven). The BJP lost not only because it fared poorly in the states, but also because its coalition partners did spectacularly badly, whereas the Congress's partners performed considerably better. The real winners were 'regional' parties: local caste-dominant parties such as the Samajwadi Party in Uttar Pradesh. The fact that the Congress has had to capitulate to coalition is indicative of what Radhika Desai has (more than a little gleefully) termed its 'slow death'. This is reflected in its decision to stand in far fewer seats than in 1999, preferring to allow its regional partners to do so instead.

The stability of its coalition government is also in question. Many of its partners have previously been bedfellows with the BJP; although its principal supporters are likely to remain loyal, it can't guarantee that regional parties won't desert them in the future. This fickleness also casts long shadows over the ability of the Congress to suture the partnerships that constitute the United Progressive Alliance (UPA) into a coherent vision for 'new India'.

So far the Congress-led UPA has had limited success curtailing the BJP's political legacy. While it has taken the symbolic steps of removing their sympathisers in high civil posts (such as Prasar Bharti, the broadcasting regulator), diplomatically it has picked up where the BJP left off. Washington and Tel Aviv have been wooed with as much ardour as under Vaipayee and Advani, despite Congress' historic fraternity with the Palestinian cause.

Its economic programme might not be as brazenly pro-middle class as the BJP-led NDA's was, but there is no sense that it has the will to reform where it needs to. Instead, it has instituted the Rural Employment Guarantee Act, which gives 100 days of manual labour to anyone in rural India, if they want it. The trouble is firstly that it pays only the minimum wage (which varies widely from state to state) and secondly that the work consigns India's poor to the kind of menial work they've been doing for centuries. In the UPA's interim budget in 2004, it allocated just Rs 10,000 crores to the reform, when estimates recommended over five times that figure. Radhika Desai justly complains that it is 'hardly an encouraging sign that the Congress is serious about consolidating support among the poor'.[70]

If neo-liberalism seems unlikely to significantly abate under the UPA's watch, then a secularist revival under the Congress seems equally unlikely. During the 2002 state elections in Gujarat, called shortly after the pogroms, Sonia Gandhi's campaign was masterminded by a former member of the RSS, Shankersingh Vaghela. Congress fielded just 5 Muslim candidates out of 203, and this in a state where 10 per cent of the population are Muslim. The Congress's historical reluctance to robustly challenge either neo-liberalism or Hindu nationalism, together with its preference to offer 'softer' versions of each, means that even if it remains in power it will only slow the march of majoritarianism, not reverse it.

Conclusion

The pathologies of Congress aside, there are social trends that might favour Hindu nationalism in the future. The most visible of these is Sanskritisation, a process by which the middle and lower castes are aping upper-caste religious behaviour by adopting the same deities, festivals, temples and rituals. Other markers of distinction, such as dress and diet, are vanishing fast. This reinvention is increasingly common in metropolitan India, where caste has been subsumed by a common (and some would argue pasteurised) Hindu identity. Though this would seem to be desirable, Sanskritisation dovetails ominously with the Sangh's dream of a 'Semiticised' Hinduism, with one god (Ram) and one dogma (the Vedas).[71] It's a dream that they have openly harboured since the agitation for the Ram *mandir* at Ayodhya; Sanskritisation promises to catalyse the process.

Given time to regroup there is every chance that the Sangh will emerge as a different animal in the coming years, having reconfigured the bad wiring between the BJP and the hardline RSS and VHP. The latter two organisations were vocal and bitter about the former's renunciation of core Hindutva issues during their term in power, in particular the failure to pursue the construction of a temple at Ayodhya, the issue which had catapulted them to popularity in the first place. The NDA's neo-liberal bastardisation of *swadeshi* didn't win them many fans in Nagpur either.[72] At election time they were scornful of Vajyapee and Advani's open courting of the Muslim vote (both donned ceremonial Muslim headgear when photo opportunities beckoned). This bad blood might turn out to be a boon for the BJP if they are able to extricate themselves from RSS patronage as a result.

Free to pursue their consolidation of a middle-class vote swelled by Sanskritisation and neo-liberalism, the BJP will serve up what no party can: a nationalist confection that appeals to both wallets and egos. If minorities and the poor are occasional casualties, so be it. The Sensex has proven resilient to Ayodhya and Gujarat. This is the logic of majoritarianism; it may not be fascist, but it does hurt. The question is whether the Left is astute enough to know how it needs to position itself, which alliances it should forge and what kind of communitarianism it should endorse to forge a credible and coherent challenge to the Hindu Right. This will be explored further in Chapter 4.

Notes

1. Achin Vanaik, *The Furies of Indian Communalism* (London: Verso, 1997), p. 261.

2. Arundhati Roy, 'The End of Imagination', in *The Algebra of Infinite Justice* (New Delhi: Penguin, 2002), p. 33.

3. Communalism, in the Indian context, refers to division and allegiance along religious lines. The riots which followed the destruction of the Babri Masjid were hence described as communal violence.

4. Aijaz Ahmad, *On Communalism and Globalization: Offensives of the Far Right* (New Delhi: ThreeEssaysPress, 2002) p. 2.

5. Ibid., pp. 2–3.

6. Ibid., p. 17.

7. Ibid., p. 6.

8. Ibid., p. 2.

9. Ibid., pp. 2–3.

10. Vanaik, *Furies of Indian Communalism*, p. 267.

11. Ibid., p. 268.

12. Ibid.

13. Ibid., p. 280.

14. Ibid., p. 274.

15. George Crane, 'Imagining the Economic Nation: Globalisation in China', *New Political Economy*, 4.2, 1999.

16. Bharatiya Janata Party, *Humanistic Approach to Economic Development: A Swadeshi Alternative* (Bharatiya Janata Party: Delhi, 1992), p. 8.

17. Swadeshi Andolan, *Struggle for Economic Freedom* (Bangalore: Sahitya Sangama, 1994).

18. Rajendra Singh, *Telegraph*, 4 May 1995.

19. BJP statement, quoted in Thomas Blom Hansen, 'The Ethics of Hindutva and the Spirit of Capitalism', in Hansen and Jaffrelot (eds), *The BJP and the Compulsions of Politics in India* (Delhi: Oxford University Press, 1998), p. 303.

20. The identification of poverty as the greatest enemy of the nation and the concern of socialism extended as the slogan of Congress from the nationalist movement's determination for the 'uplift of the poor' to Indira Gandhi's electoral promise for '*garibi hatao*' ('end poverty').

21. Politically, this was paralleled by the crisis of legitimacy suffered by the Left in the post-1968 era. Socialism, which had historically catalysed the aspirations of the colonised world, by conceiving an opt-out of the structural dependence on advanced capitalist societies, was teetering on the brink of a crisis that was cataclysmically played out by the collapse of the Soviet power bloc in the late-1980s. Where once capitalism had been apprehended as the imperialising architecture of colonialism, and socialism seized as a revolutionary challenge to the hegemony of metropolitan power (realised in the aspirations of the Bandung conference), the latter has been ideologically severed from the developmental agendas of 'Third World' nationalisms.

22. David Frawley, *Awaken Bharata* (New Delhi: Voice of India, 1988), p. 14.

23. Meera Nanda, 'Postmodernism, Hindu Nationalism and Vedic Science', *Frontline*, 21.1, 3–16 January 2004, http://www.frontline.com.

24. Ibid.

25. Andrew Wyatt, 'Re-narrating Indian Development: Economic Nationalism in the 1950s and the 1990s', http://www.bbk.ac.uk/polsoc/download/events/Narratives_Economic_Nationalism.doc. Vanaik also believes that at the same time, 'there was a synchronisation of thought at the elite level across the global space', 'in the eighties, the upper echelons of functionaries in the Ministries of Finance, Commerce and Industry were increasingly drawn into the mental orbit of their counterparts in the West'. Achin Vanaik, 'The New Indian Right', 2001, http://www.sacw.net/2002/achin_NewIndianRight.html.

26. Atal Bihari Vajpayee, quoted in *The Hindu*, 19 December 1999.

27. Vajpayee, Independence Day speech 2003, quoted in Wyatt, 'Re-narrating Indian Development'.

28. L. K. Advani, 'Globalisation on the Solid Foundation of Swadeshi', Lecture to the 71st annual session of the Federation of Indian Chambers of Commerce and Industry, 25 October 1998.

29. Praful Bidwai, 'Vision and Vitriol', *Frontline*, 10–23 April 2004. http://www.flonet.com/fl2108.com/fl2108/stories/20040423007612700.htm.

30. Radhika Desai, *Slouching Towards Ayodhya* (New Delhi: ThreeEssaysPress, 2002), p. 62.

31. Vanaik, 'The New Indian Right'.

32. Desai, *Slouching Towards Ayodhya*, p. 100.

33. This is in contrast to the hostility of militant factions within the Sangh Parivar, such as the RSS-sponsored Swadeshi Jagaran Manch (SJM) which sought to moderate the flow of foreign investments into the highly industrialised and BJP-controlled states of Gujarat and Maharahstra.

34. Wyatt, 'Re-narrating Indian Development'.

35. Ibid.

36. BJP statement, quoted in Hansen, 'The Ethics of Hindutva', p. 308.

37. Bharatiya Janata Party, *Humanistic Approach to Economic Development: A Swadeshi Alternative*, quoted in Thomas Blom Hansen, 'Globalisation and Nationalist Imaginations: Hindutva's Promise of Equality through Difference', *Economic and Political Weekly*, 9 March 1996, p. 611.

38. Arif Dirlik, *The Postcolonial Aura: Third World Capitalism in the Age of Global Capitalism* (Boulder: Westview Press, 1997), pp. 156–8.

39. Frawley, *Awaken Bharata*, p. 13.

40. Ibid., p. 12.

41. Ibid., p. 13.

42. Crane, 'Imagining the Economic Nation', p. 215.

43. Gurcharan Das, *India Unbound: From Independence to the Global Information Age* (London: Profile, 2002), p. 226.

44. This wave carrying India to the right rolled further and deeper into the heart of India's intellectual and political formations than levels of government policy. The rise of the Centre for Development Studies, headed by Rajni Kothari and boasting Ashis Nandy among its number, took place on a culturalist platform, seeking to evolve a scholarly discourse expressive of and articulated in an Indian idiom. This 'indigenisation' was an attempt, in the view of Radhika Desai (*Slouching Towards Ayodhya*), to procure the academic mainstream by supplanting the prominence and influence of Marxist scholarship, which commanded the ranks of the Indian Left.

45. Ahmad, *On Communalisation and Globalisation*, p. 12.

46. Desai, *Slouching Towards Ayodhya*, p. 36.

47. Dirlik's taxonomy of 'first worlds in third worlds' captures not only the reproduction of global inequalities at national levels, but also the collaborative role of transnational capital in sustaining the power base of national elites. So although the 'best option for Global Capitalism's control is [. . .] through the creation of classes amenable to incorporation into or alliance with global capital', it is a reciprocal gesture, given the dependence of the national bourgeois on foreign capital.

48. BJP statement, quoted in Hansen, 'The Ethics of Hundutva', p. 308.

49. 'The BJP wants to strengthen its links to the more cosmopolitan and

consuming middle class who, it is assumed, are in favour of the reforms'. Hansen, 'Globalisation and Nationalism', p. 613.

50. Das, *India Unbound*, p. 287.

51. Ibid.

52. Praful Bidwai and Achin Vanaik, *New Nukes: India, Pakistan and Global Nuclear Disarmament* (Oxford: Signal Books, 2000) p. 136.

53. Ibid.

54. 'Significantly, the coverage given by all the national dailies to the agitation against the Mandal report, which argued for reservations in jobs for backward castes, was much more intense than that given over to the anti-Muslim riots. Between August and September 1990 alone, the Indian Express devoted 12.81 times as much space to anti-Mandal agitation as to the riots (though 6 times as many lives were lost in the riots as in the agitation).' Charu Gupta and Mukul Sharma, 'Communal Constructions: Media Reality v Real Reality', *Race & Class*, 38.1, 1996, p. 5.

55. In 1987, Rajiv Gandhi passed the Muslim Women (Protection of Rights on Divorce) Bill, having opposed the legislation in 1985 and 1986. It followed immediately in the wake of the Shah Bano affair, when the aforementioned Muslim divorcee had successfully sued her husband for alimony in India's civil courts. The Bill protected the rights of Muslim husbands to withhold alimony payments in accordance with *shariat* and not secular law. Speculation on Gandhi's *volte face* include the considerations of upcoming local elections in Muslim majority areas and the rising Muslim assertiveness in the face of an increasing tide of Hindu nationalism.

56. Interview with middle-class Maharastrian family, quoted in Hansen, 'Ethics of Hindutva', p. 298.

57. This legacy (of which Nehruvianism represented only the behaviour of the State), Varma contends, imparted social sensitivity and an 'ambiguous ethical imperative as a powerful attempt to counter the fragmented and individualistic vision of the educated Indian'. Varma condenses the Gandhi–Nehru legacy into five shared values for shared behaviour: 'an acceptance of the role of ethics in society, probity in public life, and the link between politics and idealism; a belief in the vision of an industrialised India, rational and scientific in outlook and modern in the Western sense of the term; a social sensitivity towards the poor, a belief that the state and society must work towards their upliftment; a reticence towards ostentatious displays of wealth, which was seen as something in bad taste and incongruent in a country as poor as India; an acceptance of the goal of self-reliance, reflecting an optimism in India's intrinsic economic strengths and the political need to be insulated from external manipulation; a belief in a secular state, above religious divides.' Pandey observes that by the early 1990s, this legacy was in tatters, describing it as 'a world that has passed, or nearly so. There is little concern for education today, let alone the

education of the disadvantaged and the poor [. . .] The entire ruling class in India (as, again, in so much of the rest of the world) appears to have been won over by this wonderful vision. So much so that, as a commentator pointed out in the *Times of India*, not a trace of the language of welfare nor even of a reference to the poor is to be found anywhere in the Union Budget of 1992'. Pavan Varma, *The Great Indian Middle Class* (New Delhi: Viking, 1998), p. 129. Gyanendra Pandey, *Remembering Partition: Violence, Nationalism and History in India* (Cambridge: Cambridge University Press, 2001), p. 15.

58. Varma, *Great Indian Middle Class*, p. 131.

59. Hansen, 'Ethics of Hindutva', pp. 296–7.

60. Varma, *Great Indian Middle Class*, p. 183.

61. Das, *Indian Unbound*, p. 285.

62. Varma, *Great Indian Middle Class*, p. 202.

63. Chetan Bhatt, 'Democracy and Hindu Nationalism', *Democratization*, 11.4, August 2004, pp. 210–11.

64. India's former prime and deputy ministers (of the BJP), Atal Bihari Vajpayee and Lal Krishna Advani, were both schooled in RSS camps and were prominent leaders of the organisation in the 1960s and 70s .

65. Christophe Jaffrelot, *The Hindu Nationalist Movement and Indian Politics: 1925 to the 1990s* (New Delhi: Viking, 1996), p. 433.

66. Desai, *Slouching Towards Ayodhya*, p. 121.

67. A. Sivanandan, 'Poverty is the New Black', *Race & Class*, 43.2, 2001, p. 2.

68. Bhatt, 'Democracy and Hindu Nationalism'.

69. Bidwai, 'World Social Forum'.

70. Radhika Desai, 'Forward March of Hindutva Halted?', *New Left Review*, 30, p. 63.

71. See Thomas Blom Hansen, 'RSS and the Popularisation of Hindutva', *Economic and Political Weekly*, 16 October 1993, pp. 270–1.

72. The city in which the RSS headquarters is based.

Chapter 3

Spilling the Clear Red Water: How we Got from *New Times* to New Liberalism

The years hunched around 1990 were a tumultuous epoch for British political and cultural life. A decade dominated by Thatcherism and the monetarisation of social values was brought into disgraceful decline by Hillsborough, Salman Rushdie's *The Satanic Verses*, a *fatwa*, the iron lady's ignominious shuffle off centre stage and a Bradford headmaster's unexpected emergence as the champion of Middle England.

It is the last event that I want to seize on as the defining moment in the convergent crisis of mainstream anti-racism and British socialism. This crisis had been given voice in Paul Gilroy's landmark obituary 'The End of Anti-Racism' (1990) which argues that sequestering anti-racist energies in the stifling confines of local government has divested it of the dynamism, genuine radicalism and grass-roots involvement that had made it a political imperative in the first place. It was important both as a riposte and a pre-emptive strike against a resurgent centre-Right critique of multiculturalism and anti-racism.

Municipal anti-racism's dictatorial edicts on best practice were easily seized on as 'moralistic excesses' on what constituted best behaviour. The backlash from the conservative heartlands, though ostensibly an assault on the 'absurdities of antiracist orthodoxy', jeopardised the legitimacy of anti-racism as a worthwhile political project – especially in the absence of other models of how its objectives could be met.

Gilroy identified anti-racism's crisis in the confluence of a simplistic rendering of its objectives, its isolation from the larger scope of anti-racist movements, and its organisational reliance on the Labour party and local authorities. Anti-racism had become abstracted from other political antagonisms and, using Gilroy's words, had become largely perceived to be 'epiphenomenal'.

This in turn set municipal anti-racism adrift from other black interest groups that existed outside the mandates and zones of the local state in informal civil organisation. Since many community and voluntary groups operated without the patronage of the local-authority (for reasons of political or ideological dissonance, sometimes strategic purpose) there was a palpable failure to mass-mobilise towards anti-racist aims. It was responsible for what Gilroy laments as the creep of 'political inertia' in what was once an 'anti-racist movement'.[1]

Anti-racist bureaucracies had cultivated a discrete and self-contained political formation so inured in the local authority complex that it was able to 'sustain itself independently of the lives, dreams and aspirations of the majority of blacks from whose experience they derive their authority to speak'.[2]

Gilroy's intervention was necessary to undercut the growing credibility of this critique and in so doing allow the Left itself to take responsibility for the renewal of anti-racism. By certifying anti-racism's death, he opened the intellectual space for Stuart Hall and others to imagine its rebirth in 'new times'. Arguably the most telling observation Gilroy made of the moribund culture of anti-racism was the 'poverty of political languages, images and cultural symbols which this [anti-racist] movement needs in order to develop its self-consciousness and its political programme'.[3] It was into this symbolic breach that Stuart Hall and like-minded reformists from *Marxism Today* consciously positioned themselves.

As totems of black intellectualism in Britain, Hall's and Sivanandan's interventions 'mattered' in a very urgent sense. While Stuart Hall's leadership on the issue marked a significant shift in his own position, whether Sivanandan – as the icon of *Race & Class* – inclined or resisted had decisive implications for the compass of future activism. In retrospect, it would also prove to be strongly indicative of what it would mean to be black, British and political in the twenty-first century. The outcome of their tussle would reverberate beyond the cloistered corridors of the academy; this was a turf war for the soul of British anti-racism. Since community anti-racism and Marxism has developed a close symbiosis both at the level of intellectual engagement and activism, it was inevitable that the shifts in the political culture of the latter would profoundly impact the former: without an independent platform its fortunes were tied to the larger movement. Was 'new times' a window of opportunity for anti-racism to emerge out of the shadow of British Marxism, or would the old Left drag anti-racism to its political grave? Had individuals been bludgeoned under the Marxist hammer or would the end of collectivism also be the end of anti-racism?

This chapter examines the recent history of the British Left's difficult relationship with community, and heads to the dawn of the 1990s when British anti-racism was proclaimed to be 'dead'. It takes a revisionist approach to the struggles of the old Left to renew itself and looks at how this was rendered into a stark ideological choice between collectivism and individualism. The public debate between Sivanandan and Hall will be used to arrive at an explanation of why secular community was the principal casualty of this fall-out and how this ultimately would have a decisive impact on the inclination of the Left when the majoritarian reflex is at its most pronounced.

While influential socialists were reinventing themselves as individualists, others persevered with a defiant loyalty to the enduring values of solidarity. I piece together the personalisation of Left politics with New Labour's governmental communitarianism and explain how, together, they eroded the ground for secular collectivism. I argue that the Left, bereft of a home in civil society, has had fewer and fewer places from which to speak to the challenge posed by the return of assimilationism to the political agenda or to ground alternative answers to our current progressive dilemma.

'New times'

Despite their mutual antagonism, both Sivanandan and Hall agreed that 'a revolution in the productive forces' had taken place that irrevocably reconfigured not only the balance of power between capital and labour, but also the character of class struggle. Even Sivanandan reluctantly concedes that the forms of political struggle associated with industrialism have become redundant today, conceding that the working class has 'lost its economic clout, and, with it, whatever political clout it had, whatever determinacy it could exercise in the political realm'.[4]

Hall similarly diagnoses the 'decline of the skilled, male, manual working class and the feminisation of the workforce, the new international division of labour' and 'new forms of the spatial organisation of social processes' as symptomatic of the Thatcherite brave new world.[5]

Hall draws a deterministic line between the revolution in the production of forces and the conventional forms of collectivism which have been marshalled under the canopy of the working class:

> The most visible of recent changes in class relations involve the genesis of a professional and managerial class and the expansion of surplus labour which appears in a number of contradictory forms, 'housewives', 'black youth', 'trainees', ' the middle class' and 'claimants.' This surplus population must be examined in its own right as a potential class in its relationships to other classes and class fractions. However, the novelty of the conditions we inhabit is not always appropriate to the relationship that these groups make with other new social forces within the labour movement.[6]

Sivanandan concurs that the new Thatcherite economy has brought about 'greater fragmentation and pluralism, the weakening of older collective solidarities and block identities and the emergence of new identities associated with greater work flexibility, the maximisation of individual choices through personal consumption'.[7]

Both Sivanandan and Hall agree (the former more reluctantly than the latter) on the need to relocate the locus of activism from the economic. But while Hall asserts that 'new times' has 'practically and theoretically' disintegrated any simple correspondence between the 'political and the economic', thus 'throwing the language of politics more over to the cultural side of the question', Sivanandan contests his deduction:

> All the significant social and cultural changes that we are passing through today are similarly predicated on economic changes [. . .] the economic determines in the last instance still but shorn of its

class determinacy [. . .] And this is what moves the terrain of battle from the economic to the political, from the base to superstructure and *appears* to throw the language of politics over to the cultural side [. . .] The battle is the same as before – only it needs to be taken at the political/ideological level and not the economic/ political level.[8]

Socialist individualism

This juxtaposition highlights that their diagnoses are very similar even though their prescriptions may differ. In Sivanandan's reckoning the 'collapse of class determinacy' merely shifts collectivist aspirations to the political arena. Hall disagrees: without a working class to marshal, 'new times' is the death knell for collective action and economic resistance. The style of post-Marxist resistance is individualist and cultural; 'new times' is the obituary of collective anti-racism. *Marxism Today* saw socialism's political redemption in the individual, not the community.

It therefore holds a critical, but not necessarily contradictory, relationship with Thatcherite individualism. The imaginary of 'democratic citizenship' could well be conceived as the dialectical outcome of Thatcherite individualism and collectivist socialism; Hall considers both to undervalue 'new times'. Hall, Leadbeater, Jacques et al. find commendable features in both, features worth emulating. It's not surprising that the *New Times* manifesto has been retrospectively heralded as New Labour's intellectual compass.

Though the *New Times* group predictably scolds Thatcherism for promoting a culture of self-aggrandisement and social irresponsibility this is tempered by a grudging recognition that it is better attuned to 'new times' than the political Left. It is not individualism itself that *Marxism Today* was opposed to, but the decomposition of society into individual interests. Charlie Leadbeater:

> For Thatcherism, society becomes merely a meeting place for a plethora of individual wills, an area for individual satisfaction, a set of opportunities for individual achievement, advancement and enjoyment. Society is merely a tool and aid to help people achieve their pre-determined individual ends. People co-operate for purely instrumental reasons, to achieve their chosen ends more efficiently. Thus all allegiances to collective solutions become

vulnerable to break-away. People are not encouraged to feel any
sense of belonging or obligation to a wider collective'[9]

Leadbeater sees in Thatcherite individualism the foreclosure of
collectivism. In a society bereft of community spirit, atomised by a
'plethora' of uncoordinated 'individual wills', collective solutions
are doomed to inevitable fracture by the prevalence of selfish
interests. Rather than opposing individualism with collectivism
in the fear of remaining 'trapped in a stale debate', the *New Times*
collective put forward an argument for 'putting individual interests
at the centre of socialist strategy'. They justify this through a
comparison with Thatcherism which has succeeded 'by articulating
a vision of how society should be organised which has individual
morality at its centre'.[10]

What this entails is a compromise between 'radical individualism'
and 'collective action'. It means an oxymoronic reconciliation
between Left and Right, and the softening of hard Leftism to
restore public belief in the ability of collective action to meet
individual needs. According to Leadbeater, 'new times' asks for
a socialism that will not restrain individualism, but successfully
form reciprocity between individual achievement and the fulfilment
of socialist aspirations:

> It needs a socialist individualism at the core of its vision of how
> society should be organised. Socialists should not get trapped in a
> stale debate, in which they are painted as collectivists seeking to
> restrain Thatcherite individualists. They should not confine their
> case to the socially divisive consequences of Thatcherite indivi-
> dualism. They should confront it by directly offering an alternative
> progressive individualism.[11]

Responding to cultural diversity

The emphasis on individualism responds to Gilroy's detection of
burgeoning black attraction to the ethical tenets of Thatcherism.
Gilroy attributes the fracture of collective anti-racist coalitions as
the fall-out of a paradoxical dovetailing of 'the ideological gains of
Thatcherism with the shibboleths of black nationalism – self
reliance and economic betterment through thrift, hard work and
individual discipline'.[12] Thatcherism's allure for some Asian
communities was well known (memorably satirised through the

Pakistani acolytes of Thatcher's enterprise culture in Hanif Kur-
eishi's *My Beautiful Laundrette*) but it also found advocates among
Afro-Caribbeans who saw in its policies the promise of a 'stronger,
self-reliant and proud community'.[13] Solidarity, Labourism and
welfare ideologies were the collective names for black failure; the
community could only be raised on the shoulders of enterprising
individual achievement. Though this by no means represented a
majority position among black Britain, it is at least indicative that
even those who had suffered the most at Thatcherite hands were
embracing its ideas, if only because of an absence of appealing
alternatives.

It is perhaps because of this that socialist individualism is
informed by a strong 'multiculturalist' impulse. In the demise of
class determinacy – the 'theological guarantees' holding in place the
correspondences between class and political identity – Hall saw
possibilities to democratise socialism. Behind the failure of socialism to adapt to the 'new times' socio-scape has been the monopoly
of Hall's figure of 'Socialist Man':

> We cannot imagine socialism coming about any longer through
> that image of that single, singular subject we used to call Socialist
> Man. Socialist Man, with one mind, one set of interests, one
> project, is dead. And good riddance. Who needs 'him' now, with
> his investment in particular historical period, with 'his' particular
> sense of masculinity, shoring 'his' identity up in a particular set of
> familial relations, a particular kind of sexual identity? Who needs
> 'him' as the singular identity through which the great diversity of
> human beings and ethnic cultures in our world must enter the
> twenty-first century? This 'he' is dead: finished.[14]

Instead of political identities coalesced around familiar collectives
– in trade unions, shop floors and Labour party meetings – the
New Times writers favour a devolution of political responsibility
from time-honoured communities to ordinary citizens. They argued
for socialism reflective of the cultural diversification of British
society. Submitting all conflict to the banal antagonism between
the working class and the bourgeoisie perpetuates, in their view, a
resolutely Eurocentric and masculinist perspective, bludgeoning all
ethnic and gender difference under the Marxist hammer. Such a
wilful denial of Britain's cultural diversity holds socialism complicit
with the cultural racism staged so savagely by Thatcherism. By

collapsing all oppressed consciousness into the colour- and culture-blind ideological bloc of the working class (the heroic figure of 'socialist man'), unreconstructed socialism banishes itself as an anachronism to political wastelands. By drawing on an awareness of other identities, on the other hand, the Left could put more people in the frame of political involvement.

Citizenship and personal responsibility

Their progressive alternative was to make citizenship the crucible for individual responsibility and empowerment. This investment in citizenship is intended not only to advance the public recognition of difference, but also to exploit emergent zones of political responsibility. Their appeal to a culture of 'individual citizenship' is projected as an antidote to 'individual consumerism', counter-weighing Thatcherism's surfeit of consumer rights with a call for 'people to carry responsibilities'. Leadbeater asks the Left's individualism to 'foster individuality, diversity and plurality in civil society'.[15]

They proposed that the idea of citizenship as an enlarged sense of personal responsibility would democratise socialism by presenting itself as a 'social individualism'. Instead of being wielded to wrench communities apart, the Left's social individualism would be used to write 'people's interdependence', 'their mutual obligations', into a public language of common rights, with the aim of repairing bonds of social cohesion withered by Thatcherite atomism. Their notion of citizenship invests heavily in the values of independence. Expanding zones of responsibility correspondingly means enlarging the scope to act on it:

> If the Left stands for one thing, it should be this: people taking more responsibility for all aspects of their lives. Whatever issues the Left confronts, its question should be this, 'How can people take more responsibility for shaping this situation, determining its outcome?'[16]

The personal is political

This multiculturalist, individualist socialism envisaged anti-racism to be more effectively realised through the public recognition of diversity and plurality. That's why Rosalind Brunt claims that unless identity is at the heart of any transformative project, 'our politics won't make much headway beyond the Left's own political circles'.[17] Relaxing socialism's hostility to identity politics – what Brunt describes as closing the gap between the 'actual and potential political subject' – involves personalising politics.

The personalisation of politics, in turn, is believed to be made possible by the 'enormous expansion of civil society'. The diffuse and erudite modes of expression made possible by the civil social explosion have 'expanded the positionalities and identities available to ordinary people'.[18] The individual has been opened up to the 'transforming rhythms and forces of modern material life', and become politicised through an engagement with this material life, through an exposure to the politics of 'family, of health, of food, of sexuality, of the body'.[19] Hall argues that the adoption of certain modes of behaviour, of identification, position us politically at all times. Civil presence in the 'landscape of popular pleasures' is always a possible statement of *political* choice, potentially signifying dissent on any number of issues. The proliferation of diversity throughout civil society is presumed to continually undermine the marginalising constructions of cultural racism by relativising all cultural identities to the ephemeral expanse of material life.

There is concession in his celebration, though. The proliferation of new sites of social antagonism and resistance, the appearance of 'new subjects and social movements', cannot be manoeuvred into recognisable socialist positions, since they will not subordinate themselves before a 'single and cohesive' political will. Rather than coercively bending modern individuals into political shapes they would eventually reject, the Left should accept that personalised politics is the inevitable outcome of diversified social worlds, and adapt itself to this new reality.

As an anti-racist strategy this translates into a wholehearted embrace of multiculturalism. It requires unlearning the intuitive symbiosis of capital and racism by encouraging individuals to leave autonomous anti-racist imprints across civil society through choices in speech, dress and even consumption.

The *Race & Class* response

Dereliction of duty

Sivanandan was less enthused by the personalisation of politics, and he holds it directly liable for the dissipation and discrediting of anti-racist energies in the 1980s. It is held responsible for exacerbating a crisis engineered by the state. It is perceived to have catalysed the black flight from community, the intellectual's flight from class and the abdication of communal responsibility in the name of a counterfeit struggle that was being moved to higher, more democratic terrain. Responsibility for oneself superseded responsibility for the community:

> The 'personal is political' has also had the effect of shifting the gravitational pull of black struggle from the community to the individual at a time when black was already breaking up into ethnics. It gave the individual an out not to take part in issues that affected the community: immigration raids, deportations, deaths in custody, racial violence, the rise of fascism as well as everyday things that concerned housing and schooling and plain existing. There was now another venue for politics: oneself, and another politics: of one's sexuality, ethnicity, gender – a politics of identity as opposed to a politics of identification.[20]

Sivanandan refutes 'social individualism' on the basis that socialism does not concern itself with the self-determination of the privileged and enfranchised, but of the disenfranchised and deprived. Their problems cannot be relieved by creative consumption, but addressed to the state through a struggle which can only be *collectively* sustained. A socialism defining its renewal through citizenship as individual responsibility would be socialism aping Thatcherism. Socialist responsibility, he argues, is always acted out in community: it is a responsibility to the least able to self-determine their existence. Social individualism is thus oxymoronic since it supposes individual fulfilment through independence and not interdependence; quoting from *The German Ideology,* he reminds Leadbeater that Marx himself said that it was only in 'community with others' that the 'individual has the means of cultivating his gifts in all directions, only in community is personal freedom possible'.[21] Privileging the individual over the community is counter-productive to a genuinely socialist politics. 'While the personal is political may produce radical individualism, the personal is political produces a radical society'.[22]

Championing ethnicism

Sivanandan therefore depicts the post-Marxism of *New Times* as a capitulation to Thatcherism, not its alternative. As advocates of personal politics, as cheerleaders of the 'astonishing return to ethnicity', Hall and the *New Times* collective are marching to a Thatcherite beat, wholly against the interests of anti-racism. Their promotion of ethnicism, under the general programme of 'social individualism', complements the efforts of successive governments to crush the militancy of the black community by encouraging balkanisation: the old colonial ruse of divide and rule.

Sivanandan traces ethnicism back to state multiculturalism. Born in the climate of liberalism in the late 1960s, multiculturalism was later institutionalised in the Community Relations Committee and the Race Relations Board, among other government bodies. It was championed as a vehicle for Roy Jenkins' (1967) vision of integration as 'equal opportunity accompanied by cultural diversity in an atmosphere of mutual tolerance'. By the late 1970s and early 1980s it had rapidly degenerated into a corruptible and divisive force on black communities – especially those beset by the worst problems of urban deprivation. This led to inducements by local authorities (increasingly emasculated by central government) for ethnic groups to fight for local resources, as independent parties, thus creating the 'deadly embrace of either pure competition, or at best, collaborative competition'.[23] Sivanandan:

> Ethnicity was a tool to blunt the edge of black struggle, return 'black' to its constituent parts of Afro-Caribbean, Asian, African, Irish – and also, at the same time, allow the nascent black bourgeoisie, petit-bourgeoisie really, to move up in the system. Ethnicity de-linked black struggle – separating the West Indian from the Asian, the working-class black from the middle-class black [. . .] Black, as a political colour, was finally broken down when government monies were used to fund community projects, destroying thereby the self-reliance and community cohesion that we had built up in the 1960s.[24]

According to Sivanandan, the advent of ethnicism presaged not only the demise of black political culture, but also the obituary of an anti-racist culture. As the anti-racist corollary of the personal is political, ethnicism personalises racism by training resources and energies on attitudes, not outcomes. Ethnicism reflected the shift to multiculturalism as mainstream anti-racism and brought cultural responses to institutional racisms in its train. It retreats from what Alana Lentin (2004) describes as the 'state-centred critique of racism', developed out of the anti-colonial movement to a contest of opinions fought out on the hallowed ground of civil society.[25] Racism was reduced to an inadequate representation of difference; attributable to little else besides cultural misunderstanding, a fight against prejudices, not institutions and practices.[26] Ethnic headcounts became the catch-all prescription for British racism.

Socialism, not socialist individualism

Sivanandan compellingly proposes that anti-racist cultures are oxygenated by socialist values. An individualist anti-racism can never produce a socialist society because socialism is as much a culture as a programme. He argues that socialism begins and ends with identification with the oppressed, an imaginative empathy drastically foreclosed by the inward-looking nature of individualism. Socialist conscience does not necessarily arise directly from a personal experience of hardship, but the capacity to see in our own oppression the oppression of others. Socialism, in contradistinction to individualism, stimulates the cultural values of responsibility in community, unlike *New Times* self-determination whose moral compass gravitates towards the self. By politicising individual concerns it precludes universalising struggle, on which the socialist fight against racism and poverty depends. The individuation of political interest works inevitably to the exclusion of a collective agenda. The greatest liability of a socialist challenge to racism is the privileging of a singular oppression above another, precisely what the personalisation of politics encourages:

> Too much autonomy leads back into ourselves; we begin to home in on our cultures as though nothing else existed outside them. The whole purpose of knowing who we are is not to interpret the world, but to change it. We don't need a cultural identity for its own sake, but to make use of the positive aspects of our culture to forge correct alliances and fight the correct battles. Too much autonomy leads us to inward struggles, awareness problems, consciousness-raising and back again to the whole question of attitudes and prejudices.[27]

'New times': window of opportunity or closing door?

Both Sivanandan and Hall saw 'new times' as a window of opportunity for the Left to regroup after the setbacks of the

1980s. While Hall's *Marxism Today* saw signs of the redundancy of collectivism for contemporary socialism, Sivanandan's *Race & Class* read the challenge as one for collectivist rearguard action, despite the absence of ready-made class formations.

Marxism Today approaches 'new times' as a chance to renew socialism. The passing of class determinacy was not regarded mournfully in their quarters but positively seized to democratise socialism. This meant embracing innovative modes of political expression, most obviously through the expanses of civil society, redirecting individualism to socialist ends. They proposed to stage this by reclaiming the notion of citizenship. An inaugural socialist citizenship would challenge the universalising thrust inherent in its dominant construction. As Leadbeater claimed, 'Leftist individualism' would foster 'individuality, diversity and plurality in civil society'. Concurrently, it would be the vehicle through which individuals would be able to accept full responsibility for themselves, to autonomously shape their existence. The Left's ability to deliver self-determination would be the new yardstick by which it would judge its legitimacy.

This remodelled citizenship would enshrine its 'double focus' – expanded equal rights and equal practices – through a constitution or bill of rights which set out the individual's power to determine outcomes. An expansion of rights by itself would be insufficient to meet the demands of social individualism without correspondingly expanding people's capability to determine outcomes: 'beyond those to caste a vote, but also to enjoy the conditions of political understanding, involvement in collective decision-making and setting of the political agenda which make the vote meaningful.'[28]

Sivanandan, and *Race & Class* under his stewardship, had other ideas about 'new times'. For them, 'new times' was not an opportunity, but a grave threat to a hard-won political culture which reinforced more strongly than ever the understanding 'that unity has to be forged and re-forged again and again'.[29] Sivanandan retorted that despite the disaggregation and dispersal of working-class forces, socialism's constituency has enlarged even as it has been rendered invisible, excised from the popular consciousness and balkanised through the machinations of the state and the market. Sivanandan admits that by their 'very nature and location', the underclass are the 'most difficult to organise in the old sense of organisation'.[30] The imperative that arises from these 'new times' is not to capitulate to the individuation of political interest, but to form new movements and alliances. These challenges need to be made not in civil society but in direct confrontation with the state. These emergent communities of resistance 'have little sympathy with the ethics of the personal is political because this has tended in practice to personalise and fragment and close down struggles'.[31]

Rather than abandon the political culture of the working-class movement for a palatable cultural politics subverted from Thatcherism, Sivanandan argued that these new movements can only be sustained by values and traditions inherited from older struggles: 'loyalty, comradeship, generosity, a sense of community and a feel for internationalism . . . and above all, a capacity for making other people's fights one's own – all the great and simple things that make us human'.[32]

Multiculturalism's communities

Following the marginalisation of socialist forms of community, less intuitively 'oppositional' imaginaries have acquired currency, particularly during the 1990s. While Britain's new Left was busy remaking individualism in it's own image it surrendered community to conservatives on either side of the political spectrum. It is from these imaginaries of community that multiculturalism itself and its signature description of British society as a veritable 'community of communities' grew both to intellectual fashion and political favour.

Before a fuller discussion in Chapter 5 of multiculturalism's articulation of community I will take the opportunity to ground our understanding of it by way of a detour to the old-style communitarianism to which it owes a sizeable ideological debt.

To draw out the contrast between socialist ideas on community (without exalting these as the most politically responsible) and conservative alternatives to them, I want to suggestively (if somewhat schematically) describe them as rights and responsibility centred: whereas Sivanandan's communities of resistance are driven by collective rights-seeking, orthodox communitarianisms are sustained by reciprocal *responsibility*. Therefore although it is outwardly secular, it is the preference towards responsibility-centred relations that brings orthodox communitarianism and mainstream multiculturalism into ideological familiarity.

Importing communitarianism

By way of example, Amitai Etzioni's *The Spirit of Community* (1995), fêted by the Clinton regime and said to be equally influential during the early years of Tony Blair's office, addresses itself conspicuously to the social balance between rights and responsibility.

Communitarianism originated as a philosophical critique of liberalism and its excesses in libertarian legal philosophy, and its leading advocates are exclusively academic.[33] *The Spirit of Community* is the proselytising manifesto of Etzioni's Communitarian movement. Communitarianism hails itself as the recovery of America's moral voice, and Etzioni explains that 'we adopted the name Communitarianism to emphasize that the time had come to attend to our responsibilities, to the conditions and elements that we share, to the community'.[34]

His movement rails against what it perceives to be American morality's progressive atrophy, blaming the erosion of the social fabric on the supremacy of rights as cultural common sense. The Communitarian agenda addresses itself to what its proponents observe as a surfeit of individualism and a weakening of collective fellowship, or what Etzioni dumbs down to the catchphrase of a 'severe case of deficient we-ness'.[35]

He argues that immersion in a rights-oriented culture has made it impossible for Americans to even imagine responsibilities to other citizens. This has fomented two chronic debilitations in society: a poverty of civic virtues and a crippling culture of claims and dependency on the state. Etzioni proposes that redressing the former will ameliorate the pressure on the latter.

He discerns a trend towards socially responsible citizenship in American society. Sobriety checks, anti-loitering laws and drug checkpoints, all previously anathema to a rights-centric society, are now increasingly populating the social landscape. He cites these as examples of how small contributions by each of us can provide major benefits for all.[36]

This trend points Etzioni to the conclusion that a culture of responsibility is on the horizon and increasingly palatable to a society gorged on a diet of incessantly bloating rights. Etzioni prescribes his own measures to cultivate these values further. To this end, he proposes the implementation of compulsory national service for all school leavers to serve as an 'antidote to the ego-centred mentality' and as a 'grand sociological mixer' for developing shared values among people from different racial, class and religious backgrounds.[37]

Ultimately though, Etzioni tries to convince us that the most sustainable means to transmit social responsibility rests with the devolution of moral authority from the state to civil community. The community, he tells us, 'speak to us in moral voices. They lay claims on their members. Indeed, they are the most important sustaining source of moral voices other than the inner self'.[38] The restoration of the moral voice of communities (and the 'web of social bonds, the communitarian nexus that enables us to speak as a community') is the catalyst for an expanded chain of peer pressure with which to renew America's sense of moral responsibility.[39]

The Communitarian agenda sets out its opposition to state-driven moral authority by arguing that while rights discourse inhibits social cohesion, the community, by drawing people into mutual interdependence, cultivates higher orders of care and accountability. While the state can only deploy *coercive* authority on citizens to behave responsibly, the community acts with the gentle arts of moral suasion where 'people generally agree with one another about what is to be done and are encouraged to live up to these agreements'.[40]

If community morality bears an uncomfortable resemblance to the second coming of Puritanism, Etzioni assures us that 'suasion' only offers a humane alternative to recourse to state machinery. Suasion, at most, would take the form of rebuke and reproach for individuals to observe 'those values we all hold dear', voluntarily observed by the majority. 'Suasion is the acceptable face of community, coercion the unacceptable'.

It is the 'suasive' voice of community that is preferential to legislation, which does not guide behaviour, but swathes its directions in a morass of rights. He counsels us that rights 'do not automatically make for rightness'.[41] He suggests that the existence of rights is tacitly supposed to signify not only their legality but also their inherent beneficence. Acts of law are therefore inadequate motors of moral chastisement since they mislead citizens into conceiving their entitlements as worthy courses of action to be pursued without restraint or reproach. Etzioni reasons that it is only the suasive power of community – the civic religion of responsibility – which can plug the moral vacuum of rights talk.

Multiculturalism or communitarianism: what's the difference?

It is not impossible to make connections between Etzioni's communitarianism and Bhikhu Parekh's multiculturalism. After all, both employ the phrase 'community of communities' to aphorise their aspirations. Parekh is, of course, a pronounced communitarian himself.

In fact much of the disquiet around *Rethinking Multiculturalism*, even from outspoken multicultural advocates and Runnymede Report co-authors such as Yasmin Alibhai-Brown (2001), centred on Parekh's insistence that community looms large both in the social imaginary and individual consciousness. Others, such as Bernard Yack, were taken aback by his attempts to foist communal duty onto people, citing his directive for us to 'preserve and pass on to succeeding generations what they think valuable in it'.[42]

There is also an assumption at work throughout *Rethinking Multiculturalism* that multiculturalism is only viable if we conserve the integrity of our existing communities. This conservation demands staunch policing and constant nurture. Without a respect for community borders the multiculturalist dream perishes in the prevailing rubble of societal incoherence. For Parekh, like Etzioni, it is communities which perform the crucial educative task of imbuing us with respect, sensitivity and duty; immediately to our familial others, and secondarily to all members of the human race.

Thirdly, Etzioni's communitarianism, like Parekh's, has come under fire from libertarians and the 'radical-individualists' of the ACLU (American Civil Liberties Union). Just as Parekh's multiculturalism has been berated for insufficient attentiveness to 'the unequal and unjust power relationships' which exist within communities, Etzioni has too has been accused of understating the diversity of views in any given community, and intra-community democratic rights. Seyla Benhabib encapsulates this unease as the trade-off between 'internal freedoms and external protections'.[43]

As briefly mentioned above, there remain important distinctions between the secularity of Parekh's multiculturalism and Etzioni's communitarianism. The proliferation of diversified interests, otherwise derided as 'lobbies of self-interest', are counter-productive to the primary ambition of strengthening common interests. His manifesto preaches the suppression of diversity, not its expression. His pleadings for community are defined in secular, voluntaristic terms. Where Parekh instrumentally deploys community to preserve cultural difference, Etzioni coaxes us into communities of our own making. He speaks of neighbourhoods, clubs, associations and other voluntary organisations. The initiative lies with our voluntary participation in the community, just as the desires to act in the collective interest, to uphold those values 'dear to most of us', are done under no coercive duress. Parekh's communitarian message, meanwhile, is couched firmly in the discursive idiom of multi-culturalism. It is premised on the assumption that the social acceptance of community supposes the ideological triumph of cultural diversity. Here, the community is figured not as the home of 'narrative, cohesion and coherence', but as the expression of difference and plurality. Multicultural communities are not volun-taristic in the sense expounded by Etzioni, but the 'networks, institutions and practices which give sustenance to our cultural selves'.

Another axis of difference can be understood as that of the respective communitarian affinity with the nation. Though com-munitarians are ostensibly hostile to nationalism because it mili-tates against the devolution of government and decision-making to local communities, there are others (like Etzioni) for whom communitarianism is the most eloquent expression of American national pride.

In this vein, Etzioni's message has been taken up as a rallying cry to reassert America's national identity. The regeneration of core values that collectively constitute Americanness and bind the nation in cohesion has been identified as the essence of community spirit. Despite Etzioni's exhortations to 'sub-national collectivities', he continually reasserts the centrifugal impact of cohesive commu-nities on the renewal of American national spirit. Parekh, by contrast, is not concerned with the resuscitation of British nation-alism. He seeks, instead, the nation's rearticulation as a catholic shelter for a diversity of cultural perspectives, united in their commitment only to the principle of diversity itself. The common interest of multicultural Britain, as Parekh judges it, is to uphold 'the spirit of multiculturality', which does not approximate into the singularity of 'the spirit of community'.

These differences aside, orthodox communitarianism and main-stream multiculturalism remain defiantly responsibility-centred imaginaries of community, where citizens are subordinate to the will and identity of the corporate whole. In such configurations relations are not conceived of as empowering or necessarily equi-table, but as molecular constituents of a coherent whole whose stature is measured in stability and community. Even Etzioni's stress on the voluntaristic nature of civil membership belies a deeper concern for the sustenance of such relations: hence the urgent need to regenerate community in the first place. Neither is genuinely committed to inter-community diversity even if Parekh, indifferent to the fortunes of national spirit, has no interest (as Etzioni does for America) in fostering a civil constellation of micocosmic Britishness.

Neither imaginary reflects the values that Sivanandan prizes among socialism's imperilled communities of resistance: 'loyalty' or 'comradeship'; their cultural identities exist not to forge alliances but to uphold their internal coherence. Etzioni and Parekh's communities do not come together to mount challenges to the state; they are irrefutably apolitical collectives.

Governmental communitarianism

It is no surprise, then, that Blairism has been comfortable riding both ideological horses. It had been, at least until 2001, an avowed advocate of multiculturalism, whilst simultaneously trumpeting the values of communitarianism. As was argued in Chapter 1, New Labour's vaunted devolution of responsibility – influenced by the *New Times* manifesto for the Centre Left – translated into the championing of informal collective organisation, inflating 'neighbourliness' into a third space of social agency and energy. But it also served the *New Times* agenda on cultural diversity (sometimes to disturbingly sycophantic levels) by courting minority favour, especially among well-to-do Asians. By making a public show of congratulation to those immigrants who were successful enough to feature on the 'Cool Britannia' tableau, New Labour buttressed vocal support for multiculturalism with a willingness to showcase its modernising inclinations and its comfort with cultural diversity.

That's not to say it was all about peerages for prominent blacks and Asians; Robin Cook won the approbation of the *Daily Mail* as 'one of the strongest defences of multiculturalism ever made by a Government minister'.[44] During its first term in office New Labour surreptitiously dropped the 'primary purpose' clause in immigration rules, which prevented people marrying a spouse if they admitted the main purpose was to settle in Britain. Since it was directed at reducing incidences of immigration produced by 'arranged marriage' it was another feather in the government's cap for more conservative quarters of Britain's South Asian population. As Les Back et al. have shown though, New Labour's second (and now third terms) have been more hostile to multiculturalism than their first.[45] The government's mobilisation of community, on the other hand, has been so pliable that its pathologies are manifest not only in the essentialism of state multiculturalism but equally in the recently harsher line on cultural diversity.

Anthony Giddens, whose writings on 'third way' politics have received substantially more recognition than the *New Times* writers as the intellectual progenitor of New Labour, has said that the 'theme of community is fundamental to the new politics, but not just as an abstract slogan'. Keen to distance his idea of community from the overbearing moralism of communitarians like Etzioni, Giddens elaborates to assure us that ' "community" doesn't imply trying to capture lost forms of social solidarity; it refers to practical means of furthering the social and material refurbishment of neighbourhoods, towns and larger local areas'.[46]

Driver and Martell, writing around the time of New Labour's first landslide election victory, understood its communitarianism as serving two principle objectives: firstly, in the footsteps of *New Times* by offering an alternative to conservative neo-liberalism, and secondly of 'distancing the party from its social democratic past'. It offered a political vocabulary that assured big business that Labour weren't seeking to roll back neo-liberalism, only the individualistic arc pursued by Thatcherism. It was also elastic enough to 'embrace collective action' but without the dead hand of class or the state on a party of modernisers.[47] Specifically, New Labour communitarianism was able to nurture two ideological tenets of centre-Left renewal which are of interest here: a pluralist vision of governance grounded in an empowered civil society, and a conformist vision of shared national values that is the signature of current liberal conservatism.

Pluralist governance and empowered civil society

New Labour was vocal, both in opposition and during its first term, about reinventing government along communitarian lines. Though nominally incongruous with *New Times* socialist individualism this translated into a commitment to devolving responsibility to, among other non-state institutions, the individual, the family and the neighbourhood. Like *New Times* it sought to market the dislocation of obligation from the state to voluntary endeavour as empowerment. On an individual basis this became clear with the de-emphasis on state benefits and the creed of 'helping individuals to help themselves'. Collectively it has not been so obvious. While

New Labour has talked a lot about 'community responsibility' and pluralist governance, it has made little headway in actually decentralising government to any meaningful degree, or giving voluntary organisations the agency it wants them to act on.[48]

It could well be the case that there is simply too strained a contradiction between the imperatives of individual responsibility, a faith in neo-liberalism, and a desire for collective action as a support for these two priorities. As Gideon Calder has remarked, it is 'hard to hold the competing concerns for [communal] inclusion and a deregulated market in a single vision, unless one views inclusion as, first and foremost, inclusion in the economic marketplace as an empowered, self-responsible economic actor and consumer'.[49]

Rather than an alternative to Thatcherism, Tony Blair's vision of a 'stakeholder's society' has begun to resemble an ideological equation of Thatcherism + community: hard to distinguish from its predecessor in substance, but stylistically differentiated by all the nebulous merit and rhetorical purchase the latter term carries. Consistent with this view, and his anxiety for his vision to be seen to be unique, was Blair's early defiance that community was more than a rhetorical accessory; from an early stage in New Labour's career it's significance would become associated with the aspiration and renewal on which the party built its electoral platforms:

> The risk of community becoming merely a synonym for government is met by re-inventing government. Co-operation, to ensure desirable social and economic objectives, need not happen through central government, operating in old ways. Indeed, often it is better if it doesn't.[50]

The meta-ethical communitarianism of One Nation

On another level, community has found its way into New Labour's political vocabulary to stand in for an idea of order and unity that draws strength from Etzioni's ethical insistence that rights entail responsibilities, or the idea that we cannot exercise rights without regard for their consequences. But it goes further than communitarian political philosophy to suggest that values of mutuality and co-operation are not particular to specific communities, but to British society taken as whole. This is what Driver and Martell describe as the third aspect of New Labour communitarianism: its meta-ethical dimensions.[51] Blair himself has described this national moral agenda as one of 'strong values, socially shared, inculcated through individuals, family, government and the institutions of civil society'.[52]

But while it is explicitly meta-ethical, it retains the conditional shape associated with orthodox communitarian positions, such as Etzioni's. Invoked in this sense, community has been rhetorically deployed as a progressive proxy for the dislocation of rights from desired political subjectivity, and the prior insertion of responsibility in the political subject.

From the very beginning of the party's programme of renewal, this 'conditional' communitarianism has existed in parallel with the comparatively more rhetorical nature of empowered civil governance, and has been the bedrock for an increasingly strident 'One Nation' discourse.

The mobilisation of community here has also encouraged New Labour to further appropriate Thatcherism through authoritarian measures to protect and preserve 'Britain's community life', a manoeuvre exemplified by the position of successive home secretaries on both law and order and immigration (gainsaying earlier leniencies with the latter).

As we've seen through the rising salience of new liberalism, this meta-ethical invocation of rights and responsibility in the Disraelian 'one nation' has become more prominent through New Labour's terms, in response to popular anxieties over social cohesion and immigration. What began as a challenge to conservative monopolies on neo-liberal society has, gradually but inexorably, become consolidated as liberal conservatism.

Of the two communitarian notions of pluralist devolution and one-nation unity, it is only the latter that has become truly operational. On balance, and in practice, New Labour's communitarian has veered towards the prescriptive, conditional, conservative, conformist, moral and individual and eschewed the pluralist, equitable, progressive, voluntary, socioeconomic and corporate.[53] It has therefore, over time, conspicuously diverged from the devolutionary *New Times* agenda for centre-Left relevance to arrive at an association with community that compels the centralisation of executive power.

In fact, community governance and autonomy has only survived in the endorsement of multiculturalist modes of political representation. In *The Third Way* Giddens answers his own question of 'who decides where "the community" ends and the other begins' with the suggestion that 'government must adjudicate on these and other difficult questions'.[54]

This is clearly a critical aspect of community governance that is naturalised in the rhetoric of local empowerment. It is also highly amenable to those political entrepreneurs who openly seek to present themselves as 'proper' representatives of the community and who are able to reify cultural difference to that end. Nowhere in New Labour community speak is there an articulated acknowledgement of the contest between the presented unity of the community as the actor of government initiatives and the struggles on the ground to redraw boundaries or dispute given essences. There is no consideration of 'community without unity'.[55]

Overwhelmingly, community has become governmental, to borrow Nikolas Rose's (1999) typology of the new technologies of power associated with third-way politics, in relation to the management of cultural diversity. Its critical edge has been concerned with social control, not local empowerment. It is no surprise that many of the organisations claiming to speak for the religions of its major immigrant groups have come into existence since New Labour came to power.

Community has become a sector of government that has allowed politicians to pass the burden of responsibility on to self-appointed community leaders, and absolve the state of its obligations to constituent members of autonomous communities that have been left to govern themselves. Inequalities, like disputes within naturalised and territorialised communities, are disregarded, as is the general sense of concern for the well-being of community members.

Conclusion

Sixteen years after it took place, how can we judge the legacy of the 'new times' debate? In several meaningful ways, the terms of the dispute between Hall and Sivanandan are as relevant as ever. The other *Marxism Today* writers were confronting what David Goodhart and other liberal conservatives purport to be doing now: a progressive dilemma for liberals and the Left. At the time the threat came from the dominance of neo-liberalism; now it is (supposedly) cultural diversity. Both seek to respond by giving underlying sociological changes progressive political content. Both also look to frame their response through the renewal or appropriation of a political subjectivity monopolised by the Right: during 'new times' it was the individual, and now it is the community.

What is instructive here is not only the comparison between their respective positions in the vanguard of the incumbent new Left, but in the prophetic and productive nature of criticism from nominal political allies. Sivanandan, speaking for an intransigent but defiant old Left, couldn't regard *New Times* reforms as anything more than a celebration of Thatcherism. That indictment animates the savagery of his rebuttal. Part of that savagery can be located in what, at various points in the *New Times* project, appears to be disillusionment with socialism's ability to transcend the collapse of the social-democratic settlement and a capitulation to the inevitability of neo-liberal regimes. But although *New Times* may have inclined too far towards the hegemony it wanted to contest, it is also true that the *Race & Class* counter-position didn't open any plausible opportunities to arrest the marginalisation of the Left.

The significance of the debate can also be measured by the fall-out of the divisions between the old and the New Left, their impact on the fortunes of British anti-racism, and the extent to which they bolstered or moderated majoritarian tendencies. Recent events have clearly catalysed anti-racist introspection and the certainties of multiculturalism have been shaken even in its political heartlands. But by advocating the relocation of centre-Left politics from historical solidarities to the individual, it perversely served as a prophylaxis for the proliferation of cultural solidarities that eventually congealed into territorialised communities. Multicultural individualism may have become the handsome expression of a middle-class lifestyle, but in socialism's constituencies – the bottom third of society – it only bolstered culturally conservative collectivism. In its commitment to ethnicity and 'putting identity at the heart of its transformatory project', *New Times* did not anticipate that the realities of multiculturalism would mutate into ethnicism and the drift towards splintered factionalism.

It did not foster individual empowerment as the *New Times* project had hoped, but through New Labour's corruption of their legacy, nourished 'parallel cultural blocs' exempt from social scrutiny. The multiculturalist patronage they endorsed simply diverted political energy from one moribund institution to another: rejuvenating religious collectivism while killing labour collectivism. Traditional elites dammed power into their own hands and the benefits that were supposed to follow from governance through community have, in time, come to look very costly to marginal or dissenting individuals.

It could well be argued that the *New Times* reformists have inadvertently contributed to the ascendancy of liberal conservatism and majoritarian politics in general. By failing to contemplate alternative avenues of collectivism, new solidarities or communities of interest, the *New Times* reformists failed to imagine workable social anchors for their political culture, surrendering the communal ground to balkanising faith and ethnic interests granted the legitimacy of recognised community by New Labour, and awarded powers of virtual self-governance. It is this autonomy or parallel existence that now excites the majoritarian reflex, justifying the government's harder line on cultural diversity and the need for the unity of values in Britain.

While *New Times* has been retrospectively lampooned for fathering New Labour – contributors such as Geoff Mulgan took their philosophy all the way to the Downing Street Policy Unit – it is unfortunate that Stuart Hall should still be considered to be an academic apologist. Hall's condemnation of New Labour's 'humanised' neo-liberalism has been as vehement as any, and he has reserved particular derision for the ideological hollowness at the heart of Blairism. In 1998, he wrote an article that attempted to put clear red water between his politics and Blair's, and establish himself as a leading critic of New Labour in the process. He wrote that while 'Mrs Thatcher had a project', 'Blair's historic project is adjusting us to it'.[56] Many on the Left, including Sivanandan, would have said the same thing about him nine years before; the jury is out on whether liberal conservatism will be similarly judged in the future.

Notes

1. Paul Gilroy, 'The End of Anti-Racism', in John Solomos and Wendy Ball (eds), *Race and Local Politics* (Basingstoke: Macmillan, 1991), p. 192.
2. Ibid., p. 193.
3. Ibid.
4. A. Sivanandan, 'All That Melts into Air is Solid: The Hokum of New Times', *Race & Class*, 31.3, 1989, p. 29.
5. Stuart Hall, 'Brave New World', *Marxism Today*, October 1988, pp. 24–9. Neil Lazarus accuses Hall of 'presentism' in his depiction of New Times as a categorical break with the Fordist past. Lazarus contends

that in his critiques of Thatcherism, Hall is guilty of attending to the singular and autonomous significance of developments at the 'local level' and a neglect of the 'integration of capitalism as a world system'. Neil Lazarus, 'Doubting the New World Order: Marxism, Realism, and the Claims of Postmodernist Social Theory', *Differences: A Journal of Feminist Cultural Studies*, 3.3, 1991, p. 112.

6. Stuart Hall, 'The Meaning of New Times', in Martin Jacques and Stuart Hall (eds), *New Times: The Changing Face of Politics in the 1990s* (London: Lawrence and Wishart, 1990), p. 28.

7. Hall, cited in Sivanandan, 'All That Melts', p. 6.

8. Sivanandan, 'All That Melts', p. 8.

9. Charlie Leadbeater, 'Power to the People', in Jacques and Hall (eds), *New Times: The Changing Face of Politics in the 1990s*, p. 142.

10. Ibid., p. 141.

11. Ibid., p. 137.

12. Gilroy, 'End of Anti-Racism', p. 191.

13. Editorial in the *Journal* newspaper, cited in Gilroy, 'End of Anti-Racism', p. 202.

14. Stuart Hall, *The Hard Road to Renewal: Thatcherism and the Crisis of the Left* (London: Verso, 1988), pp. 169–70.

15. Leadbeater, 'Power to the People', p. 148.

16. Ibid., p. 137.

17. Rosalind Brunt, 'The Politics of Identity', in Jacques and Hall (eds), *New Times: The Changing Face of Politics in the 1990s*, p. 150.

18. Hall, 'The Meaning of New Times', p. 129.

19. Ibid.

20. Sivanandan, 'All That Melts', p. 15.

21. Ibid., p. 20.

22. Ibid., p. 28.

23. Aijaz Ahmad, 'Out of the Dust of Idols', *Race & Class*, 41.1/2, 1999, p. 19.

24. A. Sivanandan, 'Challenging Racism: Strategies for the 1980s', *Race & Class*, 25.2, 1983, p. 4.

25. Alana Lentin, 'Racial States, Anti-Racist Responses', *European Journal of Social Theory*, 7.4, 2004, p. 437.

26. Ibid.

27. A. Sivanandan, *Communties of Resistance: Writings on Black Struggles for Socialism* (London: Verso, 1990), p. 76.

28. Stuart Hall and David Held, 'Citizens and Citizenship', Jacques and Hall (eds), *New Times: The Changing Face of Politics in the 1990s*, p. 28.

29. Sivanandan, 'All That Melts', p. 24.

30. Ibid., p. 25.

31. Ibid., p. 28.

32. Ibid., p. 24.

33. Adam Crawford, 'The Spirit of Community: Rights, Responsibilities and the Communitarian Agenda', *Journal of Law and Society*, 23.2, 1996, p. 250.

34. Amitai Etzioni, *The Spirit of Community: Rights, Responsibilities and the Communitarian Agenda* (London: Fontana Press, 1995) p. 15.

35. Ibid., p. 26.

36. Joseph Kahne, 'The Spirit of Community: Rights, Responsibilities and the Communitarian Agenda', *Harvard Educational Review*, 66.4, 1996, p. 467.

37. Etzioni, *Spirit of Community*, p. 168.

38. Ibid., p. 31.

39. Ibid., p. 10.

40. Ibid., p. 44.

41. Ibid., p. 201.

42. Bhikhu Parekh, *Rethinking Multiculturalism* (Basingstoke: Palgrave, 2000), p. 160.

43. Seyla Benhabib, '"Nous" et "Les Autres": The Politics of Complex Cultural Dialogue in a Global Civilisation', in Christian Joppe and Steven Lukes (eds), *Multicultural Questions* (Oxford: Oxford University Press, 1999), p. 57.

44. Tony Kushner, 'New Labour, Old Racism?', *Jewish Socialist*, Spring, 2002, p. 13.

45. Les Back, Michael Keith, Azra Khan, Kalbir Shukra and John Solomos, 'The Return of Assimilationism: Race, Multiculturalism and New Labour', Sociological Research Online, 7.2, 2002, http://www.socresonline.org.uk/7/2/back.html.

46. Anthony Giddens, *The Third Way* (Cambridge: Polity, 1998), p. 79.

47. Steven Driver and Luke Martell, 'New Labour's Communitarianisms', *Critical Social Policy*, 52, 1997, p. 33.

48. The only real sense in which community governance has had practical applications has been the New Deal for Communities, which required that all bidding partnerships demonstrate the potential for genuine community involvement.

49. Gideon Calder, 'Communitarianism and New Labour', *The Electronic Journal: Social Issues*, special issue on 'The Futures of Community', 2.1, November 2003.

50. Tony Blair, 'The Rights We Enjoy Reflect the Duties We Owe', *The Spectator Lecture* (London: Labour Party, 1995), p. 13.

51. Steven Driver and Luke Martell, 'New Labour's Communitarianisms', p. 35.

52. G. Radice, *What Needs to Change: New Visions for Britain* (London: HarperCollins, 1996), p. 8.

53. Driver and Martell's six poles of communitarian thinking. See 'New Labour's Communitarianisms'.

54. Giddens, *The Third Way*, p. 85.

55. See J. Brent, 'Community Without Unity', in P. Hoggett, *Contested Communities: Experiences, Struggles, Policies* (Bristol: Policy Press, 1997).

56. Stuart Hall, 'The Great Moving Nowhere Show', *Marxism Today: Special Edition*, November/December 1998, p. 14.

Chapter 4

The Blame Game: Recriminations from the Indian Left

In the colonial society, community was where citizenship was not.*

The jeering, hooting young men who battered down the Babri Masjid are the same ones whose pictures appeared in the papers in the days that followed the nuclear tests. They were on the streets, celebrating India's nuclear bomb and simultaneously 'condemning Western Culture' by emptying crates of Coke and Pepsi into public drains. I'm a little baffled by their logic: Coke is Western Culture, but the nuclear bomb is an old Indian tradition?†

In the years following the BJP's ascension to power at the centre, a flurry of critiques claiming to expose the intellectual rationale for Hindu nationalism has appeared. From the philosophy of Chetan Bhatt's *Liberation and Purity* (1997) and the rationalism of Meera Nanda's *Breaking the Spell of Dharma* (2003) to the varied

* Aijaz Ahmad, *On Communalism and Globalisation: Offensives of the Far Right* (New Delhi: ThreeEssaysPress, 2002), p. 211.
† Arundhati Roy, *The Algebra of Infinite Justice* (New Delhi: Penguin, 2002), p. 33.

Marxisms of Achin Vanaik's *The Furies of Indian Communalism* (1997) and Radhika Desai's *Slouching Toward Ayodhya* (2002), they have commonly indicted the follies of Indian anti-secularism for 'sharing discursive space' with Hindutva.

It is no doubt true that the ascendancy of the postcolonial critique of modernity assigns it a powerful voice in debates around the legitimacy of state secularism in India. Since it has long since concerned itself with posing a political as well as an epistemological challenge to Western power, postcolonial reason has led in the front lines of a battle of ideological wills which has split India's contemporary Left.

Nanda, for example, writes that postcolonial studies aided and abetted the meteoric coming to hegemony of cultural nationalism and the cultivation of the religious vote bank. Its contribution to the crisis of secularism has occurred by way of its conception of minority politics in overwhelmingly epistemic terms – mandated by its institutional co-ordinates in English and cultural studies departments. Its imperative for the 'power-knowledge of the West to be deconstructed and the colonized allowed – again – to see reality through "their own" conceptual frameworks' has been appropriated by the resurgent organs of Hindutva.[1]

It is, she insists, not by way of a deliberately communal agenda but an inadvertent yet fateful surrender to a bankrupt idea of community which disabled the Left's resistance to Hindutva's assault on the secular character of Indian society.

This chapter takes a contrary position. While I am prepared to concede that anti-secularism has a misplaced faith in religious community and culture, I also argue that anti-secularism is a straw man for the established Left. I suggest that the oblique implication of anti-secularism with Hindu nationalism absolves all other intellectual and political formations of their responsibility to answer Hindutva's assault on Indian secularity. The chapter concludes that neither state secularism nor anti-secularism answers meaningfully to Hindu majoritarianism, but that the latter, like Parekh's multiculturalism, move us towards the 'politically sensitive imagination' required to rehabilitate the project of Indian democracy. Resolving the progressive dilemma involves internalising the anti-secularist engagement with popular anxieties and the consequent recognition that majoritarianism cannot be confronted at a distance.

Anti-secularism

As Achin Vanaik notes, anti-secularism is 'not a serious political force guiding any identifiable party, or organisation of any major consequence. It is rather an intellectual current which has gained ground in Indian academia, among NGO activists, and has influenced the general public discourse on matters pertaining to communalism and secularism'.[2] It had gained ground and achieved public resonance, as I intimated earlier, with the wave of Gandhian nostalgia popularised and romanticised by the Janata Party (JP) movement.[3]

The emaciation of the Nehruvian consensus (secularism, socialism and scientific temper), coupled with the dwindling influence of organised labour, handed the political initiative to a political populism which was Gandhian in inspiration. It was neo-Gandhism in turn which vivified the anti-secularist agenda. Catalysed by the popularity of the JP movement, a complex of environmental groups, academic scholars and political groups took up the Gandhian mantle. Even the Janata Sangh, boasting ministers Atal Bihari Vaypayee and Lal Krishna Advani, gained influence in the political centre as part of the ramshackle coalition that briefly deposed Indira Gandhi with its self-styled political philosophy of 'Gandhian socialism'.[4]

The reconstitution of the Indian Left and the renaissance of the anti-secular agenda can therefore be explained, partially at least, by the ideological vacuum left by the implosion of Nehruvian socialism and the crisis of credibility suffered by Indian democracy. I shall now look at the substantive aspects of anti-secularist politics.

Anti-secularists on Hindutva

A basic anti-secularist premise is the refusal to accord Hindutva *religious* status. Chatterjee rejects the possibility that the Hindu Right can be fought on the site of the secular. He argues that Hindutva's strategies have not been characterised by demands for the elevation of religious institutions or dogma to public office and law, but more accurately by a desire to firm up the definition of a national culture able to homogenise citizenship.[5] It is only within the domain of the modern that it can mobilise ideological resources to 'promote intolerance and violence against minorities'.[6]

Nandy (above all others) forcefully makes the distinction between religion as ideology and religion as faith. According to him, Hindutva is categorically barren of religious faith, mobilising demagoguery and symbolism for blatant secular ends. The instrumental bastardisation of Hinduism manufactures a 'national ideology' stripped bare of its moral, cultural and religious content.[7]

He argues that the gentrified, modernised and culturally sanitised Hinduism sold to the nation is a selective and elitist abridgment of Hinduism's ungovernable diversity. He states that Hindutva 'defensively rejected or devalued the little cultures of India as so many indices of the country's backwardness', selectively sculpting a Brahmanic, Vedantic and classical Hinduism that could aspirationally commune India's lower classes with their urbane middle-class countrymen without embarrassing the influential and wealthy diasporic communities. This 'high culture' of Hinduism was then processed, packaged and sold as the spirit of a globally competitive India. Nandy's perception of Hindutva is of a travesty of Hinduism, a religion refracted through the distorting lens of consumerism, massification and urban gigantism.

Nandy sees further evidence of this in the emptiness of the imagining of the Hindu *rashtra*. It makes no reference to 'folk traditions' of governance and is 'culturally hollow', 'nothing more than the post-seventeenth century European concepts of nationality and nation-state projected back into the Indian past'.[8] Unlike Islamic theocracies that are governed in the spirit of Islam and by *sharia* law, the imagined Hindu *rashtra* bears little resemblance to the social, cultural or moral landscapes of pre-modern India; it is merely urbanisation, remote government and secularisation re-branded 'Hindu' to enthuse 'urban, middle class' and 'expatriate Indians'.[9] It is in the modern context of Hindutva that the 'westernised middle classes' see their 'secular interests as well as private hopes, anxieties and fears well reflected'.[10] India's political culture is therefore no longer a contested field of modern or traditional values, but now:

A site of contestation between the modern that attacks or bypasses traditions and the modern that employs traditions instrumentally. This has opened up political possibilities for Hindu nationalism that were not open when the traditional idiom of Indian politics *was* the major actor in the culture of Indian politics and when a sizeable section of Indians were not insecure about their Hinduism. As we have said, Hindu nationalism has always been an illegitimate child of modern India, not of Hindu traditions. Such a nationalism is bound to feel more at home when the main struggle is between two forms of modernity and when the instrumental form of traditions – the use of religion as an ideology rather than as a faith – is not taboo for a majority of the political class.[11]

Nandy claims that Hindutva parasitically harvests the insecurities and anxieties of Hindu identity. These anxieties, in turn, have sprung from the disorientating process of urbanisation, secularisation and development. He regards Hindutva's ideology and the instrumental deployment of religion for nationalist power as inevitable by-products of Indian modernity. This 'modern worldview' has not arrived at such widespread influence as colonial legacy alone, but also through a self-conscious amnesia on the part of modernised Indians of past Indians' concepts of statecraft.[12]

Anti-secularists on modernity

Nandy contends that this modernising trajectory has sought to steamroller ethnicity under the wheels of modernisation. Ethnic groups are not brought to peaceful coexistence through political process but terminally resolved through state interventions. Ethnicity itself is perceived to imperil the integrity of a 'mainstream national culture' which is 'fearful of diversities' and 'panicky about any self-assertion or search for autonomy by ethnic groups'.

Ethnicity is therefore identified as threatening to the state and routinely subject to its 'coercive power'. There is no mediation between the community and the state; the state refusal to recognise the actual and legitimate presence of ethnic communities indicts secularism itself as 'a part of the disease'.[13]

Nandy complains that the ruling elite's obsession with statism and nationalism has not only bypassed traditional channels of political mediation, but also systematically undermined their legitimacy; both ideologically and materially. In breach of these fraternal networks, the values of Nehruvian secularism have undermined the intuitive social cohesion of 'folk' life and everyday Hindu practice:

> Inter-community ties in societies like India have come to be increasingly mediated through distant, highly centralized, impersonal administrative and political structures, through new consumption patterns and priorities set up by the processes of development, and through reordered traditional gender

relationships and ideologies which now conform more and more to the needs of a centralized market system and the needs of the masculinised modern state. These issues have remained mostly unexplored in existing research on violence in India.[14]

Nandy's lament for 'reordered traditional gender relationships' (read female emancipation) and the breakdown of 'traditional communities' (read caste mobility) flays his veneer of counter-cultural radicalism and exposes the beating heart of communitarianism in his writing.

In common with other work on the evils of development, Nandy professes a desire to rehabilitate older imaginings of the individual's relation to society – imaginings ordered predominantly in terms of responsibilities, not rights. Hence the obituaries for traditional community relations stand in for broader cultural values of obligation and duty, selfless sacrifice in the name of a transcendent greater good like the community, society or the universe – precisely the kind of reasoning used to acquire caste submission.

The chief actors Nandy identifies with state development are the 'modern' and 'semi-modern' middle classes. Though there is a confused conflation in Nandy's writings between the bourgeoisie and the middle classes, he generally distinguishes between the nexus of 'Anglicised elites' and urban middle classes who propagated modern liberalism during the independence movement and the recent explosion of a politicised middle class eager for status 'disproportionate to its size and its need for an ideology of state that would legitimate that access'.[15] Though he struggles to separate one demographic formation from the other, he is more hostile to the older class since he considers the later entrants to be innocent victims reaping the whirlwind of Westernisation. Their ideological support of Hindutva is excused on the grounds of the traumas of disorientation, displacement and marginalisation, attributable to the globalising missions of the Anglicised elites.

As the principal actors of radicalism and nationalism, Nandy reckons that the middle classes are favourable to any interpretation of communal violence that 'even partially hides their complicity'. The middle classes, the Left and nationalism conterminously represent the canker of secularism in the anti-secularist imagination. The growth of one feeds the others, strengthening the definition of the 'national mainstream culture' and marginalising those minorities which might be perceived as impediments to India's evolution from backward to modern society.[16]

Nationalism is generally depicted as having an exclusively middle-class appeal since they are the only demographic which is literate in the scientised concepts of secularism, history and the nation state. It holds no currency for the Indian masses according to Nandy. Between Left and Hindu nationalism, the latter is considered to have greater allure for the modern middle classes, since they are the group most discomfited by the alienations of modern life and social relations and which requires the palliative of a Hinduism compatible with their desires for upward mobility.

The citizens of the Hindu *rashtra* are likewise exclusively metropolitan Indians or those constantly exposed to what he terms the 'modern idiom of politics', those with 'one foot in western education and values', the other in simplified versions of classical thought now available in commodifiable forms in the urban centres of India'.[17] Hindutva offers a palatable and 'pasteurised Hinduism' to help make sense of the 'schizophrenia of dislocation', the 'reality of uprooting, deculturalation and massification'.[18]

The only distinction Nandy permits between secular and Hindu nationalism is one of intellectual origins: while secularism legitimately derives from modernity, Hindu nationalism is modern India's 'illegitimate' child.[19] Hindutva exists as an embarrassment to state secularism, testifying to its inadequacies in politically managing India's diversity. From an anti-secularist standpoint secularism can never be a viable inoculation against communal violence because it begets the very conditions under which society becomes communalised. The coercive bludgeoning of ethnic demands by state machinery in 'turn leads to deeper communal divides and to the perception of the state as essentially hostile to the interests of the aggrieved communities'.[20]

Nandy thus explains Hindutva as a distorted representation of the religiosity suppressed and censored by secularist dogma. Psychologically, Hindutva's secular derivations are interpreted to unveil the 'ideologues of religious violence' as representatives of the 'disowned self of South Asia's modernised middle classes'.[21]

It's on this basis that Nandy exonerates the agents of Hindutva from any deliberate wrongdoing in the *Ramjanmabhoomi* agitation. He categorically affirms that 'in the story we have told' [of *Ramjanmabhoomi*] 'there are no villains,' and 'even those who look like villains in our story turn out to be messengers carrying messages they themselves cannot read'.[22] They cannot read these messages presumably because they themselves inhabit such 'invaded, fragmented and destabilised' territory that they are marginalised in the very place they stand. Hindutva's lumpen minions cannot be held accountable for their own alienation since criminalising these 'unhappy, torn, comic-book crusaders for Hindutva as great conspirators and bloodthirsty chauvinists is to underwrite the self-congratulatory smugness of India's westernised middle class and deny its complicity in the Ramjanmabhumi stir'.[23]

So while Nandy refrains from assigning blame to the perpetrators of communal violence, he is ready to implicate those whom he believes are culpable for their alienation. The proxy institutionalisation of the 'modern' idiom of politics by the West's 'brain children' has by and large been conducted against the intuitive will of the Indian people.

Secular imperialism

This conflict between secularism and democracy goes to the heart of Nandy's rhetoric and reason. By arguing that secularism is undemocratic, Nandy is free to present 'critical traditionalism' as a kind of heroic, popular anti-fascism. He does this firstly by stressing how secularism has censored the public expression of religiosity, effectively disenfranchising 'average Indians' as political actors, and secondly by claiming that it is only 'democratisation itself [that] has put limits on the secularisation of Indian politics', as 'average Indians' have challenged the 'anglocratic' monopoly of the national imaginary.[24]

By rhetorically identifying secularism as an intellectual beachhead of missionary colonialism he is able to embed it within teleologies of progress. Bruce Robbins agrees: 'the word secular has a long history of serving as a figure for the authority of a putatively universal reason, or (narratively speaking), as the ideal end point of progress in the intellectual domain'.[25]

Nandy's critique is sympathetic to the tirades against secularism issued in the wake of the Rushdie *fatwa*. As Ziauddin Sardar and Merryl Wyn Davies declare in *Distorted Imagination*, 'standing up to secularism has thus become a matter of cultural identity and survival for non-Western societies'.[26] Defying the 'secular hegemony', rhetorically figured as the cultural expression of Western power, is a struggle for ideological sovereignty waged as fiercely as the political and territorial battles fought throughout the Muslim world. Because secularism must 'subjugate' all 'systems of belief' it is the 'imperial power par excellence, totalitarian since it determines you can have any belief you choose, so long as it is not useful in negotiating the future of society'.[27]

Anti-secularists correspondingly observe in the modernising state technologies and ideological resources with which to brutalise society. The secularisation of society has alienated the masses by stigmatising minority and even popular cultures in the public sphere, while the regime of individual rights has rationalised social relations so that 'traditional intercommunity ties' have been lost to development, depriving civil society of indigenous channels of political mediation.

Although Nandy is less forgiving in his critique of modernity than more moderate anti-secularists who might interrogate secularism within the conceptual framework of postcolonial 'catachresis', a common anti-secularist premise is that communal violence and ideology arise and are exacerbated by the power of the modernising, secularising state.

All, to varying degrees, subscribe to the view that the Indian state's attempts to 'create a nationality', fortifying the contours of a mainstream national culture by disciplining minorities into compliant cultural positions, has promoted intolerance towards minorities. What is evident in the anti-secularist reading of Hindutva is its recognition as a novel form of discrimination (peculiar to modern regimes) where religious difference operates as racial difference and without precedent in traditional India. Anti-secularists like Chatterjee, who quotes Sarkar's observation that 'the Muslim here becomes the near exact equivalent of the Jew', typify this sociological viewpoint.[28]

With the exercise of 'political modernism', where the culture of the majority 'usually comes to enjoy some primacy in the culture of an open polity', genuine multiculturalism cannot exist and liberal imaginaries are unable to cope with collective cultural rights. The anti-secularist imagination thus sees tragic causality between nationalism and ethnocide:

The title [*Creating a Nationality*] represents the awareness that the chains of events we describe is the end-product of a century of effort to convert the Hindus into a 'proper' modern nation and a conventional ethnic majority and it has as its underside the story, which we have not told here, of corresponding efforts to turn the other faiths of the subcontinent into proper ethnic minorities and well-behaved minorities [. . .] even the partial achievement of these goals is a minor tragedy, for its consequences cannot be anything but ethnocide in the long run.[29]

Anti-secularists conceive of communal violence as an asymmetrical exchange between the 'West' and the 'non-West'. The West here is not figured as a political bloc but as a psychological, epistemological and above all ideological presence in decolonised space. As Nandy himself explains, the ubiquity of the West is its most insidious aspect since 'the west is now everywhere, within the west and outside; in structures and in minds'.[30] These exchanges are asymmetric because they take place on sites of domination and conquest supported by the invasiveness of the nation-state. In this scene of occupation, traditions and traditional cultures are depicted as vulnerable, exposed and endangered species constantly buffeted by relentless torrents of modernisation which decimate 'time worn Indian realities', razing institutions, communities and relations in the process.

The effects of the ideological colonisation of state and civil society have been the dislocating fragmentation that characterises the lives of 'average Indians'. The displacement of 'folk Hindu' religiosity from everyday life by processes of secularisation has left a conspicuous vacuum. Into this vacuum, misguided efforts have been made to habilitate forms of religion which are commensurable with Indian modernity, often for political gain. Hindutva is one such example of this distortion; religion refracted through rationalist modernity. It does not truthfully capture traditional religiosity but abridges, corrupts and compresses Hinduism into a compromised palliative to ward off the blandness of modern life.[31]

Anti-secularists argue that the displacement of the traditional to the modern and the religious to the secular has been so comprehensive that it could not have been achieved through coercion alone but only by coercion braided with consent. It has been premised on the hegemonisation of a rationalist, 'scientised' view of society and history which preaches social evolution and the succession of the traditional by the modern. The religious, the traditional and the communal are assimilated to this world view as inferior and primitive pathologies of an inadequately rationalised society.

It follows then that the only way Nandy believes it possible to preserve the elements of a traditional society (and thus to defer the psychological conditions under which Hindu nationalism attains salience) is to be *irrational*. That which cannot be assimilated to the rationalist world view cannot, in his opinion, be subject to rationalisation.

Nandy seeks to oppose the 'imperialist dogmas' of secular rationality with a radical mode of dissent 'articulated in a language that will not be fully comprehensible to the other side of the global fence of academic respectability'.[32] This counter-cultural inscrutability is emphasised in the prefatory lines of *The Intimate Enemy* where he commends 'those who dare to defy the given modes of defiance'.[33]

Nandy's attitude is that the most radical act of minority defiance is to challenge the subjection of cultural practices to rational evaluation. The refusal of scrutiny to group outsiders becomes an act of resistance in itself, its most potent gesture to refuse the eye of the West (its 'oculus mundi') the right to gaze on 'subaltern' society. In *The Intimate Enemy* Nandy exhorts the non-West to throw down a challenge to the West by evolving a singular discourse of resistance which would remain unintelligible on the other side of the imperial divide. Europe or the West has to be provincialised and only incubating native cultures, values and processes can do this. 'Critical traditionalism' defines itself as the imperative of the non-West to:

> Talk to itself and of itself through its own language, so as to initiate a contemporary, unapologetic discourse concerning itself. This involves relearning the flexibility and dynamics of its own traditions and history. Only when its thought and debate are grounded in its own conceptual universe can it hope to create a new relationship with the Western world and author its own postmodern reality. This new discourse may require a fresh definition of our institutions, especially in the area of knowledge generation and transmission. [. . .] These structures must revive a plethora of languages outside the Western imperium, each with its own vocabularies and concepts.[34]

It is obvious that Nandy considers 'critical traditionalism' not only to be a personal discourse of opposition, but also a grand pedagogy for the oppressed, an insurrectionary cultural and discursive practice empowering the non-West to resist the colonisation of its collective mind by the state, multinationals, Western non-governmental organisations and cultural imperialism as a whole. Instead of being passive receptacles of Western culture, the aggregated Southern oppressed can take arms against the 'imperium' by 'reviving languages' that assert their subjectivity as autonomous cultural actors.

Anti-secularist communitarianism

Partha Chatterjee's arguments for the legislative autonomy of religious communities in 'Secularism and Toleration' are a continuation of Nandy's anti-secularist politics. But whereas Nandy is concerned with the relation between India and the West in general terms, especially in *The Intimate Enemy*, Chatterjee's article directs those insights to the exploration of political possibilities within the 'domain of modern state institutions as they now exist in India'.[35] The move is one from a critique of Indian modernity at large to an inquiry into how community – and therefore citizenship too – can become an instrument of resistance to the intrusions of the nation-state. Though it may be indirect, the article does answer to Hindu nationalism, written as it was at the height of a BJP campaign for the imposition of a uniform civil code through the dissolution of Muslim personal law.

Chatterjee's proposal for the juridical sovereignty of minority communities arises through a heuristic opposition between secularism and toleration. Since he discerns no obvious hostility between Hindutva and secularism, he, like Nandy, deduces that 'secularisation and religious toleration may sometimes work at cross-purposes'.[36]

Chatterjee models his insights into the intrusions of state power on Michel Foucault's notion of governmentality. He tellingly employs governmentality for the express purpose of evading the stringency of concepts of sovereignty and rights and to entertain the 'shifting locations of the politics of identity and difference'.[37] Through governmentality, Chatterjee communicates the dynamics of rationality and resistance more artfully than Nandy. Nested within the freedom to practise is the freedom to exercise cultural difference and in that act, to broach the power of governmental technologies. Resisting the disciplinary hegemony of state authority by 'literally declar[ing] oneself unreasonable' politicises irrationality by claiming inscrutability as a normative right:

What is asserted in a collective cultural right is in fact the right not to offer a reason for being different. We have our own reasons for doing things the way we do, but since you don't share the fundamentals of our world-view, you will never come to understand or appreciate those reasons. Therefore leave us alone and let us mind our own business.[38]

The notion of governmentality refers to a form of disciplinary power which permeates the state–civil-society border. It is Foucault's attempt to capture the ubiquity of modern power. The governmentalisation of the state is a process comprised of juridical sovereignty on the one hand, and governmental technology on the other. In practice, the latter envelops the former since technologies of governmentality pivot on the expansion of rationalisation. Chatterjee thus describes its mode of reasoning as 'a certain instrumental notion of economy and its apparatus an elaborate network of surveillance'.[39] To participate in that mode of reasoning is to recognise the legitimacy of governmental power, and accede to a form of self-discipline. Exercised as it is through representation and reason, governmentality legitimates and perpetuates itself through a flexible 'braiding of coercion and consent'.[40]

Chatterjee argues that resisting the ubiquity of governmental discipline can only be premised on liberation from the technologies of disciplinary power. He proposes that given the envelopment of juridical sovereignty by technologies of governmental power, to evade the latter is to be placed beyond the scope of the former. The assertion of minority cultural rights is one of those sites where a disjuncture between the two can occur if the technologies of governmentality are successfully resisted. Social actors win autonomous sovereignty where this is accomplished; Chatterjee suggests that the only way to achieve sovereignty is 'literally to declare oneself unreasonable'.[41]

Since 'the respect for cultural diversity and different ways of life finds it impossible to articulate itself in the unitary rationalism of the language of rights', collective cultural rights come down to the right to refuse to justify cultural practice in the dominant ethical idiom.[42]

To this end Chatterjee asks why, 'even when one asserts a basic incommensurability in frameworks of reason, does one nevertheless say we have our own reasons?'[43] When a community, religious or otherwise, declares itself unreasonable, Chatterjee asserts that it refuses to submit to the disciplinary power of the state. By refusing to engage with administrative discourse the community cocoons itself from the incursions of governmentality.

Toleration appears as the social acceptance of that 'unreasonableness'. The community's right to autonomy is still predicated, despite its rightful unreasonableness to outsiders, on its accountability to its own members. Chatterjee qualifies the group's insistent right not to give reasons for doing things differently with the caveat that it explains itself adequately in its chosen forums.

Anti-secularism versus multiculturalism

The communitarian sympathy between Chatterjee's anti-secularism and Bhikhu Parekh's multiculturalism is fairly obvious here. Chatterjee's advocacy of self-governing communities operating on their own societal ethics echoes Parekh's working principle of 'operative public values'. These 'constitute the primary moral structure of a society's public life', which though 'never sacrosanct and non-negotiable' provide the 'context and point of orientation for all such discussions'.[44] These values both regulate the relations between its members and form a complex and 'loosely knit whole and provide a structured but malleable vocabulary of public discourse'.[45] Consistent with Nandy's critique of liberal modernity, Parekh identifies 'historically inherited cultural structure[s]' which inform its conduct in public life'. Modifying that structure in the name of political modernisation can result in 'widespread disorientation, anxiety and even resistance'.[46]

In these recognisably communitarian arguments both Parekh and Chatterjee are attempting to relativise liberalism by presenting the case for fairness in non-liberal societies. But whereas Parekh's stipulation for 'non-liberal operative public values' is the observation of a minimum of universal prohibitions (slavery, torture, rape), Chatterjee's only reservation is for (democratic) accountability *within* the community.

The difference between Parekh and Chatterjee (and by extension Nandy) is an urgent one. While Parekh is comfortable with the existence of cultural diversity within a discourse of rights, or of similarity with difference, Chatterjee is more circumspect about the rational scrutiny of cultural practice, since this would be tantamount to a submission to disciplinary power.

This is not to deny that Parekh has no discomfort with secularist principles. His stem from a belief that India's national democratic culture cannot be guaranteed by state recognition of individual rights without acknowledging its singular religiosity. The Indian state has to recognise that religion oxygenates India's very way of life. To deny the centrality of religion is to 'make people speak in secular languages' introducing 'self-alienation' and subjecting them to 'disadvantages', 'by requiring them to speak in a language different to the one in which they think'.[47]

For Parekh secularism can only be a 'simple-minded solution' to the problem of communal conflict since by universalising the operative public values of liberal societies, it conceals its cultural bias. The 'great political project' of Indian democracy, by contrast, requires a 'historically sensitive imagination, a culturally attuned intelligence, and a shrewd sense of political possibilities.' He perceives little evidence of these qualities among the acolytes of the BJP, nor among their secular opponents 'whose thinking has advanced little since Nehru's death'.[48]

He doesn't go so far as to state that these values are incommensurable with those from other cultures, only that that these are articulated in distinctive idioms and may privilege values other than those universalised by the liberal world view. Integral to his commission for intercultural dialogue is the supposition that it is possible to appeal to universal values as long as that appeal is mindful of cultural definitions of reason so that they are related to the 'moral and cultural structure of the society concerned'.[49]

Debunking the anti-secularist critique of modernity

Critical blindness to the injustices of tradition

Anti-secularist ideas for religious toleration are flawed for two overriding reasons. Firstly, they grossly caricature traditional communities as fair societies and are critically blind to the infringement of rights which occur under the sign of the community. Secondly, they overstate the evaporation of communal institutions in Indian modernity, oversimplify the rationalisation of social relations as comprehensive individuation, and overestimate the secularisation of Indian politics.

The most obvious fallacy propagated by anti-secularism is the egalitarianism of traditional Indian society. Anti-secularists' silence on caste oppression and gender inequality speaks eloquently of

their biased portrait of traditional or 'folk' values. The commonplace cruelties of all pre-modern societies merit no comment from
any anti-secularist critic, unless cited in remonstration with the
exaggerations of 'modernist' and secular critics.

Meera Nanda argues that postcolonial epistemologies, such as
those articulated in the name of anti-secularism, have disarmed the
Left by simplifying the epistemic victimhood of the non-West. By
failing to register the suppression or syndication of a multiplicity of
traditions in the coming to supremacy of a dominant cultural idiom,
they have neglected the illiberalism of those 'minor' national
cultures:

> The problem, however, lies in that what appears to be marginal
> from the point of view of the modern West, is not marginal at all in
> non-Western societies which haven't yet experienced a significant
> secularisation of their cultures. Local knowledge that Western
> critics assume to be standpoints of the 'oppressed' are in fact
> deeply embedded in the dominant religious/cultural idiom of non-
> Western societies [. . .] Those who appear to be 'innocent' because
> of their victimization by the West. The problem is that those who
> appear as 'victims' from a global anti-Enlightenment vantage
> point are actually the beneficiaries of traditional cultural legitima-
> tions.[50]

The populism that animates anti-secularist politics has propagated a critical blindness to the multiple sites of power and
minority; the corollary of a polity that bows before the religious
is an intelligentsia prostrate before the popular. Achin Vanaik's *The
Furies* accuses Nandy of 'applying the critical edge of his thinking
overwhelmingly to modernity' and the same could be said of many
of the populists who smother secularism under a litany of sins
against the popular, whether this is cast as cultural imperialism,
elitism or even atheism. Crucially, this has not been willingly
balanced against an assessment of what the popular or the traditional (themselves often casually conflated) *exclude*.[51]

The genuflection to the popular, what Edward Said regards as the
'dangers and temptations' that Orientalism poses in postcolonial
modernity, is a capitulation to the seductions of community and
filiation, at the expense of the critical task of heeding the spectre of
minority which haunts the very invocation of the popular. It renders
invisible the dialectical production of majority and minority which

foreshadows the victory of the popular. Amir Mufti identifies this as the great danger of populism, since it

> Reinforces and naturalises, in the name of a numerical (that is, quantitative) majority of abstract citizens – as against the tiny minority that is the national elite – the privileges of a cultural (that is qualitative) majority. In this sense as well, its procedures are no different from those of official secularism, which declares a formal equality of all citizens but at the same time normalizes certain cultural practices as representative of 'the people' as such.[52]

The anti-secularist imagination ignores that the inverse of identification with the popular, as with the elite, is a necessary alienation or exclusion from it. What is overlooked by a critical privilege of the 'operative public values' of a society is an awareness of those oppressed by those values and a corresponding concern of how power is held accountable under regimes of community values. Secularism does not only allow for a relationship between 'politics and ethics separated from religion', as Vanaik argues, but also for a relationship between individuals and authority independent of religious interference. Secularism can therefore be seen to prefigure the endowment of citizenship. Kelly concludes that despite its best intentions, Parekh's core principle of operative public values, which underwrites Nandy and Chatterjee's demands for societal inscrutability, is simply 'too communitarian':

> It places too much emphasis on 'how we do things around here' in order to address concerns about the impartiality and the false neutrality of liberalism, with its unfortunate history of imperialism. Parekh's theory has nowhere to go but the internal view of a particular society and culture. Yet it is precisely the authority of such internal perspectives that multiculturalists wish to challenge in their quest for recognition and inclusion'.[53]

Political claims for absolute cultural difference do not advance minority interests but those of traditional hierarchy. The resources for dissent within traditional societies are inherently limited and it is precisely their overwhelming character which is definitive.[54] And, as Chetan Bhatt contends, the expression of the epistemological, ethical or moral exceptionalism of any culture is a familiar symptom of all contemporary forms of religious authoritarianism.

He argues that endorsing these cultural claims of incommensurability by placing them beyond the analytic reach of reason plays into the hands of reactionary religious movements. A progressive anti-fundamentalism would insist on subjecting them to a putative universal critique:

> In fact, the claim to dissimilarity, difference, closure and uniqueness is a foundational declaration of religious and racialist movements and it is this authority that they now use to disavow critical assessment or political challenge. Versions of Spivak's argument that reason is Eurocentric [. . .] or Bhabha's arguments on foundational incommensurability are rehearsed by those same movements as legislative norms.[55]

Caricaturing India's secularisation

The second, definitive flaw in anti-secularist reasoning derives from its overwhelming caricature of the secularisation of the Indian polity and by extension of the demise of communitarianism in Indian society. The first point to be made is that India's political culture has not been profoundly relocated from the contested field of 'modern or traditional values' because the modern has never been conceptually free of the traditional (particularly the religious). Hindu nationalism cannot therefore be a psychological 'reaction' to the secularisation of either polity or society because neither has been seriously undertaken.

Jawaharlal Nehru posed the development issue as one of moulding the nation in the enlightened image of the state. This explicit paternalism understood the ignorance and superstition of the masses as the primary obstacle to national development. In public announcements, the Nehruvian state made no efforts to conceal its condescension to the Indian masses. In the draft of the first Five Year Plan (1951), it was stated that '[Certain] conditions have to be fulfilled before the full flow of the people's energy for the task of the national reconstruction can be assured. The ignorance and apathy of large numbers have to be overcome.'[56]

The 'conditions' Nehru refers to here are those which allow 'the people' to appreciate the rational drive of the developmental state. It is a call for the 'enlightenment' of the masses as a prerequisite for the modernisation of the nation. For the masses to realise the direction the nation was to take, it needed to share the state's vision of progress. The core values of 'scientific secularism' (which became synonymous with Nehruvianism) were intended to be drip-fed to the people through a national infrastructure spearheaded by education and health-care programmes. The state's adoption of Western scientific methods in medicine and engineering were intended to be exemplary of the spirit of scientific secularism.

But while outwardly disassociated from the state and regarded as an obstacle to collective social progress, religion was still publicly pronounced as a determinate influence on 'inner' development.[57] Religious consciousness (of which Nehru became increasingly associated with in his later years) was advocated for the progress of the individual.[58] Though this does not necessarily contravene secular principles, it diminished the prospects for embedding a secular polity. The spectacle of state officials undertaking Hindu rituals in public office – an occurrence that continues to the present day – exemplifies the pollution of the secular by the religious. Political discourse in India has always been sacralised to some extent:

> Nehruvian socialism mostly meant a formal nod to secular ideals, with very little principled commitment to them. There is substance to these concerns. As I will argue here, the battle for secularism and humanism was never joined at the terrain of culture; the secularists – and here not just the Nehruvian liberals but all other left intellectuals share the blame – never adequately challenged the pervasive and reactionary influence of religious thought on the hearts and minds of Indians.[59]

The 'scientific temper' which the Nehruvian era promised to usher in may never be fully accepted into Indian society, while the inadequate secularisation of Indian public office persists. This 'democracy under the spell of *dharma*', 'secularism without secularists' has perpetuated secular genuflection to religiosity. In a political culture held hostage by divinity, the progressive encroachment of the Hindu Right on state power has only consolidated its 'saffronisation'. Indian secularism, like India's unique modernity as a whole, remains, an 'unfinished project'.[60] Judgements on its progress will also depend on perspective; for many people India cannot, and should not, aspire to the absolute expulsion of religion from the public sphere.

The persistence of Indian community

So while secularism is not the rampant demon anti-secularists would like us to believe it to be, neither is it the agent of communal dissolution. The supposedly irreversible decline of communitarianism in modern society, and in particular intercommunity relations capable of moderating communal violence, is ably contradicted by Ashutosh Varshney's flawed but illuminating sociological study of the geographic distribution of Hindu and Muslim communal violence, *Ethnic Conflict and Civic Life: Hindus and Muslims in India* (2002). Varshney's analysis carries insights into how secular, affiliative networks are able to confound the majoritarian agenda.

He argues that the debate over secularism has neglected the ground-level civic structures which organise communities locally. As Varshney states in his methodological outline, this has been the organising principle for his own study. The methodological inadequacies of previous studies have been the 'scale of aggregation' with an unwarranted focus at the national and global level of analysis. Sociological orthodoxies focus exclusively on why ethnic violence occurs, and ignore the comparative question of why it occurs in some places but not others. His conclusion is that we look no further than the institution of organisational civil life:

> Where such networks of engagement exist, tensions and conflicts were regulated and managed; where they are missing, communal identities led to endemic and ghastly violence. As already stated; these networks can be broken down into two parts; associational forms of engagement and everyday forms of engagement. The former ties are in organisational settings; the latter require no organisation. Both forms of engagement, if intercommunal, promote peace, but the capacity of the associational forms to withstand national level 'exogenous shocks' – such as India's partition in 1947 of the demolition of the Baburi mosque in December 1992 in full public gaze by Hindu militants – is substantially higher.[61]

What emerges with greatest poignancy from the study is that of all associations, those that most successfully immunise societies from ethnic violence promote *interdependence* between its members. Exemplary of this are trade unions that unify religious groups

with common working interests.[62] Where communities are localised around industries and economic activities which employ
communities in mutually binding occupations and do not allow
them to segregate along religious lines, they tend to be less riot-
prone.

The crucial factor in their success appears to be the intractability
of this interdependence. Where Varshney finds a predominantly
Hindu proprietary class employing a Muslim workforce in the
textile industries of Ahmedabad for example, violence is against
the interests of both parties. Since the skills of the workforce are not
easily transferred (due to accumulated dexterity on the part of the
weavers) it's not possible to simply switch from a Muslim to a
Hindu labour force:

> Mass level intercommunal civic structures thus have the effect of
> moderating the communal right wing. Where is the room for a
> passionate argument for Muslim disloyalty to the nation and a
> 'targeting' of Muslims for 'punishment' if one depends on Mus-
> lims for profits, for a living, for civic order?[63]

This is starkly realised in cities that bear deep socio-economic
stratifications. The cartographic distribution of violence in the
Gujarati city of Surat demonstrates the importance of civic engagement. Whereas the Old City, suffused with guilds and professional
networks, was quick to stabilise itself in the immediate breakout of
violence, the slums and shanty towns in the 'new' areas of the city
were several times more riot prone. The lack of civil institutional
infrastructure meant that no communication took place between
the ethnic factions in the slums.

Other conclusions Varshney draws are contestable. His unwillingness to take sides in the modern–traditional debate would seem
to be refuted by his own evidence; the most successful forms of civil
engagement are those coalesced around industrial interdependence
that is also predominantly urban.[64] The trade union movements
have been central to the fortunes of violence-control in his case
studies; that they affiliate on voluntary rather than religious
grounds is crucial.

The creation of social space where individuals can act as
secular citizens is a unique feature of modern civil society but
neglected by the anti-secularist imagination, where state power
is conceived to be contested or negotiated solely through the

historical community. In fact, civil society allows us to conceive of alternative ways of constituting life together and of innovating relations that are fluid, multiple and reciprocal. It is the imagination and enactment of these communities that can debunk exclusionary rhetorics of ethnic or religious nationalism by demonstrating how lived relations contradict imagined boundaries of incommensurability or intolerance.

In defence of the anti-secularist position

Anti-secularism's fixation on the colonial frontier as the site of cultural violence means it is fighting a battle which has long been lost, and against forms of power which have long been eclipsed by sophisticated mutations of nationalism which have instrumental sympathies with shape-shifting capitalist regimes. The traditional communities it shelters behind in the hope of insulation from modernisation's whirlwind are warped recollections of a stagnant imagination, as distorted as the rehabilitations of a Vedic golden age summoned by Hindu nationalism from India's prehistory. They exist only in corrupted and de-legitimised forms where integralism – like that of the fabled Hindu *rashtra* – rules sovereign over individual rights. In confrontation with the majoritarian nexus between neo-liberalism and Hindutva it is only 'resistance identities' that are able to register the complexities of contemporary oppression and deprivation without herding everything under the rubric of cultural imperialism that can emerge as the sites where effective challenges can be made.

But in spite of its obvious oversights and weaknesses, it would be facile – and wrong-headed – to brand anti-secularism as Hindutva's epistemological seedbed. Through its affiliations with environmental, intellectual and artistic movements it is able to bring swathes of the 'new' Left under its political compass. It has also been adopted by an influential faction within the subaltern studies project, part of what Vinayak Chaturvedi (somewhat generously) characterises as the 'problem of conceiving an agenda of how to re-imagine Marxism within the cultural logic of capitalism'.[65]

This reorientation of that project from 'Thompsonian social history' to the post-structuralist critiques of 'cultural studies' confirmed a distinct wariness to Marxism, due as much to a withering of class-consciousness – conceded both by Achin Vanaik and Sumit Sarkar – as much to the European provenance of Marxism.[66] This 'critical engagement with the enlightenment', though locally aligned with the dubious politics of anti-modern neo-traditionalism, cannot be isolated from a global scepticism of liberalism and Marxism, undertaken not in the name of postcolonial epistemology but in the fall-out of political failure. Liberalism, for example, cannot easily accommodate group rights into its normative vocabularies of justice. Nor, as Dipesh Chakrabarty points out in 'Radical Histories and Question of Enlightenment Rationalism', can it speak to the religious inspiration of public ethics.[67] These, remember, are exactly the criticisms ranged against the inadequacy of liberal rights by multiculturalists in Britain and Canada.

This sense of political failure is no different even if more acute in India. As Vanaik explains, the rise of authoritarian nationalism is best seen as the 'consequence of the collapse of the postcolonial project institutionalised in 1947'. Its decline, and that of the Congress, has been 'the condition for the rise of the Sangh Combine'.[68] Even more specifically than that, the failure has been that of failing to join the battle for secularism and humanism 'at the terrain of culture' for which, as Nanda correctly observes, 'all Left intellectuals share the blame'.[69]

I am arguing therefore that anti-secularism should not be summarily dismissed as a hothouse for Hindutva, as in Radhika Desai's Marxist *Slouching Towards Ayodhya* (2002) or Meera Nanda's rationalist *Prophets Facing Backwards* (2002) and *Breaking the Spell of Dharma* (2003), but regarded as the begged question of the organised Left's arid response to Hindu nationalism. It has proven far easier to demolish the rational and rhetorical bases of anti-secularism and decry the defection of anti-secularists to a 'shared discursive space' with Hindutva than to interrogate the failure of the Left to capture the Indian public imagination and consequently to check the ascendancy of cultural nationalism. I want to suggest that anti-secularism, like multiculturalism, is provocative but not debilitating.

Resolving the progressive dilemma will demand that the Indian Left acknowledge that it has to engage with popular religiosity, if not religion itself. It also has to accept that anti-secularism, taken as a whole, is not complicit with Hindu nationalism; 'sharing discursive space' can also imply contesting discursive space. That is a potentially more useful means of reframing the promise (if not the historical contribution) of the anti-secularist position. It could be argued that abstaining from appropriated political terrain is tantamount to complicity. The first necessary step in resolving the progressive dilemma is pledging to confront majoritarianism where it asserts itself; the next is to judge by what means to do so, and how to align that intervention with a political creed.

The difficulty of embedding constitutional principles in civil society does not warrant their dissolution, as anti-secularists would advocate, but neither can these principles bypass the lived values neglected by austere advocates of 'pure' secularism. Engaging secularist humanism 'at the level of culture' so that they may be 'owned' by social actors requires a concession to the worldliness of the anti-secularist position.

It demands a recognition from the orthodox Left that culture and religion are not merely structuring categories of thought – 'false consciousness' – but also lived experiences. Anti-secularist priorities draw attention to the need for a 'culturally attuned intelligence' through which human-rights values might be popularised.[70] Secularist sensibilities, meanwhile, enable us to judge the distinction between a defence of the 'politics and ideology of secularism in cultural terms', a 'civilisationally anchored understanding of pluralist democracy' and the appropriation of those standards by cultural nationalism.[71]

Orthodox Marxist ideas on secularism

To expand on what I've alluded to here as the rootedness of the Left in infertile ground, I shall detail Marxist strategies to reverse the mass communalisation of state and civil society. Orthodox Marxism has made recourse to state nationalism in answer to the 'secularism' question. Its commitment to secular individualism has often meant a *de facto* endorsement of a secular nationalism, since it is only on the terrain of nationalism that Gramsci's 'national popular' will can be mobilised, and on this terrain that the forces of 'a fully articulated fascist national project' have been arrayed.[72] Aijaz Ahmad has made the fullest articulation of this project in *Lineages of the Present* (2000) and the anthology of essays *Of Communalisation and Globalisation* (2003).

In the breach of civic cultures lie what Ahmad describes as 'cultures of cruelty', global and historical accompaniments to right-wing movements. These cultures of cruelty, dormant but structurally immanent in all capitalist society, both feed into the objectives and are routinised by the Right. Ahmad defines the values of these 'cultures of cruelty' as the reflexes of an atrophied moral outrage, the numbed normalisation of brutality:

I mean a much wider web of social sanctions in which one kind of violence can be tolerated all the more because many other kinds of violence are tolerated anyway. Dowry deaths do facilitate the burning of women out of communal motivations, and together, these two kinds of violences do contribute to the making of a more generalised culture of cruelty as well as a more generalised ethical numbness towards cruelty as such. And when I speak of right wing politics and the cultures of cruelty, I undoubtedly refer to the cultures of cruelties that the Hindutva right wing is creating, methodically and in cold blood, in pursuit of what strikes me as a fascist project.[73]

Both civil and state forms of violence generate what he terms an 'ethical numbness' of which majoritarian organisations and dominant classes are the main beneficiaries because while their 'sheer scale and persistence' promote 'moral numbness', they also 'maintain a rigid wall that separates the powerful from the powerless'.[74]

Such permissiveness to violence, Ahmad argues, is suggestive of an endemic illiberalism or an absent 'culture of civic virtues'. He suggests that staving off the threat of 'cultures of cruelty' on the nationalist stage requires the Left to pose an alternative nationalism to strengthen a culture of civic virtues, grounded in liberalism and a commitment to secularism.[75]

Ahmad sets great stall by the democratic pedagogies engendered by Leftist nationalism which, by bearing the 'revolutionary value of secularism', would be counterposed to the counter-revolutionary compulsions of Hindutva's fascist project. A commitment to Left-wing secular nationalism can best guarantee a culture of civility because India's oscillation from the Left to the Right is historically dependent on the inclination of the centre:

Whether a culture of civic virtues or a culture of hate and cruelty prevails in our country has depended, in general, on the actual balance of forces among these competing visions, which we could also describe as visions associated with the Left, the Centre, and the Right, respectively. Whether or not the Right can be contained will depend, in other words, on whether or not the Centre will hold and incline, for its own survival if not anything else, towards the Left.[76]

He argues that India's political culture is rigidly hinged on the currency of competing nationalisms because the structures of capitalism are mature relative to processes of state formation (especially overburdened in India by the competing claims of class, gender, regional and religious affiliations) to the point where periodic crises erupt from this disjuncture. Ahmad suggests that to resolve these crises an 'ideological cement of a nationalist kind is an objective necessity'.

If the demand for this ideological cement is not met by the Left, then it will almost certainly precipitate the collapse of the liberal centre and an 'aggressive kind of rightist nationalism will step into that vacuum'.[77] The Left's horizon therefore *must* be nationalist in scope to contest the rostrum from which the Right stage-manages India's political culture. Ahmad ascribes the impotence and invisibility of anti-fascist mobilisations in recent years to their 'dispersed' and 'mutually discrete' character and their essentially local provenance, which bear 'none of the advantages of initiative that moments of concentration bring'.[78] The imperative for the Left is to wrest the initiative from the Hindu Right by instituting secularism at the very apex of the national frame – the state – from where it can 'take hold of national culture through an organized political force'.[79]

Vanaik in *The Furies* similarly proposes that resistance against the political formations of Hindutva can be organised through a coalition appearing as the 'third force in Indian politics'. He believes such an alliance would synergise the identity politics of an assembly of oppressed groups – Dalits, peasants, and women. Vanaik does not exclude the class determinations of India's oppressed either, acknowledging that such a coalition would be inadequate unless it were joined with the 'class politics of reform, welfare and empowerment'. He suggests that it is only through such an integrated alliance that the deep process of communalisation in the polity could be staunched and ultimately reversed.

Critiquing the state secularist response

There are suppositions in both Vanaik and Ahmad's argument that need to be debunked. The first is that any variant nationalism is culturally arid and mobilised solely on the basis of rationality and ethics. The second (related) premise is that civil society is the *de facto* reflection of the state.

Ahmad's conceit of Leftist nationalism as the font of cultural civility runs counter to Edward Said's of the secular by suggesting that nationalism can offer a clean transcendence of religious or ethnic difference. Said's 'catachrestic', idiosyncratic rendering of the secular derives from his deeply held belief that any worthwhile critical imperative draws its strength from its externality to power. The secular consciousness is to be cherished because it stands as a permanent critique of 'the mass institutions that dominate modern life'. No such critique is ethically possible from within the nationalist frame. It is through this reasoning that Said, contra Ahmad, and Vanaik, does not oppose the secular to the religious but to nation and nationalism. He sets the ideal of 'secular interpretation and secular work' against

> submerged feelings of identity, of tribal solidarity [. . .] geographically and homogenously defined. The dense fabric of secular life [. . .] can't be herded under the rubric of national identity or can't be made entirely to respond to this phony idea of a paranoid frontier separating 'us' from 'them' – which is a repetition of the old sort of orientalist model. The politics of secular interpretation proposes a way [. . .] of avoiding the pitfalls of nationalism.[80]

Ahmad's depiction of the bonds of secular nationalism as inviolably affiliative is based on a selective arrangement of India's democratic history. In answer to Spivak's declaration that 'no adequate referent' for 'democracy, socialism, constitutionalism and citizenship may be advanced from postcolonial space' tacitly coded as they are with the 'legacy of imperialism', Ahmad attests that the 'precise aim of the anti-colonial movement was to institute citizenship and to put in place a constitutionality that was derived not from colonial authority but from a constituent assembly'.[81]

But Ahmad's is a history of convenience: crediting the *Swaraj* movement to its liberal inspirations camouflages the popular purchase afforded by the catholic but irreducibly 'filiative' rhetoric of Gandhian culturalism. The Congress vision of a free India was, after all, the progeny of a compromise between bourgeois and popular nationalisms. Nehru's ode to the survival of India's cultural spirit in *A Discovery of India* (1960) is a testimony that even his secular socialism was coloured by cultural sensibilities.

The point is that Ahmad deliberately disregards that nationalist community – in India as elsewhere – is not ethnically neutral. It is impossible to propose a Leftist secular nationalism which can overwrite the rhetoric of cultural singularity which brought the nation into being. Nor can it successfully invoke a 'national popular will' without invoking those same fraternal instincts.

There is a wilful suppression in that argument, too, of the bourgeois moorings of Indian secularism. Ahmad's resolution cannot answer back to Faisal Fatehali Devji's pseudo-anti-secularist complaint that secular nationalism has been thoroughly appropriated by the ruling elite so that it has come to resemble a 'kind of state fundamentalism, a sort of self-legitimising mode of coercion that ends up generating its own nemesis in the communalism it demonises'.[82] It's also vulnerable to accusations from religious minorities who feel as coerced into elite secularity as they are threatened from the 'assimilative pressures of the Hindu right wing', something consistently unregistered by the 'scholarly imagination'.[83]

This kind of accusation is invited by the all too narrow identification of secular nationalism with the state in Vanaik's and even Ahmad's prescriptions. Both Vanaik's parliamentary solutions and Ahmad's determination to seize the initiative through an appropriation of 'state power' through which national culture could 'be taken hold of' typify the paternalism of the Left, reminiscent of Nehruvianism's early personality.[84]

The secular remains something abstract to be declared, dictated and disseminated rather than acted, performed and owned. For secularism to acquire the currency of Gramscian 'common sense', the Left has to contest symbolic space between religious communities and the state: namely that of embattled civil societies. This is the ground on which secular identities can be formed, the power of the state negotiated and citizen action asserted.

Even if a secularist state were able to arrest and possibly even reverse the deep communalisation of the polity and its agencies, it remains unclear how this might transform everyday domestic life, where as Ahmad argues, the sanction for state barbarism is acquired.

As Ahmad observes, the Sangh Combine is not anticipating a 'frontal [electoral] seizure of power' but preparing the ground for a 'hurricane from below'.[85] The cultures of cruelty he speaks of, those routinised, desensitising acts of class, caste and gender violence, foreshadow the brutality of the state. It is commonplace social violence that shoulders the kind of 'authoritarian personality' on which a fascist project rests.[86] The Sangh Parivar has long realised that state control alone cannot guarantee the mandate for its actions and has correspondingly sought to impose its presence throughout civil society where it can be a more immediate influence in the intimate spaces of the local community and the family. While it is true to say that Hindutva has only achieved its current influence because of its nationalist scope, it is equally important to recognise that it has only been able to sustain nationalist ambitions by cultivating the molecular development of majoritarian 'common sense'. It has done that by gradually capturing those social spaces able to mediate between communities, preventing individuals from evolving secular identities as citizens.

The corollary of 'mass level intercommunal civic structures', 'moderating the communal right wing' is the escalation of communalisation, communal violence and the consolidation of Hindutva power.[87] It is no coincidence that all authoritarian regimes have systematically sought to destroy or colonise the spaces in which such forms of civil engagement can take place (the same can be said of totalitarian Marxist regimes).

Mumbai's Hindu extremist *Shiv Sena*, for example, has formed a tight communal-criminal nexus that binds slum-dwellers – predominantly male youth – into forms of 'civic engagement' which promotes anything but secular identities (the gang-rape of Muslim prostitutes is an example of their bonding activities).[88] The tentacles of the RSS *shakha* network are another such associational structure (an example of the 'cadre-based political parties' Varshney refers to) which militates against the interests of intercommunal dialogue and the evolution of secular identities.

The *Shiv Sena*'s activities are consonant with the foundational aims of Hindutva, which are to transform the deepest levels of civil society by circumventing the irritating safeguards of constitutionality and legality. The creeping emergence of religious public spheres has exposed the authoritarian not the democratic potential of civil society, where the prevailing order is not 'determined by rights and the free association of individuals, but one governed by responsibilities, individual sacrifice, order, conformity, 'man-moulding', discipline and collective strength for a greater purpose, namely the Hindu nation'.[89]

The absorption of secularism into cultural common sense is contingent on the inclination of these spaces of civil engagement since the organisation of the Hindutva complex is well advanced of the Left, which has long depended on the now defunct and moribund Congress organisations. Varshney avers that 'the BJP has filled the organisational void created by the Congress. It has the cadres and the ideological commitment'.[90]

Conclusion

I submit that for success in a long-term 'war of position' with Hindutva, Ahmad's and Vanaik's imaginaries of secular nationalism are, to borrow the former's own description, 'necessary, but insufficient'. The innovative propagation of ideas that Ahmad identifies in the RSS's sixty-year strategy is the implied but unspoken conclusion of his own analysis.

The proliferation of initiatives such as Mumbai's *mohalla* committees, forums for dialogic co-operation for slum-dwelling Hindus and Muslims and the police, is integral to the ownership of the secular by citizen-actors. Though these committees were initiated at the behest of the Deputy Commissioner of Police to moderate the fall-out of the VHP's Ayodhya campaigns, they have since proliferated into diverse cross-community activities such as sports events and inter-religious festival celebrations.[91]

Innovative activities such as the *mohalla* committees, which bring individuals out of ethnic or religious community into forms of civic community, encapsulate the spirit of socially owned secularism. The task for the Left is to personalise the 'secular' as the Right has personalised the communal. Expanding the national project of secularism will invariably necessitate the democratisation of those concepts into forms of performance and action that are collectively achieved.

By outlining anti-secularist and Marxist responses to Hindutva I have sought to frame their differences in terms of their articulations of community, and the scale and scope of their collective interventions. Anti-secularists privilege the community but efface the national (or global) while Marxists have typically been fixated by national concerns without adopting a molecular approach to the cultivation of secular reflexes. Neither 'answer to the new political configuration of our times', since while state secularists lapse into the 'easy recuperation and celebration of the older socialist and nationalist utopias' anti-secularists lurch towards the 'outright rejection of the possibilities of decolonisation and global solidarity'.[92]

As damningly, anti-secularists believe that religious harmony arises from communal relations that have no place in twenty-century-first century India. Those relations flourish in arcadian social worlds that are unattainable because the sociological transformations of the last sixty years are irreversible. For many that is a good thing.

Besides, as *mohalla* committees and economic intercommunal traditions have demonstrated, there is no mutual exclusivity between the modern and the communitarian. The Hindu Right has no monopoly on constituting collective life in India; it goes on every day in a multitude of ways that long-standing cartographies of communities have failed to register. That failure, paradoxically, gestures towards the fertile spaces into which an engaged anti-majoritarianism can hope to grow.

Notes

1. Meera Nanda, *Prophets Facing Backward: Postmodern Critiques of Science and Hindu Nationalism* (New Brunswick: Rutgers University Press, 2003), p. 158.

2. Achin Vanaik, *The Furies of Indian Communalism* (London: Verso, 1997), p. 152.

3. It is little coincidence that the BJP was thrown together in an uneasy alliance in the ramshackle coalition which briefly deposed Indira Gandhi in the 1977 elections, and that Jayaprakash Narayan endorsed Hindutva's electoral rise to power.

4. A creed which survived long into the 1980s as that of the BJP's forerunner, the Janata Party.

5. Partha Chatterjee, 'Secularism and Toleration', *Economic and Political Weekly*, 1994, p. 1768.

6. Ibid.

7. Ashis Nandy, Shikha Trivedy, Shail Mayaram, Achyut Yagnik, *Creating a Nationality: The Ramjanmabhumi Movement and Fear of the Self* (Delhi: Oxford University Press, 1995), p. 59.

8. Ibid., p. 63.

9. Ibid.

10. Ibid.

11. Ibid., p. 78.

12. 'Hindu nationalism has always held in contempt the memories of Hindu polity as it survives in the traditional sectors of the Hindu society'. Ibid., p. 62.

13. Ibid., pp. 19–20.

14. Ibid., p. 21.

15. Ibid., p. 23.

16. Ibid., p. 18.
17. Ibid., p. 63.
18. Ibid., p. 77.
19. Ibid., p. 20.
20. Ibid.
21. Ibid., p. viii.
22. Ibid., p. ix.
23. Ibid.
24. Nandy, quoted in Radhika Desai, *Slouching Towards Ayodhya* (New Delhi: ThreeEssaysPress, 2002), p. 115.
25. Bruce Robbins, 'Secularism, Elitism, Progress and Other Transgressions', *Social Text*, 40, Fall, 1994, p. 27.
26. Merryl Wyn Davies and Ziauddin Sardar, *Distorted Imagination: Lessons from the Rushdie Affair* (London: Grey Seal, 1990), p. 32.
27. Ibid., p. 12.
28. Sarkar, quoted in Chatterjee, 'Secularism and Toleration', p. 1768.
29. Ashis Nandy, *The Intimate Enemy: Loss and Recovery of the Self under Colonialism* (Delhi: Oxford University Press, 1988), p. vi. The unique endowments of citizenship are neglected in anti-secularist opinion on modernity. Citizenship is characteristically conceived of in negative terms, as status to be retracted or withdrawn by racist regimes, but very rarely discussed as an empowering principle. It is not distinguished from the rationalisation of social relations nor favourably compared with traditional modes of community membership. It is never, then, perceived as a possible means with which to interrogate state power since it is ideologically associated with the proliferation of rationalising secularisation. Because it represents the dislocation of individuals from community to nation, intuitive filiation to coerced affiliation, citizenship is dismissed as little more than the pathology of an atomising modernity.
30. Nandy, *The Intimate Enemy*, p. xi.
31. Ironically, this is the same explanation for the resurgence of Hindutva given by Gurcharan Das in his ode to neo-liberalism *India Unbound*. 'Without a God or ideology, bourgeois life is reduced to the endless pursuit of cars, VCRs, cell phones, and channel surfing'. Gurcharan Das, *India Unbound: From Independence to the Global Information Age* (London: Profile, 2002), p. 308.
32. Nandy, quoted in Desai, *Slouching Towards Ayodhya*, p. 81.
33. He has expanded on this elsewhere. For instance he has written '[we share] a conviction that professional and academic boundaries will have to be crossed to make sense of the problem, and the belief that the social pathologies in this part of the world will have to be grappled with on the basis of the inner strengths of the civilisation as expressed in the ways of life of its living carriers [. . .] It is not meant not so much for specialists

researching ethnic violence as for intellectuals and activists trying to combat mass violence in the Southern societies unencumbered by the conceptual categories popular in the civilized world'. Nandy et al., p. xi.

34. Nandy, *The Intimate Enemy*, p. xi.

35. Chatterjee, 'Secularism and Toleration', pp. 1776–7.

36. Ibid., p. 1769.

37. Ibid., p. 1774.

38. Ibid.

39. Ibid.

40. Ibid.

41. Ibid., p. 1769.

42. Ibid., p. 1773.

43. Ibid.

44. Bhikhu Parekh, *Rethinking Multiculturalism* (Basingstoke: Palgrave, 2000), p. 263.

45. Ibid., p. 293.

46. Ibid., p. 263.

47. Ibid., p. 323.

48. Bhikhu Parekh, 'Making Sense of Gujarat', *Seminar*, 417, 2002, p. 31.

49. Parekh, *Rethinking Multiculturalism*, p. 293.

50. Meera Nanda, *Breaking the Spell of Dharma: The Case for Indian Enlightenment*, (New Delhi: ThreeEssaysPress, 2002), p. 175.

51. Sumit Sarkar: 'What regularly happens in such arguments is a simultaneous narrowing and widening of the term secularism, its deliberate use as a wildly free-floating signifier. It becomes a polemical target which is both single and conveniently multivalent. Secularism, in the first place, gets equated with aggressive anti-religious scepticism, virtually atheism, through a unique identification with the Enlightenment'. 'The Decline of the Subaltern in Subaltern Studies', in Vinayak Chaturvedi (ed.), *Subaltern Studies and Mapping the Postcolonial* (London: Verso, 2000), p. 311.

52. Amir Mufti, 'Auerbach in Istanbul: Edward Said, Secular Criticism, and the Question of Minority Culture', in Paul A. Bove (ed.), *Edward Said and the Work of the Critic: Speaking Truth to Power* (Durham: Duke University Press, 2000), pp. 248–9.

53. Paul Kelly, 'Identity, Equality and Power: Tensions in Parekh's Political Theory of Multiculturalism', in Bruce Haddock and Peter Sutch (eds), *Multiculturalism, Identity and Rights* (London: Routledge, 2003), p. 106.

54. Vanaik, *Furies of Indian Communalism*, p. 177.

55. Chetan Bhatt, *Liberation and Purity* (London: UCL Press, 1997), p. 35.

56. The Government of India (1951), cited in T. B. Hansen, *The Saffron*

Wave: Hindu Nationalism and Democracy in Modern India (Princeton: Princeton University Press, 1999), p. 47.

57. 'What then is religion (to use the word in spite of its obvious disadvantages)? Probably it consists of the inner development of the individual, the evolution of his consciousness in a certain direction which is considered good. What the direction is will again be a matter for debate. But, as far as I understand it, religion lays stress on the inner change and considers outward change as but the projection of this inner development. There can be no doubt that this inner development powerfully influences the outer environment'. Jawarharlal Nehru, in Sarvepalli Gopal (ed.), *Jawarharlal Nehru: An Anthology* (Delhi: Oxford University Press, 1980), p. 473.

58. For more on this, see Michael Brecher, *Nehru: A Political Biography* (Oxford: Oxford University Press, 1959).

59. Meera Nanda, *Breaking the Spell of Dharma*, p. 175.

60. Jurgen Habermas, 'Modernity: An Unfinished Project', in Maurizio Passerin d'Entrèves and Seyla Benhabib (eds), *Habermas and the Unfinished Project of Modernity: Critical Essays on 'The Philosophical Discourse of Modernity'* (Cambridge: Polity, 1996), p. 51.

61. Ashutosh Varshney, *Ethnic Conflict and Civic Life: Hindus and Muslims in India* (London: Yale University Press, 2002), p. 9.

62. Varshney sketchily draws some correlations between the demise of trade union activity and the levels of communal violence. The Keralese Marxist E. M. S. Namboodiripad, writing in 1979, had himself written glowingly of the ability of trade unions and Kisan *sabhas* to 'bring people together in joint struggles on economic, political as well as socio-cultural issues cutting across all differences of castes, religious communities and other sectarian groups'. E. M. S. Namboodiripad, 'Caste Conflicts vs Growing Unity of Popular Democratic Forces', *Economic and Political Weekly*, February, 1979.

63. Varshney, *Ethnic Conflict and Civic Life*, p. 215.

64. This can be attributed to the intellectual debts he holds to Ashis Nandy, and by extension to the Centre for the Study of Developing Societies.

65. Vinayak Chaturvedi, 'Introduction' to Vinayak Chaturvedi (ed.), *Subaltern Studies and Mapping the Postcolonial* (London: Verso, 2000), p. 311.

66. Vanaik (1997) mourns the working class as 'deradicalised and demoralised in the post WWII era' while Sarkar (2000) admits to the withering of 'hopes of radical transformation through popular initiative'.

67. Dipesh Chakrabarty, 'Radical Histories and Question of Enlightenment Rationalism', *Economic and Political Weekly*, 8 April 1995, p. 753.

68. Vanaik, *Furies of Indian Communalism*, p. 284.

69. Nanda, *Breaking the Spell of Dharma*, p. 175.

70. Parekh, 'Reflections on Gujarat', p. 31.

71. As in the Sangh Combine's declaration that India is 'secular' by virtue of being Hindu. Varshney, *Ethnic Conflict and Civic Life*, p. 84.

72. Aijaz Ahmad, *On Communalisation and Globalisation* (New Delhi: ThreeEssaysPress, 2003), p. 36.

73. Ibid., p. 81.

74. Aijaz Ahmad, *Lineages of the Present: Ideology and Politics in Contemporary South Asia* (London: Verso, 2000), p. 230.

75. 'In India, at least, it has not been possible to uphold ideas of constitutional democracy or socialist equality without a prior politics of secular civility. The opposition between secularism and fascism, in a country such as ours, is thus not incidental but integral'. Ahmad, *On Communalisation and Globalisation*, see p. 5.

76. Ahmad, *Lineages of the Present*, p. 291.

77. Ahmad, *On Communalisation and Globalisation*, p. 23.

78. Ibid., p. 37. 'It was the collapse of a Left-liberal kind of nationalism that provided the major opening for a fascist kind of nationalism, which set out, then, to exploit the weaknesses of that earlier nationalism and to formulate a different national agenda', ibid., p. 23.

79. Ibid., p. 36.

80. Edward Said, interview by Jennifer Wicke and Michael Sprinkler, in Michael Sprinkler (ed.), *Edward W. Said: A Critical Reader* (London: Blackwell, 1992), pp. 232–3.

81. Aijaz Ahmad, 'The Politics of Literary Postcoloniality', *Race & Class*, 36.1, 1995, p. 5.

82. Faisal Fatehali Devji, 'Hindu/Muslim/Indian', *Public Culture*, 5.1, Fall, 1992, p. 5.

83. Omar Khalidi, 'Muslims in Indian Political Process: Group Goals and Alternative Strategies', *Economic and Political Weekly*, 2–9 January 1993, p. 51.

84. Ahmad, *On Communalisation and Globalisation*, p. 36.

85. Ahmad, *Lineages of the Present*, p. 299.

86. Ibid.

87. Varshney, *Ethnic Conflict and Civic Life*, p. 215.

88. For more on the 'provincialisation' of Mumbai by the Shiva Sena, see Thomas Blom Hansen, *Wages of Violence: Naming and Identity in Postcolonial Bombay* (Princeton: Princeton University Press, 2001).

89. Chetan Bhatt, 'Democracy and Hindu Nationalism', *Democratization*, 11.4, August 2004, pp. 145–6.

90. Varshney, *Ethnic Conflict and Civic Life*, p. 242. Varshney's ambivalence to the Sangh is another major cloud over his study. Throughout *Ethnic Conflict* Varshney exonerates politicians and places respon-

sibility on the shoulders of the citizens. His colourless assessment of the BJP attests to the negligence he pays to nationalist imaginations of India. He even goes so far as to describe Hindu nationalists as 'bridge builders'.

91. Rustom Barucha, *In the Name of the Secular: Contemporary Cultural Activism in India* (Delhi: Oxford University Press, 1999), p. 83.

92. Rashmi Varma, 'Provincialising the Global City: From Bombay to Mumbai', *Social Text*, 81, Winter, 2004, p. 83.

Chapter 5

Making a Case for Multiculture: From the 'Politics of Piety' to the Politics of the Secular?

In its lack of critical spirit, today's multiculturalism is the antithesis of what once could more rightly have claimed the name. The possibility of gaining a critical vantage on one's own society by learning about an alien one [. . .] is almost entirely foreclosed by its complacent cult of difference.*

In short, Britain is a community of communities, a community with a collective sense of identity most certainly, but also including within it many communities with a more or less developed sense of their own identity.†

The honour of being the British symbol of dignity and poise has been monopolised by half-German nobility for the best part of sixty years, but it seems she now has a rival for her crown. And what an unlikely rival she is. First seen (for most of its viewers) on a reality TV show that had been posting historically low ratings, her bullying

* Gopal Balakrishnan, 'The Politics of Piety', *New Left Review*, 7, 2001, p. 159.
† Bhikhu Parekh, 'The Future of Multi-Ethnic Britain: Reporting on a Report', *The Round Table*, 362, 2001.

at the hands of three D-list celebrities catapulted her to the bosom of the great British public.

Since capturing *Celebrity Big Brother*'s very own crown, Shilpa Shetty has been as lionised outside the house as she was victimised inside it. She was booked to speak at a Commonwealth Day speech in the presence of a host of dignitaries. She has been courted by Tony Blair, lauded by Keith Vaz. *The Guardian*'s Stuart Jeffries gushed that Shetty is no less than the 'embodiment of civility, articulacy and reserve'. She even inspired *The Sun* to launch an anti-bigotry campaign, which thanked her for awakening the nation to the 'evils of racism'.[1]

The elevation of a Bollywood actress to the pinnacle of British social virtue is, on the one hand, indicative of the progressive trivialisation of racism in Britain. The commonplace discrimination of ethnic minorities – the institutionalised failing of Afro-Caribbean boys in our schools, for instance – plays second fiddle to an argument over wastefulness with Oxo cubes. On the other hand, her treatment at the hands of three white housemates seemed to confirm the terminal demise of Britain's tolerance for cultural difference. Even since her departure from the house, the British media has seemed almost embarrassed by Shetty's otherness. That could be why she hasn't been portrayed as a cultural mirror to British xenophobia, as an outsider reflecting our moral blemishes through exemplary alterity, but as the size-zero embodiment of what we could be if we only tried. Her virtues have been so singularly Anglicised that what might have been depicted as a culture clash has simply been cast as a melodrama between the national good and bad. Into the breach of our dwindling fund of common values steps Shilpa Shetty: the Indian who's an icon of all that's best about Britain.[2]

The *Big Brother* controversy comes at a time when British multiculturalism has been obituarised with gleeful relish. Trevor Phillips, Melanie Phillips, David Goodhart and even BBC news anchor George Alagiah have all taken the opportunity to throw brickbats in its direction. If multiculturalism truly is an anachronism, a pariah across the political spectrum, then where else should the Left turn?

This chapter will argue that multiculturalism's demise is symptomatic of the Left's allergy to culture in general, and an assumption that political solidarity can only ever be imperilled by it. It is this assumption that stunts progressive responses to majoritarian ideology. By reviewing responses to Bhikhu Parekh's *Rethinking Multiculturalism* (2000) I explain why the orthodox Left is wrongly discomfited by culture, before showing why multiculturalists are equally culpable for advocating a notion of culture that is politically misplaced and unproductively narrow. The chapter concludes by suggesting why multiculturalism's attentiveness to the complexity of belonging can nonetheless illuminate the shortcomings of cosmopolitanism as a utopian political horizon, gesturing to the right sort of interventions that the Left, in Britain, India, and beyond, have to make.

The Left and 'culture'

The established Left's discomfort with culture is never more eloquently expressed than in its judgements on theories endorsing the public recognition of cultural identity. Such theories have, in recent times, been monopolised by those who claim to espouse the philosophy of 'multiculturalism'.

For good reasons, Bhikhu Parekh's *Rethinking Multiculturalism* (2000) stands totemic among such philosophies. Even more recent and politically responsive descendants, such as Tariq Modood's *Multiculturalism* (2007), are indebted to Parekh's insistence that cultural difference, above all other forms, should be regarded as sovereign.

It is philosophical multiculturalism's stand on culture as much as difference itself that this chapter will seize as its simultaneously most enabling and disabling feature. I also argue that established positions on the Left have been indifferent (and occasionally hostile) to multiculturalism not only because of worries that diversity imperils political solidarity but equally because they have long histories of aversion to issues of identity and belonging. It is culture itself that confounds many on the old Left, which explains why their default response is to retire to the supposedly utopian ground of cosmopolitanism.

Before delving into the nature of the Left's critiques of multiculturalism, I'll take a moment to discuss the context of *Rethinking Multiculturalism*'s publication. Unlike many other books on multiculturalism, Parekh's contribution to the field wasn't a dry philosophical mediation on the relative shortcomings of universalism. In fact, it was overshadowed by the fruit of Parekh's other professional position that year: the *Report on the Future of Multicultural Britain*, commissioned by the Runnymede Trust. Parekh was its

chair. Despite sustained protests at accusations of his disproportionate influence on its outcome,[3] Parekh became instantly synonymous with it; it was popularly referred to as 'The Parekh Report'.
In retrospect, this may be something he regretted.

Criticism of the *Report* was pointed. Predictable hostility from
usual suspects on the Right was compounded by the government's
initial unwillingness to recognise its authority, preferring to insist
on its unofficial standing. Parekh himself believes the *Report*
suffered by following so quickly on the heels of the Macpherson
Report since, by sharing its 'vocabulary' and 'assumptions', it
became an 'obvious proxy target' for conservatives who, having
to bend over to Macpherson out of political sensitivity, were eager
to lynch a 'black manifesto' without such immunity.[4]

Though defenders of the commission would argue it was the
victim of media distortion – at no point did the report state that
the term Britain had 'racist' connotations, as was commonly
misrepresented – it was so widely ostracised that very few such
champions existed. Except in the most faithful heartlands of
bleeding-heart Britain, the 'Parekh Report' was a hapless pariah,
condemned for beating even the most modest expressions of
patriotism and national identity with the overbearing stick of
political correctness.

But it was not only a sitting target for the tabloid press: it also had
divisive consequences for the race-relations industry itself. Raj
Chandran of the Campaign for Race Equality derided the report
as a sad indictment of 'politically correct politicians and public
figures [who] have a masochistic urge to flagellate themselves, and a
sadistic notion to insult their fellow countrymen and women'.[5]

Much of that criticism was carried out at a relatively low level of
abstraction. This is mainly because the *Report*, designed for a lay
audience, made little attempt to justify its political and philosophical underpinnings. It is for that reason that *Multiculturalism* holds
more answers than its media-friendly counterpart, since it is, in
effect, a full-length explanation of exactly what terms such as 'a
community of communities' mean, and why the distinction between
that description and one of singular national identity is so important from a perspective that values cultural diversity.

Because of its comparatively high level of abstraction, *Multiculturalism* was subjected to less rabid hostility than the *Report*
but was still assailed from a battery of positions across the intellectual spectrum. Criticism was focused around interrelated and

contingent areas. These were the closeted portrait of cultural community, the espousal of communal 'duty', the imbalance of intra-group equality, the surreptitious validation of piety and the reckless discrediting of liberalism and anti-discrimination. If some criticisms were qualifications of an otherwise welcomed intervention in the field, others drew long question marks over its political sense.

In retrospect the boiling point of all critical opinion on *Multi-culturalism* was its perceived emphasis on the legal personality of communities at the expense of individual rights. Pluralised public ethics, with their tacit approval of in-group values, carry such a threat. Of all liberal principles, it is equality that is most conspicuously set in opposition to difference. And it is equality that many critics, avowedly liberal or otherwise, believed was imperilled by recognition of difference. Seyla Benhabib encapsulates this unease as the trade-off between 'internal freedoms and external protections'.[6] Benhabib takes the bottom line to be that 'if our goal is the preservation of ethnic, cultural, and linguistic diversity for its own sake, we risk sacrificing moral autonomy to aesthetic plurality'. 'Feminist' multiculturalists such as Gurpreet Mahajan have been among those to express disquiet about the privileging of cultural recognition above individual sovereignty.[7]

While Bernard Yack takes exception with the call of loyalty to the ancestral culture rather than concern for the immediate cultural community, citing Parekh's invocation of our duty 'to preserve and pass on to succeeding generations what they think valuable in it', Alibhai-Brown is troubled by the fixity Parekh attributes to 'cultural' community itself. She believes Parekh's vision of 'a community of communities' flirts perilously with communal involution, culminating with a sense of culture as whole, integrated and beyond reproach. She remonstrates that 'we may not all be fundamentalist liberal individuals, but that does not mean that we all belong to a community'.[8] Benhabib likewise suggests that to arrive at Parekh's communitarian multiculturalism we have to 'homogenise' and 'flatten out' the contradictions and struggles, and ignore 'the interpretative strands and contestations which constitute culture'.[9]

Liberals on multiculturalism

For many avowed liberals, meanwhile, Parekh teeters on the brink of being 'simply too communitarian': floundering on contradictions between an ostensibly relativist, communitarian approach and a commitment to egalitarianism. Kelly avers that this relativism assumes that societies are all as tolerant of difference as ideal liberal democracies are, leaving unaddressed 'the unequal and unjust power relationships which exist within [them]'. Since Parekh 'rejects the possibility of an appeal to universal principles or norms as a way of reconciling or arbitrating between cultural groups', 'moral and political issues can only be addressed from the internal perspective of a moral and political tradition'.[10] Yack wonders whether this is the point at which liberals should 'abandon' Parekh's multiculturalism.[11]

One of the most sustained and belligerent liberal critiques of multiculturalism is Brian Barry's, in *Culture and Equality* and 'The Muddles of Multiculturalism' (2001). Barry contends that Parekh's multiculturalism undermines measures for anti-discrimination. It does so, he argues, by scapegoating the liberal establishment as the cradle of cultural intolerance and thereby weakening the foundations on which anti-discrimination rests.

Taking refuge in the beneficence of the liberal tradition, Barry defends it from Parekh's assault on its cultural bias by defining it as a principle of fair treatment and equal opportunity, rather than neutrality. He claims liberalism has been far more successful in removing the punitive disadvantages of ethnic minorities through principles of equal treatment and policies of anti-discrimination. He asserts that the problems thrown up by the uniform exercise of liberal law have been 'relatively few'. He even concludes that 'western liberal societies may be the only ones in which it has ever been widely believed that there is anything wrong in treating outsiders less well than the already established population'.[12]

Barry's suspicion of multiculturalism rehearses well-worn liberal apprehensions of the rights of vulnerable individuals in non-liberal cultures. The danger of multiculturalism (of pluralising the public culture) is to allow reactionary cultural minorities, under the patronage of diversity, to mistreat with impunity women, children and those who deviate from their prevailing norms.[13]

But the critical distance liberals such as Barry attempt to place between themselves and the communitarian aspects of multiculturalism can only be sustained in the artifice of polemical argument. The essentialism of the liberal critique of multiculturalism disregards the obvious truth that Parekh's, like all mainstream multiculturalisms, is fundamentally a conservative theory that ethically defers to prevailing societal norms.

In fact, it is multiculturalism's very implication with liberal strategies that attracts so much scepticism from anti-racist campaigners. Multiculturalism and the politics of recognition, in the mild doses advocated by thinkers like Parekh, are perfectly compatible with the aspirations of the liberal establishment; that's precisely why it has become the British state's staple anti-racist policy since Roy Jenkins' era.

A politics pivoted around cultural or racial recognition carries little destabilising threat to the social order (but then neither does it promise significant anti-racist amelioration). Barry's conclusion that Parekh is agitating for public policy that will splinter Britain into communal division distorts the latter's vision from a compromise between collective and individual rights to an exclusively communitarian projection of our social future. It is deaf to Parekh's repeated stress that the evolution of British public culture rests on a conception of the nation as *both* a community of citizens and a community of communities.

Barry is therefore disingenuous when he polarises multiculturalism from liberalism, and Parekh is at pains to express his belief that the two can co-exist without conflict or compromise. His dialogically constituted multicultural society upholds the 'truth of liberalism and goes beyond it'. Such a society 'is committed to both liberalism and multiculturalism, privileges neither, and moderates the logic of one by that of the other'.[14]

Exalting multiculturalism as a fully grown ideology is to demand too much of a relatively limited set of ideals. What Barry wilfully overlooks is that Parekh does not disavow liberal values themselves but understandably contests the presumption of liberal superiority above other 'operative public values'. Multiculturalism seeks to debunk liberal exceptionalism, not liberalism itself. Parekh insists that liberalism needs to retain its 'critical thrust' and not be 'emasculated' since it is so deeply embedded in the 'operative public values' of Western societies.

Nonetheless, and for its own good, he recommends that uncritical genuflection give way to critical reflection. Making the considered point that any cultural viewpoint is dangerous when universalised, Parekh argues that liberalism needs to be tempered with an alternative perspective from which to moderate its excesses and imagine 'alternatives'.[15]

The blind conviction of champions such as Barry in liberalism's inherent righteousness fails to acknowledge the tradition's poverty in engaging with the significance of culture and cultural diversity. Liberalism classically conceives of culture as passive, of non-liberal societies as unable to fulfil the good life, and of liberal values as universal. This residual colonial superiority haunts political theory and its mandate for justice in a multicultural society. It fails to grasp the benefits of cultural diversity for society as a whole. Advancing the debate to meet the needs of our multicultural societies, Parekh argues, involves the 'need to go further and make a positive case for cultural diversity, showing how and why it is worth cherishing, and that it benefits not just minorities but society as a whole'.[16]

By not recognising the legitimacy of alternative cultural values, liberal societies have a higher propensity for illiberalism because they absolutise their own values. Further, it invests liberals with the arrogance to presume that all who refuse to share such values 'are victims of false consciousnesses'.[17] The merits of liberal society are precisely its tolerance and inclusivity, not an authoritarian will to autonomy, individualism and self-creation. To play up the latter aspects at the expense of the former is to mischaracterise liberalism's real strengths.[18]

Without a broadened and pluralised conception of human and societal nature able to accommodate the non-liberal figure of the community into the public personality, liberalism will continue to project a social horizon fashioned in the image of middle Britain. It will continue, in short, to make the bourgeois white male the subject of justice and the bearer of rights. It will be a poor servant to those individuals who wish to participate in secular ways that are beyond the scope of liberal institutions and imaginaries. Since they do not accept that liberalism exhibits the exclusionary features of a culture, its advocates are able to excuse its practices from the scrutiny they afford those of other cultures.

Socialists on multiculturalism

It would be disingenuous, though, to portray liberalism as the only intellectual formation of the Left that's averse to culture. Liberal discomfit with cultural identity may be prodigious but it is certainly not unique. Those who claim to speak in the name of socialism have been equally hostile to multiculturalism, and though their complaints are outwardly incongruous with the liberal critique, they inevitably converge around an elective disengagement with culture.

Gopal Balakrishnan's seething disownment is a prime example of the socialist distaste for multiculturalism. His denunciation stems from his reading of it as simply an ideology of affirmative action, incapable of imagining what it would take to achieve 'real social equality', a 'stealth liberalism capable of integrating variously devout immigrants into unevenly secular European societies'. 'Transformed into a new grand theory of political society, with its own view of human nature, theory of justice, and so forth, multiculturalism tends to decay into a form of pious and wishful thinking'.[19]

Because he interprets Parekh's definition of communal cultures as a fusion of 'ethnicity and religion', he suggests multiculturalism's sole ambition is to smuggle religiosity through Western society's back door. He sees multiculturalism as a warped hybrid of liberalism and religion, each as counter-revolutionary as the other, and equally abhorrent to the genuine Left.

He aligns himself with Nancy Fraser when he points to multiculturalism's moral stress on 'difference' as counter-productive to the socialist ideal. Both surmise that the transformation of the deep structures of political economy and culture require dissolution of group differences. It is on the basis of this reasoning that Fraser advocates a political combination of socialism and deconstruction.[20] Liberal welfarism and mainstream multiculturalism are 'analogous' affirmative strategies to injustice: making surface corrections to inequitable social outcomes without disturbing the underlying framework that generates them.[21]

While both Balakrishnan and Fraser are within their rights to question the 'transformative' scope of multiculturalism, there is a characteristically academic disdain in their critiques for cultural environments and their influence on political literacy and engagement. Both regard religious or ethnic community and identity at worst as something to be 'put out of business', at best as 'false consciousness', but either way, unworthy of being sensitively accommodated to the matrix of human-rights culture.

They forget that cultural minorities coalesce into communities because others in their community have suffered the same hardships that they are confronted with. It is critical to remember that inequalities and inequities are not arbitrarily diffused through society. Barry may be right to guard against assigning all disadvantages to ethnic origin, but racism, xenophobia, Islamophobia and other forms of bigotry remain determinate engines of economic and social injustice. 'Denizens of the same ghetto' have little consolation but their own fraternity and little goodwill but from those who, having suffered with them, are enjoined to fight in solidarity. Communities in struggles against human violations are, in the words of Upendra Baxi, 'the primary authors of human rights'.[22] In discriminatory environments, community is defined as much by shared struggle as by received cultural identity. Fraser seems to forget that ethnic minorities have had to organise separately – to assume the identities of communities – in response to their experiences of racism, exclusion and discrimination.[23]

Fraser's stated contradiction between ethnic or racial identities and transformation implies that any resistance conducted on the basis of that identity militates against social justice and is therefore devoid of any 'significant' virtue even if it might achieve 'surface' gains.[24] By doing so she ignores those many struggles for material equalities – such as single-issue campaigns against prejudiced policing or inadequate housing – that are conducted in the name of distinctive cultural groups. And as Iris Young counter-argues, most of these struggles self-consciously involve issues of 'cultural recognition and economic deprivation' but do not constitute these as 'totalising ends'.[25] Assertions of cultural identity are often the only means to secular justice. As she goes on to suggest, anti-racist, feminist and anti-gay movements, herded together under the rubric of 'identity politics', are better understood as conceiving of recognition as a means to socio-economic justice.[26]

The logic of domination, realised in stigma and demonising practices, dictates that people come to think of themselves and others in terms of identity experiences, which they hold in community and which alienate other identities at the moment of experience. The communitarian identity assumed for the historical moment is that of a 'minority community'. They effectively become the 'resistance identities' that Castells, in the second volume of his trilogy *The Information Age: Economy, Society and Culture* (*The Power of Identity*, 1997) writes about as the compelled antithesis of domination power. Neera Chandoke, in her account of contemporary majoritarianism, describes how communities with 'stigmatised identities' will attempt to revalue their formerly stigmatised identity and endeavour to 'change the power equation in society'. Through this process, members of that community will become differentiated from others 'despite many commonalities that may create bonds of solidarity, as well as subsume differences within the community'.[27]

Fraser's partnering of deconstruction with socialism exemplifies the stupefying obliqueness of materialists to cultural belonging. The logic from which she deduces that deconstruction should be socialism's 'cultural analogue' reinforces the position that cultural difference has to be obliterated before formal equalities and liberties are affirmed. Deconstruction is touted as the 'deep restructuring of the relations of recognition' where ever-new constructions of identity and difference are 'freely elaborated and then swiftly deconstructed'. The 'transformative recognition' politics of deconstruction are comfortable with the 'transformative redistribution' politics of socialism because both 'undermine existing group differentiations'.[28]

But its 'utopian image', as Young responds, is 'a world of political ends and objectives that is eerily empty of action'.[29] More than that, it is an imaginary abstracted from lived struggles against injustice – particularly racial justice – which are acted inside deeply specific historical and cultural coordinates. They are also acted in community with others, communities which cannot be sustained without 'the bonds of recognition, reciprocity and connection'.[30]

The projection of fluid identities is the kind of fantasy that can only be nurtured in academic discourse. Fraser's argument betrays not only an arid imagining of socialism but a fallow apprehension of cultural belonging too. Bleeding cultural identity of its weight, it insidiously views it as something dissoluble (considering its dissolution a worthy ambition). Fraser is mistaken to think that we can shed our cultural identities like clothes as though our social lives are revolving wardrobes from where we can pick and choose from a shiny confection of attractive suits.

The inadequacy of philosophies of formal equalities such as Fraser's is that they only begrudgingly engage with questions of cultural difference, and then only on their own universalist terms. That she is only able to analogously extrapolate racial justice from socialist strategies exposes how heavily difference is subordinated to universality in her way of thinking.

It is no surprise then that liberals and socialists have been dogmatic in their refusal to accept that their own solidarities could be *cultural*. It is anathema to their sensibilities that they might carry distinctive identities, present obstacles to inclusion or behave communally. In the absence of self-reflexivity, liberalism and socialism consistently abstract their solidarities from the particularities of belonging that collectively inform their world view. Perhaps it takes a 'multicultural' sensibility to recognise the parochialism in their values or the absolutism for which both commonly indict other solidarities.

The Indian Left and Hindutva

It might appear as if I am highlighting these shortcomings for polemical point-scoring. I want to stress that it is driven, on the contrary, by a conviction that the Left's cultural engagement will determine our collective political future. It may be difficult for those on the British Left to comprehend the long-term prognosis for an oppositional politics that abstains from issues of culture and belonging. The same cannot be said of the Indian Left, whose tribalism has effectively crippled coherent resistance to the majoritarianism of the Sangh Parivar.

The cost of electively disengaging from culture has been profound: in the absence of a coherent response, Hindu nationalists have successfully shifted India's political centre to the Right. While the Congress Party has prevaricated over its secularity, while caste-based parties have become increasingly assertive and individualistic, and while the Communist parties look incapable of renewing themselves, those sympathetic to Hindutva have made systematic efforts to communalise the state and civil society. Though these have not always been successful, and the BJP has been toppled from parliamentary power, it is indisputable that Indian secularity has never looked as precarious as it has in the past ten years.

The Indian Left has not been slow to point fingers, and as we have seen, the recriminations have been bitter. Belatedly, the major factions have come to some kind of self-realisation that it has been a historical indifference to the question of culture that has been decisive. Meera Nanda laments that the failure has been to join the battle for secularism and humanism 'at the terrain of culture'. She remarks that it is as failure for which 'all Left intellectuals share the blame'.[31] Aijaz Ahmad, meanwhile, has reflected that Hindutva's rise to power has come on the back of a growing 'culture of cruelty' which licenses permissiveness to violence and moral numbness. He suggests that staving off the threat of such cultures requires the Left to pose an alternative nationalism to strengthen a 'culture of civic virtues', grounded in liberalism and a commitment to secularism.[32]

As inadequate as they are, neither of these responses is commensurate with a cosmopolitan sensibility that desires to obliterate cultural identities in favour of an idealistic belonging to globality, or a deconstructive will for disposable identities. In the face of majoritarian projects like Hindutva, the utopianism of old political horizons seems hopelessly moribund. The Indian Left has had to revise its relationship to culture accordingly; the globalised consequences of the war on terror have meant that many democracies, including Britain and Holland, have endured a rightward drift on issues of multiculturalism and national identity that have to be responded to as urgently.

The trouble with Parekh's culture

The danger is that, in our haste to address these issues, we adopt the wrong approach by embracing outwardly progressive but politically inappropriate models of culture. Such a temptation is grave when we already have ready-made answers to the dilemma of cultural difference: philosophies of multiculturalism. What I will argue here is that multiculturalism is as much a part of the problem as it is a part of the solution, but that its flaws are completely misrepresented by the established Left.

We have seen that Parekh's philosophical multiculturalism is well placed to expose the cultural obtuseness in theories of formal equality. It is not so adept, however, at interrogating its own assumptions. In fact, what is striking in *Rethinking Multiculturalism* is an unflinching conviction in its conception of culture. The assurance with which Parekh privileges one manifestation of culture above all others repeats itself in virtually all subsequent theories of cultural diversity. Troublingly, it also underwrites state multiculturalism.

Parekh on culture and community

It is a passage where Parekh expounds on the reciprocities between culture and community that goes furthest in illuminating his understanding of culture, and the kind of solidarities that he imagines arising from the political application of multiculturalist principles. It reveals his belief that while certain forms of culture are able to sustain community, others are ultimately too fragile.

To be precise, Parekh is heavily sceptical about the possibilities of evolving communal identities and the ability of *experienced* culture to sustain bonds of community between people. This scepticism derives entirely from how he conceives both culture and community, and their role in sculpting individual and collective identities.

For him, culture is something we inherit, not something we make, and it is communities of inherited rather than emergent culture that concern him.

Parekh describes cultural community as 'a body of people united in terms of a shared culture'.[33] He argues that it is possible to retain aspects of culture while being estranged from the overarching community, as in the case of economic migrants and refugees. It can also cut the other way when individuals dissent or renounce cultural values but remain communally bound because they are 'deeply attached' to the community (or, as likely, economically and socially dependent on it).

While cultural communities might not be determining or constitutive of human personality, Parekh is not shy of suggesting that they are the *principal* factor in human beings' social evolution. 'To be born and raised into a cultural community is to be deeply influenced by both its cultural content and communal basis'. Individuals' behavioural characteristics and inclinations arise almost in imitation of others in their immediate cultural circle since 'culture catches them at a highly impressionable and pliant stage and structures their personality'. The depth and breadth of these impressions strike deep roots and become an inseparable part of their personality.[34]

Parekh is insistent that the way that cultural communities frame human existence, from the cradle to the grave, makes them a qualitatively different experience from voluntary forms of association. They are neither 'instrumental' nor dispensable when they satisfy extrinsic interests. As 'historical communities' sustained by 'long collective memories of struggles and achievements and well-established traditions of behaviour' they are also not ephemeral creations. They imbue their members with 'a sense of rootedness, existential stability and the feeling of belonging to an ongoing community of ancient and misty origins'.[35]

But what is glaringly absent from Parekh's account, with its heavy privileging of inherited over secular relations, is a worldly sense of community as experiential and evolving. Though he is rightfully scathing of the liberal tendency to conflate cultural communities with voluntary associations, he over-determines and overplays the inherited characteristics of historical community relative to its participatory and experiential dimensions. Despite the many qualifications he makes to insist on the negotiable nature of this inheritance his insistence remains a begged question. Why is

Parekh at such pains to defend 'historical' community above all others?

After all, it not as though historical communities and their identities – as he defines them – are on the verge of social extinction, or are even in decline. Religious and ethnic associations dominate British civil society and are the principle forums through which minority politics (in particular) are convened. The forms of association which have perversely become scarce, as historical communities flourish, are those communities 'of resistance' which transcend sectarian identities for common secular goals.

State or philosophical multiculturalism: what's the difference?

Parekh's priority of historical communities is also problematically redolent of state multiculturalist *policy*, which, in the British context at least, has financially rewarded the pursuit of cultural recognition. Parekh's multiculturalism has nothing to say about this; it finds itself in awkward agreement with the patronage of inherited culture.

In fact Parekh's multiculturalism quietly endorses the legacy of multiculturalist policy: the formation of ethnically defined fiefdoms managed by a class of community ambassadors who arrogate representative authority to themselves. In his obituaries of anti-racism, Sivanandan indicts state multiculturalism as the architect of its demise, holding it accountable for deflecting the 'political concerns of the black community into the cultural concerns of different communities'. Cultural politics 'spelt the death of a more generalised political culture', 'leading to people fighting each other over these issues that transgress their identities', rather than 'opposing the larger tyrannies of the state that affect them all'.[36]

The ravages of state multiculturalism are the outcomes of privileging and patronising cultural communities; they are policy corollaries of prioritising inherited cultural identities above experienced social identities. Since Parekh has no concern for experiential solidarity, why should a poverty of political literacy bother him when minorities have the compensation of cultural lattitude? Because Parekh's multiculturalism practically endorses the state rationalisation of cultural diversity, it offers us no alternatives whatsoever to the policy disaster of state multiculturalism.

Secondly, though Parekh is convinced of the compelling nature of 'intercultural dialogue' it remains a politically empty and programmatically abstract concept. Parekh believes that, compared to liberalism, intercultural dialogue can better realise the aspirations of deliberative democracy. He says this is so because it imbues us both with a sense of empathy and a critical view of ourselves – a perspective of 'immanent transcendentalism'. The inhabitancy of the Other's perspective allows the transformation of our own. He describes the process of conversation as to be 'beyond oneself, to think with the other and to come back to oneself as if to another'.[37]

Parekh contends that the willingness to empathetically inhabit alternative perspectives is a value neglected by liberal pedagogies. The faculties of 'imagination', 'sympathy' and 'sensitivity' all rank low in the liberal imagination but feature highly in Parekh's multiculturalist one.

Parekh's autopsy of the escalation of tensions between the liberal establishment and the Muslim community through the Rushdie affair is transparently concerned with vindicating such an argument, and typifies his tendency to attribute all conflicts between majorities and minorities to a poverty of cultural literacy so that intercultural dialogue becomes a sovereign remedy.

According to Parekh, it was the poverty of cultural literacy on the part of both parties that exacerbated the fractiousness of the conflict and prolonged stalemate over the issue. The exchange between liberal backlash and Muslim outrage during the Rushdie affair was rendered partially intractable because costs and rights were conceived of in peculiarly liberal terms on one side and peculiarly Islamic values on the other, since 'both groups knew little about each other's way of life and thought'.[38] Without a cultivated 'bicultural literacy', reasons were apprehended within each community's own cultural horizons and misunderstood. The true cost of each demand was misrepresented and it was this, Parekh contends, that stymied a resolution to the conflict, costing British society as a whole 'the opportunity to develop a self-understanding adequate to its multicultural character'.[39] He believes that a negotiated compromise could have been reached only if both parties had been sufficiently bicultural or had made a genuine effort to enter into each other's way of thinking.[40]

But Parekh's account of the episode is partial and biased to his own multiculturalist mandate. It elides the need for secular common ground by arguing that greater cultural knowledge could have averted the crisis. By doing so he fails to indict multiculturalist policy for perpetuating structural disadvantages of political literacy which left Muslims as *a community* with very few actors who could meet liberals on secular terms (especially since leadership was monopolised by traditional elites).

Muslim demands for editorial amendments and restrictions on publications were predominantly mediated through references to religion, faith and community that were incongruous with the liberal recourse to free speech. Liberal critics of the Muslim response, such as Fay Weldon, Roy Jenkins and senior journalists at the *Sunday Telegraph*, were able to monopolise secular reason. The discursive hierarchies between the liberal establishment and the Muslim communities were made to stand in for wider civilisational disparities between barbaric Islam and the British mainstream, giving succour to arrogant brow-beating about how best to civilise British Muslims from their book-burning barbarism to Britain's exalted democratic values.

Bradford's Muslims in particular were politically isolated in the debate and unable to form alliances with other faith or civil-society groups because their representatives were unable to reach across the cultural boundaries of their 'community' as secular citizens. Through multiculturalist policies they may have been politically 'recognised' but they were nonetheless impotent; able to mobilise as a faith community but unable to address the state on the basis of their rights. Despite their rhetorical multiculturalist construction as a community, this didn't make them 'integrated collective actors' able to exercise community rights.[41]

Minorities might instinctively appreciate the 'spirit of multiculturality' as a means to impress their views in the public sphere, but it is less obvious why it should be compelling to the majority. Multiculturalism offers no incentives for hegemonic voices to compromise their power and authority beyond the platitudes of the inherent virtues of cultural diversity. Neither does Parekh specify the purpose of intercultural dialogue, nor how it might structure anti-racist resolutions. Without a substantive constitutional programme for action, multiculturalism becomes the backdrop for peacock politics; talking shops without discernible aspirations or outcomes.

Indian anti-secularism and Hindutva

If philosophical multiculturalism has been critically impotent when addressing the obliteration of secular collectivism in Britain, analogous intellectual positions in India have been indicted for far greater political culpability. There, the rising intellectual currents of what has been collectively described as 'anti-secularism' have historically dovetailed with the ideological rise to power of Hindu majoritarianism.

As we saw in Chapter 4, even though anti-secularism cannot be simply reduced to an indigenous Indian multiculturalism, they share enough common features to make a compelling comparison. Though there are several points of confluence, it is a common privileging of inherited culture and its corollary of historical communities that stand out as their most politically disabling features. Anti-secularism and multiculturalism come together on many levels but it is their unequivocal articulation of culture that is most curious, especially when set in relief against the resurgence of cultural nationalism across the world.

The inherited cultures which draw most protection from anti-secularists are overwhelmingly religious (as they are in Parekh's multiculturalism). A common anti-secular concern is therefore the preservation of religious communities' cultural autonomy from conformity to secular values. Anti-secularists are wedded to the notion that religiosity oxygenates the Indian way of life – a point that Parekh himself has made on several occasions. In fact, it is the only type of culture that anti-secularists ever speak of with optimism or enthusiasm. They are scathing of national culture, sceptical of socialist culture, and silent on experienced culture. They see no future in solidarities ordered along any one of those axes.

In fact, just as multiculturalists like Parekh are rendered ideologically complicit with a state multiculturalism that divides and rules, anti-secularists are similarly implicated in the exaltation of religious community. So while anti-secularists have been as vocal in their condemnation of Hindu nationalism as other ideological factions on the Indian Left, they have been just as busy dismantling the ranks of secular opposition to it. It may not be deliberate, but this surrender to religious culture has been fateful and partly responsible for the Indian Left's capitulation to Hindutva's assault on Indian secularity.

The problem that confronts both anti-secularists and multiculturalists is that they ultimately find themselves on the wrong side of the political fault lines – even if they don't recognise it themselves. While philosophical multiculturalism endorses state multiculturalism, anti-secularism rationalises state majoritarianism. This is because both multiculturalism and majoritarianism originate from the premise that we prefer our 'own kind', and that kind is always defined in terms of inherited culture.

Inherited versus experienced cultural identities

The privilege multiculturalists and anti-secularists afford inherited cultural identities therefore also marginalises and devalues the merits of emergent secular identities. These emergent secular identities derive from inhabitations of minority that have social rather than historical origins. Philosophical multiculturalism simply forecloses on the possibility of new political alliances formed by individuals' re-articulation of communitarian ties.

Examples from Britain might be those communities of affinity that mobilised for justice for the murders of Stephen Lawrence and Ricky Reel, the wrongful imprisonment of Satpal Ram and the death in prison of Zahid Mubarek. In India, Mumbai's *mohalla* committees exemplify how even deeply entrenched communal divisions can be sublimated by civic community.[42]

These are participatory, experiential and secular communities. They are communities that resist facile categorisation as voluntary associations even though their contributions to political culture might outlast their communal basis. These are the novel kinds of 'resistance identities' that Castells principally relates to collective victims of racialisation and demonisation, but which differentiate their members from more orthodox 'inherited' cultural communities by creating bonds of experiential solidarity.

It is also obvious that these are not disposable communitarian identities that can be casually discarded once they have outlasted their usefulness. Individuals' participation and identification with these communities have deep influences on how they understand themselves and the society around them. Unlike historical communities for whom a critical understanding of society can be a low priority, political consciousness underwrites the shared culture of such communities of resistance.

In short, the recovery of secular solidarity – and with it the prospect for coherent political resistance – is as unlikely to be realised with those who only recognise inherited culture as it is with those who disavow culture altogether. Whether one position is taken or the other, genuine political agency remains corralled by historical elites or traditional hierarchies. Whichever approach is chosen the political consolidation of ethno-religious difference is also left *in situ*, just as alternative axes for political solidarity remain unexplored.

The real challenge – which neither ideological camp is ready to accept – lies firstly in enabling individuals from marginalised historical communities to realise some kind of political autonomy, and secondly in providing an ideological/organisational counter-balance to the incentivisation of ethno-religious solidarity by regressive state policies. Where does such a project begin?

Secular multiculture

What I'm proposing is that multiculturalism is as inescapably a part of the solution as it is irrefutably a part of the problem. I'm not declaring it the salvation of a secular political culture: it is a useful starting point, but not a full stop. Philosophical multiculturalism – Parekh's in particular – pushes us in the right direction by debunking universalist assumptions about political engagement. Political solidarity *can* be ordered around culture, inherited or experiential. Banal as that statement may seem, it is potentially profound for our advocacy of secular solidarity and culture; properly applied, it promises to democratise and enrich the cultural matrix of political activism in general.[43]

Though Parekh problematically dwells on cultural difference and understates global principles of the common good, this shouldn't obscure the significance of his critique of universalism. Even if his focus lies elsewhere, his insights are instructive for those concerned with the devolution of political agency, while his attentiveness to the complexities of attachment and cultural identity exposes the orthodox Left's chronic blindness to such issues.

Parekh might like to tout his theory of multiculturalism as cosmopolitanism's conceptual inverse, but I believe this is too simplistic a role for it to adopt. At face value it is true that Parekh appears so obsessive about filial communities that he fails to consider how such communities project themselves onto the world, how individual members articulate themselves as secular actors, or how other political solidarities might spring from alternative social axes.

But when approached with other critiques of cosmopolitanism in mind, multiculturalism opens up more suggestively for the possibilities of constructing an alternative means of connecting cultural identity with political solidarity. Even though Parekh and others see cultural recognition as the end of the political rainbow, there's no reason why we shouldn't take multiculturalism's attentiveness to identity and build something more ambitious with it.

To expand on these somewhat cryptic remarks, the sensibilities of what Françoise Vergès describes as 'creole cosmopolitanism' moots the possibility of reconciling internationalised attachments with the particularities of cultural difference. It also disproves assumptions that inhabitations of 'cultural' minority produce exclusively parochial political values. Vergès speaks of 'creole cosmopolitanism' as motivated by a longing for 'access to the universal' in the place of a delimited 'territory on which to speak'.[44]

Nothing suggests that such political desires are localised in the historical conditions under which creole cosmopolitanism came into being; they are potentially common to all cultural minorities. While orthodox cosmopolitanism eschews localised forms of belonging entirely, in favour of a higher commitment to the flux of global rootlessness itself, it is entirely possible to defend secular principles from the particularities of local positions without strain or contradiction.

A globalised sensibility born in the coordinates of inherited cultural identity is not necessarily more fragile than orthodox cosmopolitanism; assertions of cultural identity do not preclude a willingness to connect with the world. Put simply, there is nothing intrinsic about collective cultural identity that inspires parochialism or insularity. You can be as attached to a certain world view as you like but still retain a desire to 'access the universal', to cross communal boundaries to speak truth to power, to inhabit the subjectivity of human rights. It is what militates against the *realisation* of that desire that has to be confronted, and this is another way to frame the challenge facing the contemporary Left.

This is why, even if Parekh's multiculturalism may offer us no indications of what culturally informed human rights solidarities might look like, he takes us closer to actualising them by alerting us to the poverty of universalistic assumptions about political engagement. His theory tells us that human nature and identity cannot be explained by recourse to their universal and particular dimensions, but instead by dialectical interplay between the two. Since 'humans belong to a common species not directly but in a culturally mediated manner', 'their similarities and differences are both important and dialectically related'. We therefore 'acknowledge the obligation to respect both their shared humanity and cultural differences'.[45]

Importantly, this need not translate into a relativist rejection of global norms. On the contrary, Parekh's dialectic forecloses on the very possibility of absolute difference. As human beings endowed with common characteristics and needs, we are all entitled to fundamental human rights; as culturally different beings we are entitled to have our differences respected too. Joseph Carens' counter-concept of 'justice as even-handedness' argues from this premise that to treat people fairly, we must regard them concretely, with as much knowledge as we can obtain about who they are and what they care about. In answer to the preference of abstraction inherited from John Rawls' totemic *Justice as Fairness* (1971), Carens suggests that instead of trying to 'abstract from particularity', we should 'embrace' it, but in a way that ensures fairness to all different particularities.[46]

Until we acknowledge that universal principles of empowerment can never become popularly owned until they are tuned into the cultural and religious languages through which we articulate our everyday lives, they will remain the exclusive domain of those blessed with liberal privileges. Individuals within historical communities will remain alienated from the means with which to interrogate either the leadership that appropriates collective personality for personal gain or the state power that only recognises them as constituents of ethno-religious collectives. Perversely, unless we are able to bring human rights into conversation with 'culture' we will never see its widespread inhabitation or, consequently, the recovery of secular solidarity.

If it seems illogical that secularity should be borne of culture, experiential or inherited, it is worth considering the views of Stuart Hall on the possibilities offered by 'multicultural political logic'. Hall recognises this as a reforming pressure on liberal-constitutional models, involving the 'expansion and radicalisation of democratic practices in our social life' and the diversification of public-sphere activity, where cultural identities are not attenuated in secular activities but actively retained. Through the process of democratic reaffirmation, a 'diversity of new public spheres' must be constructed in which 'all the particulars will be transformed by being obliged to negotiate within a broader horizon'. He appeals for this space to 'remain heterogeneous and pluralistic, and for the elements negotiating within it to retain their *différance*.[47] This last point is crucial. Contrary to conventional wisdom, diversity does not have to be sacrificed to enable expansion or radicalisation.

This is what I mean by 'secular multiculture': a new framework for the Left's engagement with culture, where cultural difference co-exists with secular association. Secular is used here as Edward Said thinks of it: not as opposed to religion, but to the nation, against 'all paranoid frontiers separating "us" from them'.[48] Nurturing the tension between 'multicultural political logic' and the ethics of the secular can revitalise a public sphere beggared by state multiculturalism's skewing of political agency towards traditional elites.

Secular multiculture in action: examples from Britain

When we examine the trajectory of minority politics in Britain this 'secular multiculture' appears to be increasingly prominent, transforming the character of the alternative public sphere in the process. What was once dominated by the politics of inherited identity has given way to solidarities animated by cultural identity but anchored in human rights.

Throughout the 1980s and early 1990s separatist ethnic movements mushroomed while multiethnic pressure-group activity declined. Because of their localised and politically incoherent nature, they were unable to wield much institutional influence and are historically weak actors in campaigns against state racism.

Recent developments offer hope that the sectarian tide is slowly being turned as new political actors have emerged out of the wreckage of multiculturalist policy. The enquiry into the murder of Stephen Lawrence catalysed the formation of 'hybrid' ethnic minority politics which Shukra et al. have characterised as a 'transitional public sphere'. These social movements determinately retain 'black perspectives' ordered through 'self-organisation'.[49] Unlike traditional sectors of the ethnic-minority political sphere, they prosecute their objectives through appeals to human-rights standards and so have acquired a legitimacy that is not contingent on state patronage.

Pioneers of the transitional public sphere, such as the National Civil Rights Movement, are purpose built to act on legislative initiatives such as the Macpherson Report and the Human Rights Act, linking the judicial system with 'family-led campaigns about specific cases of racial justice'.[50] The charter of the National

Assembly against Racism is likewise founded on a commitment to human rights in policing and asylum legislation.

The judicial awareness of actors in the transitional public sphere has also been instrumental in the molecular expansion of human rights and political literacy among organised ethnic minorities. Operation Black Vote, for instance, has initiated its own political education programmes, while the Black Racial Attacks Independent Network has counselled community organisations on how to apply the Human Rights Act in their own work. This is not to deny that the mismanagement of the transitional public sphere could present as many obstacles as opportunities for the radicalisation of ethnic-minority politics. The vulnerability of smaller groups to alienation from wider networks potentially stifles dissent; the professionalisation of senior echelons in these movements is another source of compromise; while the inclusion of state agencies such as the police forcibly moderates agendas.

These innovations in minority politics display a novel syncretism that dismantles state-orchestrated distinctions between inherited and experiential cultural identities. Though they may not have done enough to subvert the hierarchies of political patronage that exist at present – it is still the leadership of religious community organisations that the government courts for approval – their very existence offers an alternative axis along which to order political solidarities, disincentivising the political consolidation of ethno-religious difference. They allow citizens the opportunity to form new political alliances by rearticulating existing communitarian ties without having to sever them.

Conclusion

If this chapter seems to be ending on an optimistic note, I want to correct that. The new political solidarities gestured towards are merely glimmers of hope. They carry distant promise, not immediate salvation.

Cultural identity has become the ideological fault line of the global struggle between humanity and cruelty. It is apparent not only in India, which has lurched as perilously close to a state renunciation of secularism as at any point in its democratic history, but also throughout the world, as cultural nationalism has risen in ideological complement to counter-terrorism and neo-liberalism. Global politics today is as much defined by the exploitation of anxiety and the cultivation of paranoia as anything else. Holland is the latest country to bear its teeth in a majoritarian grin.

We cannot hide from it, any less than we can hide from race, the nation or identity itself.[51] The escalating radicalisation of cultural identity – whether from the state or those arraigned against it – is always bad news for the powerless.

Our collective political future therefore hinges on whether the leaders of oppositional politics are savvy enough to get their hands dirty by plunging into the murky waters of belonging. The time has come to recognise that our emerging political actors will be multi-culturalism's children: citizens who refract their political interests through the lens of their inherited cultures without being bound by them.

While the Left ties itself in knots weighing the priorities of redistribution against the demands of recognition, clinging desperately to the dream of a cosmopolitan future, the merchants of majoritarianism hunt the big game of cultural identity. They know that manipulating desires for belonging delivers a far bigger payout than factionalised navel-gazing. It's a lesson the Left could be learning for a long time.

Notes

1. Sadhavi Sharma, 'Worshipping a Bollywood Actress? How Backward', *Spiked*, 26 February 2007.

2. Trevor Phillips, chief of the Commission for Equality and Human Rights, has said it took Shetty to remind us 'what we most value about being British'.

3. 'The report is entirely their creation, and I only hope that the understandable but regrettable tendency to identify a report with a commission's chair will be studiously resisted'. Bhikhu Parekh, preface to The Runnymede Trust Commission on the Future of Multi-Ethnic Britain, *The Future of Multi-Ethnic Britain* (London: Profile, 2000).

4. Bhikhu Parekh, 'The Future of Multi-Ethnic Britain: Reporting on a Report', *The Round Table*, 362, 2001, pp. 679–80.

5. Raj Chandran, 'An Insult to All our Country', *Daily Mail*, 11 October 2000, p. 7.

6. Seyla Benhabib, '"Nous" et "Les Autres": The Politics of Complex Cultural Dialogue in a Global Civilisation', in Christian Joppe and Steven Lukes (eds), *Multicultural Questions* (Oxford: Oxford University Press, 1999), p. 57.

7. Gurpreet Mahajan, 'Rethinking Multiculturalism', *Seminar*, 484, 1999, p. 61.

8. Bernard Yack, 'Multiculturalists and Political Theorists', *European Journal of Political Theory*, 1.1, 2001. Yasmin Alibhai-Brown, 'Rethinking Multiculturalism: Cultural Diversity and Political Theory [Review]', *Political Quarterly*, 72.3, 2001.

9. Benhabib, '"Nous" et "Les Autres"', p. 57.

10. Paul Kelly, 'Identity, Equality and Power: Tensions in Parekh's Political Theory of Multiculturalism', in Bruce Haddock and Peter Sutch (eds), *Multiculturalism, Identity and Rights* (London: Routledge, 2003), p. 104.

11. Yack, 'Multiculturalists and Political Theorists', p. 112.

12. Brian Barry, 'The Muddles of Multiculturalism', *New Left Review*, 8, 2001, p. 52.

13. Brian Barry, *Culture and Equality: An Egalitarian Critique of Multiculturalism* (Cambridge: Polity, 2001), p. 284.

14. Bhikhu Parekh, *Rethinking Multiculturalism* (Basingstoke: Palgrave, 2000), p. 340.

15. Ibid., p. 128.

16. Ibid., p. 98.

17. Ibid., p. 112.

18. Ibid., p. 113.

19. Gopal Balakrishnan, 'The Politics of Piety', *New Left Review*, 7, 2001, p. 159.

20. Nancy Fraser, 'From Redistribution to Recognition? Dilemmas of Justice in a "Post-Socialist Age"', in Cynthia Willett (ed.), *Theorizing Multiculturalism: A Guide to the Current Debate* (Oxford: Blackwell, 1998), p. 41.

21. Ibid., p. 31.

22. Upendra Baxi, *The Future of Human Rights* (Oxford: Oxford University Press, 2002), p. 89.

23. Kalbir Shukra, Les Back, Michael Keith, Azra Khan and John Solomos, 'Race, Social Cohesion and the Changing Politics of Citizenship', *London Review of Education*, 2.3, November 2004, p. 190.

24. Fraser, 'From Redistribution to Recognition?', pp. 31–3.

25. Iris Marion Young, 'Unruly Categories: A Critique of Nancy Fraser's Dual Systems Theory', in Willett (ed.), *Theorizing Multiculturalism*, p. 65.

26. Ibid., p. 51.

27. Neera Chandhoke, *Beyond Secularism: The Rights of Religious Minorities* (New Delhi: Oxford University Press, 1999), p. 31.

28. Fraser, 'From Redistribution to Recognition?', pp. 38, 36.

29. Young, 'Unruly Categories', p. 65.

30. Stuart Hall, 'The Multi-Cultural Question', in Barnor Hesse (ed.), *Un/Settled Multiculturalisms: Diasporas, Entanglements, 'Transruptions* (London: Zed Books, 2001), p. 236.

31. Meera Nanda, *Breaking the Spell of Dharma: The Case for Indian Enlightenment* (New Delhi: ThreeEssaysPress, 2002), p. 175.

32. Aijaz Ahmad, *On Communalisation and Globalisation* (New Delhi: ThreeEssaysPress, 2003), p. 5.

33. Parekh, *Rethinking Multiculturalism*, p. 154.

34. Ibid., p. 156.

35. Ibid., p. 162.

36. A. Sivanandan, *Communities of Resistance: Writings on Black Struggles for Socialism* (London: Verso, 1990), p. 84, and Campaign Against Racism and Fundamentalism, 'Fighting our Fundamentalisms: An Interview with A. Sivanandan', *Race & Class*, 36.3, 1995, p. 74.

37. Michaeflelder and Palmer, quoted in Parekh, *Rethinking Multiculturalism*, p. 337.

38. Ibid., p. 305.

39. Ibid.

40. Ibid.

41. A notable exception was the pressure group Women Against Fundamentalism who demonstrated democratic agency neither to endorse nor defend Western liberalism or Islamic values, but used the affair to draw attention to women's issues of household inequality, prostitution and education. In the words of Homi Bhabha (1995), their intervention was one of 'reconjugating, recontextualizing, translating the event into the politics of communities and public institutions'. They are a good hybrid example of a cultural and affinity community, sharing a common historical culture but also an experiential culture born in oppression. Bhabha, 'Translator translated', interview with W. J. T. Mitchell, *Artforum*, March 1995, p. 114.

42. Though the committees were initiated at the behest of the Deputy Commissioner of Police to moderate the fall out of the VHP's Ayodhya campaigns, they have since proliferated into diverse cross-community activities such as sports events, and inter-religious festival celebrations.

43. Rustom Barucha, *In the Name of the Secular: Contemporary Cultural Activism in India* (New Delhi: Oxford University Press, 1999), p. 99.

44. Françoise Vergès, 'Vertigo and Emancipation, Creole Cosmopolitanism and Cultural Politics', *Theory, Culture & Society*, 18.2–3, 2001, pp. 171, 179.

45. Parekh, *Rethinking Multiculturalism*, p. 124.

46. Joseph Carens, 'Justice as "even-handedness"', *Seminar*, 484, 1999, p. 49.

47. Hall, 'The Multi-Cultural Question', pp. 235–6.

48. Edward Said, Interview by Jennifer Wicke and Michael Sprinkler, in Michael Sprinkler (ed.), *Edward W. Said: A Critical Reader* (London: Blackwell, 1992), pp. 232–3.

49. Kalbir Shukra, Les Back, Azra Khan, Michael Keith and John Solomos, 'Black Politics and the Web of Joined-up Governance: Compromise, Ethnic Minority Mobilization and the Transitional Public Sphere', *Social Movement Studies*, 4.3, 2005, p. 42.

50. Ibid., p. 38.

51. Paul Gilroy, 'Joined-up Politics and Postcolonial Melancholia', *Theory, Culture & Society*, 18.2–3, 2001, p. 166.

Conclusion

This book has explored the current struggles over the progressive dilemma. As we've seen, the terms of this dilemma are themselves contested, with competing assertions of where the real fault lines in today's global politics lie. There are those on the Left for whom class remains the great dividing line and, less archaically, those who persist in the belief that the real dilemma is whether progressive politics aligns itself with redistribution or whether it allows recognition to obscure its mission.

This book has been unequivocal in its assessment of the challenges facing oppositional politics amid the various tussles for pre-eminence and priority. These challenges are the result of extensive and cumulative sociological shifts in democratic society that have global implications. The de-territorialisation of religion, mass demographic upheaval through immigration, redrawn political sovereignties and relentless urbanisation have made these shifts ubiquitous and analogous even if they are not directly comparable. They have presaged the globalisation of the progressive dilemma.

The challenge comes from the anxieties, fears and dislocations bred by these various sociological shifts. What's important to note is that these popular responses are not novel; they have and will continue to recur in the career of democratic society. What is novel is how these responses are framed. Through the democratic world (except perhaps homogenous societies like Norway) we are living in times that are not only characterised by cultural diversity but supposedly threatened by it too. This threat extends not only to national security but also, arguably, democratic survival itself.[1]

At no other point in recent memory has the diversity of cultural identity become such a vexed issue for liberals and the Left. Though those who espouse progressive politics ordinarily shy away from matters of culture and identity because of the anti-universalism they carry by association, it is fast becoming impossible to contest extremist and even conservative ideologies without such a clearly articulated position on such issues. This is the essence of the progressive dilemma; should the Left bring cultural identity under its compass to steer it in ideologically agreeable directions, or should it abstain from ideas that have no place on a progressive agenda?

This conclusion will tease out the global lessons from the three instances of the progressive dilemma examined in this book: the contest over 'new times', the right response to Hindutva, and Britain's post-multiculturalist future. It will then look at whether the conditions that have compelled the introspections of the Left are abating or intensifying, and how this is impacting on the ground, specifically referring to the fortunes of Britain's next generation of political actors. My final remarks will be reserved for recommendations, both for future political directions and necessary intellectual labour.

Progressive dilemmas

Post-multicultural Britain

David Goodhart's conservative liberalism coherently maps shifting social attitudes to diversity, mirrored in government policy. His proposals for 'second-tier' or 'earned' citizenship concretise ideas that have been floating around Whitehall in recent years.

It responds to popular anxiety about the erosion of national culture and the withering of reciprocal obligations, preoccupying causes for the neuroses of Goodhart's national subject.

His typically conservative liberal answer to the crisis of multiculturalism is to reinvigorate British identity through a highly conditional communitarianism whose signature is a higher obligation-to-entitlement ratio among newcomers than settled citizens.

I have argued that in practice such a conditional and conformist regime of British community is likely to worsen the forms of exclusion that inspire popular majoritarianism in the first place. The conditions of progressive nationalism's two-tier citizenship would do little to address what I've termed the 'reciprocity of belonging' among groups most vulnerable to discrimination, and reinforce the ideological construction of majorities and minorities. By privileging the sensibilities of ideological majorities, Goodhart's new liberal imagination of national community therefore articulates a profoundly inequitable concept of citizenship. It only entrenches – and worse, legitimates – the deprivation of some of Britain's most vulnerable groups by insisting that government should reserve its focus on the 'anxious and the liberal'. It relegates rampant Islamophobia, the institutional failing of Afro-Caribbean schoolboys, and chronic discrimination in mental-health services to the waste bin of government priorities. Its strongly conformist bent would equally make the civil-political exclusion of national Others, such as Muslims, refugees and Eastern European immigrants, that much starker.

Goodhart's progressive nationalism alerts us to the dangers of an unmeasured response to popular anxieties, particularly when it sets a new baseline for political discourse. The liberal conservative disavowal of multiculturalism has effectively opened a vitalising intellectual (and ultimately political) space where majoritarianism can expand with licence. Goodhart's major achievement, despite the overblown condemnation of some commentators, was to make it credible to dispute the intrinsic merits of cultural diversity. That he did so by invoking economic reason and identity loss made it both controversial and appealing.

But it is not only the conditionality and the conformism of Goodhart's Britain that panders to majoritarianism. It is also deeply conservative, and this is most evident in its defence and naturalisation of xenophobia. It is this communitarian dimension that is redolent of the pluralist but prescriptive nature of Bhikhu Parekh's multiculturalism. Both clearly make a case for the preference of 'our own': in Goodhart's case that means settled Britons; for Parekh, those who share our ethnic, linguistic or religious inheritances. In both cases the constitution of that shared identity is naturalised. We like our own instinctively, and so we dislike those whom we perceive to be different with equal conviction. As both have vehemently asserted, that doesn't make us racist.[2]

What it does mean is that our inherited or long-standing communitarian ties are existentially significant. The agreement between multiculturalism and Goodhart's new liberalism makes the 'progressive dilemma' a much larger issue of where the line between liberals and communitarians should be drawn, if at all. It also shows how vulnerable multiculturalism is to co-option by nominally majoritarian arguments such as Goodhart's. Take Parekh's qualification of the rights of minorities to pursue their own vision of the good life, their duty to defer to the 'operative public values' of host societies.[3] At no point does he define how 'operative public values' come into existence, or how they can disputed. They exist because they carry majority backing.

How is this different to Goodhart's insistence that minorities must concede more, culturally, than national majorities? Multiculturalism, philosophically and politically, isn't distinct or progressive enough to deserve saving; as Alana Lentin concludes, it is an unworthy prize for anti-racists in particular.[4]

'New times'

If neither multiculturalism nor its liberal wannabe successors can provide the equitable, empowering community that can contest the appeal of the majoritarian, then the Left has to be wary of governmental communitarianisms that operate in ways which effectively shrink the space for citizens to act beyond the scope of their state-defined communities, and thereby bolster majoritarian grievances.

The legacy of the 'new times' dispute is evidence of the setbacks the Left can inflict on itself when it misjudges its interventions. For the contributors to the *New Times* project such interventions were necessary if the Left was going to claim any influence on post-Thatcherite Britain, where the neo-liberal hegemony was making the Labour party increasingly irrelevant. The Left had to wake up to the singularity of the Thatcherite enterprise, and the massive economic and social changes it simultaneously represented and shaped. This meant relocating its politics to the sites of emerging political energy. It meant abandoning the collective for the individual, and embracing the conspicuous diversity of the British Left's new constituencies.

For Sivanandan and *Race & Class* the choice was equally stark: submit to sociological fatalism or reaffirm the Left's faith in the constitutive role of political agency. *New Times'* 'Thatcherism in drag' was not a critique, but a celebration that bowed to the inevitability of the empirical transformations wrought by neo-liberal governmentality. Though Sivanandan grudgingly agreed with Hall's description of the material conditions which precipitated the collapse of the social democratic settlement, he saw 'new times' as an opportunity to regroup, not reinvent. A socialism that exalted the individual as the locus of political subjectivity not only betrayed the solidarity, co-operation and mutualism that had inspired its hard-won victories against capital, but also its true constituencies. If socialism's purpose was not to unite the oppressed in harmonised struggle, then how could it meaningfully seek to offer an alternative to the brutalising, anti-social legacy of Thatcherism?

The 'new times' debate therefore rehearses many of the themes that recur in all progressive dilemmas: a universal consensus on extensive sociological change; the acknowledgement that right-wing ideologies are bending those changes to their advantage; a fear of marginalisation among reformist factions on the Left; an attempted appropriation of ideological/discursive territory, followed by condemnation from other voices on the Left, some of whom claim to be the guardians of genuinely progressive values.

But it also illustrates how challenging the parameters of the Left's mandate can debilitate as well as invigorate its political relevance, both in the present moment and in the future. This is apparent in two ways. In the first instance it is perhaps only in retrospect, with the advent of third way politics and the demise of multiculturalism, that the 'new times' debate has become useful to the development of a progressive politics. At the time neither its proposals nor the ensuing critiques of its position halted the advance of the neo-liberal hegemony, or arrested socialism's accelerating irrelevance.

Secondly, both sides in the debate were overhauled by an emerging ideology that was comfortable inhabiting the space between Thatcherism and the Left, even if it inclined more obviously towards the latter. Although neither the *New Times* reformers nor the old Left could have forecasted New Labour's communitarianism in either its multiculturalist or One Nation forms, they were nonetheless unprepared for the impact third way politics would have on civil society. It did not consolidate the market individualism that the Left as a whole anticipated for a politics that at times threatened to drift vacuously between the progressive and the conservative, but inaugurated a 'governance through community' that would have dire consequences both for the community solidarities that Sivanandan prized, and the individual agency that Hall hoped for. Third way politics effectively immobilised the Left; the result was a balkanised civil society where opportunities to negotiate and displace entrenched communitarian ties had shrunk to the size of territorialised cultural differences.

Hindutva and India's Left

Unsurprisingly, given the scope and scale of the threat offered by an ascendant Hindu nationalism, the progressive dilemma in India has been framed in more dramatic terms. The Left has had to proceed delicately but decisively, neither of which it has so far contrived to do in any sustained manner. Perhaps the greatest imperative, though, has been to act in unity, which has proven to be the greatest challenge by far.

Oppositional politics has been haemorrhaging vitality at every opportunity. It has not been helped by introspective hand-wringing, accusations of complicity and above all a failure to resist Hindu nationalism in direct confrontation.

It is easy for outsiders to attribute these failings to attritional division – compulsions of ideological chauvinism. But as my account of the progressive dilemma has shown, the right response is frequently elusive and cannot be isolated either from the complexity of sociological change or the dexterity of its majoritarian appropriation.

Hindu nationalism has certainly been nimble enough to dodge the slingshots of secular reason. Even more worryingly, it has occasionally (and maybe increasingly) proven impervious to caste politics. The fact remains that India's long-standing commitment to diversity is threatened after enduring a prolonged slide towards state communalism. The Sangh Parivar is a clear and present danger to India's secularity – and even to the robustness of its liberal democracy – because it presents the only national vision for contemporary India. It frames such a vision in fiercely conditional, conservative and conformist terms. India is not a society but, according to Hindu nationalism's messiah M. S. Gowalkar, 'a corporate personality'.[5]

The persistence of a majoritarian vision of Indian society will have acute consequences for Indian citizens, exacerbating the inequalities of a society where only a thin tranche is enjoying the spoils of globalisation. It is no coincidence that a majority of India's minorities are also among its most deprived and discriminated, and in particular that such a large proportion of Muslims live in relative poverty (and also among its poorest states). For these groups Indian citizenship is purely nominal; the routine failure to discharge constitutionally mandated governmental duties relegates them to a fractional enfranchisement, or what Chetan Bhatt has sharply observed as being akin to 'infra-citizenship'.[6] There is a direct correlation between the limited stakeholding of the poor and of minorities in civil society – including their participation in 'mass intercommunal structures' – and the nature of this citizenship. If India is suffering a crisis of genuinely democratic citizenship, then the decline of secular collectivism is partially responsible for it.

To some extent India's secularity will always vacillate because it is not secular in the European sense. India's constitutional *sarva dharma sambhava* does not require state separation from religion but 'equidistance' to all religions. Equally, as Chetan Bhatt has pointed out, the obverse implications of the operational regime of Indian secularism could also mean 'equiproximity to religions and promulgation of each'. In this 'vitalizing political space' the state has only been able to recognise and respect religion by apprehending it demographically, as a community of believers, which leads in turn to the actualisation of social groups.[7]

In addition, the failure of government to meet the constitutional rights of individual citizens has similarly given rise to the assertion of caste identities assuming the personalities of distinct social communities making aggregated political claims. This is why it is customary for Indians to remark that they do not cast their vote, but vote their caste. In many respects caste therefore performs as ethnicity does in other parts of the democratic world (and most noticeably in the absence of class anchors).

Parallel to Britain, this concretisation of inherited identity into socio-political collectivism has accelerated the decrepitude of a political culture dependent on secular collectivism. It was a culture nurtured by organisational outposts of the Congress Party that served as the 'mass intercommunal structures' that Varshney eulogises for their ability to moderate interreligous tensions, but which are long since moribund, as the party itself has fallen from hegemony. In their absence hardline Hindu nationalist groups from the VHP to the Shiva Sena have monopolised civil social sites of collective activity (at least in an organisational sense).

For these reasons it is probably inconceivable that a progressive politics could win popular appeal if it were culture-blind. Anti-secularists have insisted that any political culture that disregards 'the religious inspiration of public ethics' is destined for the margins of Eurocentric elitism. This might be so, but the Left doesn't have to incline as far as Hindu nationalists do to win a broad mandate. Nor does it have to play within the parameters of the culture or community it favours. The Left should be less concerned with marking its distance from culture and more engaged with deconstructing the naturalisation of cultural solidarity that goes under the name of Hindu nationalism. The Indian middle classes have made their anxieties over national identity plain; the Left has to offer alternatives axes for solidarity and more equitable, empowering and pluralist communitarianisms if it is to meaningfully contest Hindutva. And this contest has to be situated both nationally and locally.

Recent developments

Britain

At the end of Chapter 5, I remarked that Britain's emerging political actors will become 'multiculturalism's children'. By that I meant the second and third generations of immigrant descent who have been raised in multiculturalism's distinctive political environment. It is these actors who will reap the consequences of the Left's resistance against majoritarian imaginaries, and who will have to find the resources to undo the reversals of fortune that might take place if those interventions are misjudged. Recent developments tell us a lot about the obstacles multiculturalism's children face, prior to those interventions, to establish themselves as independent political actors in contemporary Britain. They also map the terrain on to which a progressive politics has to assert itself if it is to win their hearts and minds.

A survey conducted for a 2006 report by the conservative-leaning think tank Policy Exchange was accompanied by a poll whose headline figures garnered far more column inches. The poll revealed, among other things, that 37 per cent of 16- to 24-year-old Muslims would prefer to live under *sharia* law, compared to 17 per cent of those surveyed over 55. Another often repeated figure was the third of 16- to 24-years-olds who believed that those converting to another religion deserved execution (under a fifth of those under 55 shared that view). Unsurprisingly, 86 per cent of young Muslims said that religion was the most important thing in their lives.[8]

These figures were seized upon as evidence that British-born Muslims are more sympathetic to political Islam than their parents and grandparents, and reinforced the perception that British Muslims are Muslims first and British second. Taken in isolation from the report – which painted a more complex but not necessarily accurate portrait of contemporary British Muslim identity – such polls vindicate the government's persistence with multiculturalist policies that respond to the existential dependency of second and third generations on race and faith. Headline figures such as these make it easier for the government to engage with young Muslims through their religious identity, rather than as ordinary, diverse citizens.

But it is not only Muslims who are being marginalised by multiculturalism. In December 2004 Gurpreet Kaur Bhatti's play *Bezhti* was cancelled amid protests by some Sikhs, who claimed offence by the theme and setting of the play (and one scene in particular, which takes place in the re-creation of a *gurdwara*). On the opening night the theatre was encircled by hundreds of protesters, three of whom were arrested for criminal damage. The decision to cancel was taken with the blessing of the Commission for Racial Equality.

Following the play's closure a minister in the Home Office, Fiona Mactaggart, blithely implied that death threats against the playwright would probably increase sales. That they forced Bhatti into hiding and the withdrawal of the play in Britain altogether doesn't exactly bear that out. She also happily endorsed the protests as evidence that if 'people feel this passionately about theatres', it 'is a good sign for our cultural life'. Her shamelessly opportunistic remarks spoke eloquently about the fickle nature of British multiculturalism, veering from protection from offence to derogation from shared values depending on the needs of the political moment. It panders to minorities and placates majorities equally well, free of a commitment to upholding the sanctity of civil rights.[9]

It is extremists or conservatives who monopolise the alternative public sphere, a legacy of government patronage and a callous, uninformed tabloid media who trade in the hard currency of shock and controversy. Multiculturalism has abetted this monopoly by systematically disenfranchising a silent majority from the public sphere in favour of token representation that is seldom representative. Even those who have been consulted have felt betrayed, disappointed by the government's failure to incorporate their views or manipulated to serve a pre-meditated purpose. Some are left with the impression that consultation mechanisms are only there to fulfil obligations on paper, not to inform government decisions. Nonetheless organisations or individuals are reluctant to withdraw from the process for fear of being excluded from dialogue altogether.[10]

It is no surprise that multiculturalism has begot a silent majority. Beyond headline polls are figures that are far more revealing, and speak of the widespread desire for public-sphere democratisation and diversification among 'multiculturalism's children'. For example, a MORI poll conducted in August 2005 told a rather different story about British Muslims, comparing their social attitudes to those of the public overall.

Ninety per cent of Muslims believed that immigrants should be made to learn English – compared to 82 per cent of the general public. Similarly, 76 per cent said immigrants should be made to pledge their primary loyalty to Britain, higher than the 73 per cent overall figure. Most revealingly, 65 per cent of Muslims thought that imams should be made to preach in English, almost double the proportion of the general public. Unfortunately these kinds of statistics rarely feature in the media's depiction of minority attitudes towards Britain, which tends to favour alarmist revelations of pervasive radicalisation, as the Policy Exchange poll indicates. It therefore makes it that much easier for the government (and increasingly New Conservatism) to blame disaffection and alienation among minority youth on 'cultural malaise' rather than exclusionary causes, such as low educational achievement and disproportionately high unemployment among young Pakistani and Bangladeshi men (a problem that extends even to highly educated Muslim women).[11] Once again, multiculturalism serves as an excuse for state failure, while simultaneously obscuring persistent levels of discrimination.

The current challenge for anti-racists, and the progressive Left, is how they should distance themselves from multiculturalism without pre-empting the ascendancy of a majoritarianism that masquerades under the equitable language of social or 'community cohesion' that threatens to stigmatise all expressions of cultural difference and identity.[12] This book has concluded that it can only succeed if two conditions are met. Firstly, progressive politics has to insist on the right to respect private differences of race, faith or ethnicity without allowing those differences to be politically inflated into a primary mode of address for so-called ethnic minorities. Secondly, the Left has to consistently advocate the equality of inherited and experienced cultural relations, and oppose governmental attempts to grant the legitimacy of community status only to the former. Governance through community has to be just that; not governance through interlocutors who are hostile to dissent and devolution.

Enforcing these conditions demands that the British Left negotiate its discomfort with culture, and particularly the culture of settled and new immigrants. It has to confront the truth that principled aversion will not make the elephant in the room disappear: it only allows the Right to claim them as their domain, their property. Once that becomes too entrenched, the opportunity to steer them in progressive directions may be lost, or at best severely compromised.

India

Today, the gravest threat to Indian secularism is complacency. It is folly to confuse the electoral defeat of the BJP with the ideological demise of Hindutva, but the organised Left in India will have practically done just that if it fails to capitalise on the opportunities afforded by the disarray precipitated by those losses. The Sangh Parivar is in organisational crisis at present, but given time to regroup can pose a resurgent appeal, especially to the middle classes that it served so well at the head of the NDA coalition. The big question is what the Left can offer as an alternative. Will it be pragmatic and throw its hat in with caste politics in a bid to break up the Hindu nationalist/Congress duopoly, or can it pursue an idealistic vision of a pluralist, progressive India without recuperating obsolete Nehruvian shibboleths?

The extent to which India's marginalised groups have had to actively seek state recognition of their difference to secure the basic conditions of citizenship makes it natural for the Left to align itself with them, even if, as I have argued, their politics entrenches and accentuates division between the similarly oppressed. Dalits and lower castes (or OBCs, to use the political shorthand) have had to organise separately to obtain ordinary civic privileges, and that can only be done by asserting the legitimacy of a heritage of oppression.

But it has also led to hostility between lower castes occupying similar positions in the social order, as the consolidation of caste identity has intensified. Each of the major sub-castes has now fabulated elaborate caste-origin myths that exalt its ancestry as near descendants of the divine. The Yadavs, who predominate in Bihar and Uttar Pradesh, claim to be descended from Lord Krishna, who is depicted in Indian epics as a cow-herder (the Yadav caste function). On the one hand these ethnic myths illustrate the pride that caste heritage now inspires in modern India. On the other they speak of the deep 'ethnification' of caste, and the inter sub-caste enmity this begets. For every caste alliance there is now is a caste rivalry, and this is making caste politics less about unity under oppression than fragmented division for social dignity. There is consequently less scope for India's lower castes to form a coherent front against Hindu nationalism, or for the government to address them on the basis of common citizenship rather than caste identity. As we've seen, this has both benefits and costs but whether it can ward off majoritarianism in the long term remains to be seen.

It would also, therefore, be wrong to fête caste politics for repelling the advances of Hindu nationalism. Social trends, such as Sanskritisation, and economic trends, such as middle-class growth, conspire to make Hindutva's unifying message increasingly more relevant for increasing numbers of upwardly mobile, urban castes.

Indian Muslims are caught in much the same bind: the failure of state and federal governments to provide them with the basic provisions of citizenship have compelled them towards (outwardly) militant expressions of Islamic identity, but which in turn inspire majoritarian condemnation for separatist behaviour.

A good example is the accusation that Bihar's Sunni Muslims are fomenting regressive Islamic tendencies by preferring to send their children to the state's stronghold of *madrassas* rather than state schools. But this stereotype, common to Muslims across North India, obscures the fact that state schools are poorly run and barely functional: government statistics show absenteeism among *teachers* runs to one third on any given day. Only 3 per cent of Bihar's state schools have electricity.[13] It is no wonder that Muslim parents, like their Hindu counterparts, feel as though they don't have a choice.

Majoritarianism doesn't only compel enclavism but can also become a self-fulfilling prophecy when it provokes radicalism. It is a truism that groups that are targeted because of ascribed identities inevitably cleave to those identities with an intensity they didn't hold before. This has never been more apparent than in BJP-governed Gujarat, scene of the pogroms described in the

Introduction. While at one time Muslim and Hindu Gujaratis were interlinked, interdependent in the ways that Varshney commended as insulation against communalism, they have gradually become autonomous and segregated as the industrial composition of the state economy has shifted towards the service sector. But the division between the two communities has become profound in the wake of the 2002 pogroms. Muslims have begun to respond to their demonisation in predictable, understandable but disheartening ways. It is particularly apparent in their dress code: Muslim women have forsaken the sari for the *salwar kameez*, while Muslim men are now prone to grow beards and wear white caps. They wear their difference with distinction. With the exception of the doctors implicated in the recent airport bomb plots in Britain, India has contributed hardly any terrorists to global *jihadist* movements. Perversely, Hindu nationalism might be worse for Indian security than Kashmiri separatism; it might also send scores of poor, disenfranchised and persecuted Muslims into the welcoming arms of political Islam.

The conundrums of political and cultural identity facing Indian minorities suppose that majoritarianism remains latent in Indian society. As I outlined in Chapter 2, Indian majoritarianism runs deeper than Hindu nationalism. But it is Hindutva that can render the majoritarian mindset into a coherent ideology, and ideologies survive electoral defeats. As I've also insisted, the electoral setbacks suffered by the BJP were not as severe as they superficially appear, and certainly didn't constitute India's renunciation of Hindutva. If anything it served to warn the BJP that deviating too far from its core constituency and playing at appeasing all India's vote banks jeopardises their biggest electoral dividends.

Consider the Sangh Parivar's continuing footholds in Indian society: control of its largest trade union, its largest student union, and controlling interest of its largest network of daily and weekly publications.[14] All this and the BJP still commands a quarter of the national vote. The Sangh Parivar's long march is far from over, but its 'war of position' now moves into a defining phase following the recriminations between the RSS and the BJP after the 2004 elections.

Two post-election events encapsulate the difficulty in forecasting the longer-term fortunes of Hindu nationalism. Only a few months after the BJP-led National Democratic Alliance was deposed from the political centre, one of orthodox Hinduism's most celebrated priests was arrested on suspicion of murder in Tamil Nadu.[15] BJP leader L. K. Advani, never slow to exploit popular emotions (it was his *rath yatra* that set the *Ranjanmabhoomi* campaign in motion) raised the familiar cry of an embattled Hinduism under threat, once again. He even went so far as to stage a hunger strike outside the *Lok Sabha,* India's lower chamber in New Delhi. But far from rallying Hindutva's foot soldiers into a confrontation with Congress's 'pseudo-secularists', the protest was a resounding failure and died with a whimper. The potential flashpoint between competing ideologies never occurred. Advani himself was subsequently replaced as leader of the party.

In contrast to the indifference which met the Shankarcharya's arrest, the Hindu hardline Shiva Sena went on the rampage through Mumbai in July 2006 for much the same reasons as Advani had sought to mobilise mass protest two years earlier. In this incident a statue of the late wife of Shiva Sena leader Bal Thackeray was vandalised. Like Advani, Sena spokesperson Manohar Joshi described the vandalism as 'against Hindus and Hinduism', arguing that the rage of supporters was natural. In February 2007 the Sena achieved victories in local Maharashtra elections in partnership with the BJP which secured a five-year term of government in Mumbai.

That they did so on the platform of Hindu/Maharastrian chauvinism indicates the enduring appetite for saffron politics, even in India's most urbane metropolis. It is far too soon to discount Hindutva from India's future, and there is nothing to suggest that Congress can offer a comparably seductive vision of global prestige for the rapidly expanding and expectant middle classes. Unless those who would speak for India's minorities are not vigilant – and proactive – there is no guarantee that atrocities on the scale of Gujarat in the spring of 2002 will not bring Indian democracy into further disrepute.

Concluding remarks

Chapter 5 concluded that cultural identity has become the fault line of the global struggle between humanity and cruelty, and those who would align themselves with the former ideal cannot elect to abstain from its definition. Our collective political future is being fought out on the site of the cultural, and the solidarities it engenders.

There are of course many issues and right-leaning reversals that oppositional politics has to contend with in democratic societies, at both national and global levels. Prominent among these would be the renunciation of welfarism, the corrosion of democratic protections, pervasive corruption and diminishing accountability. None of these are a direct consequence of 'culture'. That they can all be redressed in isolation from each other, with specific campaigns fought in particular ways, is not in doubt. But the reason that many of these governmental behaviours have been made permissible is because they are mirrored by social attitudes which themselves are induced by anxieties about how collective life should be constituted. So what becomes critical is why these anxieties arise, and how collective life is not only re-imagined but also differently practised. This is why culture becomes so integral to how the Left positions itself at this crucial juncture in the life of democratic society.

There are those on the intellectual Left for whom culture elicits exasperation, and others who regard it with studied indifference. For the former camp, culture is experienced as frustration, because they see it as amorphous, nebulous and ultimately vacuous; it substitutes for everything and nothing. Since it is not reducible to language, religion or ethnicity it is disregarded for its hermeneutic redundancy for the social sciences. But that quite often is the point about culture in either its most progressive or regressive forms: it often exceeds both articulation and social recognition. This is because culture is lived, and made, and so inextricable from personal and collective identities. The Sangh Parivar's exploitation of majority anxiety is not explicable by its resort to religion itself, but to the manipulation of religiosity, the fear of its annihilation and its consequences for the existential well-being of its ideological constituency. Stripping culture down to its constitutive units neglects the crucial fact that it only becomes significant in the context of people's lives.

For even more, culture is a superficial irritant. The protection of cultural diversity is seen as the icing on democracy's cake, a decorative flourish without substantive political importance. In Fraser's words, multiculturalism is not 'transformative' and cultural identity has to be put of out business for the serious work of material distribution to begin. Such intellectuals feel the need to purge culture from their political universe, as though it can be easily and cleanly severed from their respectable objectives. They want to divorce culture from inequality, but this is just as wrong-headed.

I have argued that do so means wilfully blinding themselves not only to the manipulation of cultural identity that makes hegemony possible, but equally to the persistent appeal among their so-called constituencies. If humane politics exists to serve the powerless and speak truth to the powerful, then how can it excuse itself from one of the primary sites of power itself?

Parekh and other multiculturalists may labour the point without perspective, but cultural identity endures even when it may embarrass the cosmopolitan desires of our intellectual elite. Not all of us can disregard our inherited influences with the kind of carefree abandon that Fraser appeals for, and a sizeable proportion wouldn't want to. Besides, there is no contradiction between cultural attachment and universal aspiration; we have to be able to accommodate and even advocate the cultivation of multiple identities.

It compels us to move culture to the centre of political calculation. I'm referring here to a tactical emphasis, not on the concept of culture itself – because it is abstract, over-determined and discursified to death – but on the licence for abuse and inequality that it brings. Paul Gilroy has talked about the need to make race political enough.[16] Since culture is now being made to perform racially, it too has to be made political enough, and not shunted to the peripheries of our collective consciousness. At the same time we have to be vigilant that culture and race do not get conflated so that we come to think of the former as an 'unhelpful fiction', rather than a constructive concept that is wholly consonant with the aspirations of a politics of humanity.

This is just as hard and Herculean as it sounds, and mainly because the Left ceases to exist with any conviction in itself. What we have, to borrow *New Times* speak, is an assortment of subject positions that define themselves in antagonism not only to inhumanity, but sometimes even more eloquently to other avowedly progressive voices. It is almost impossible to assemble these broken shards into a productive coalition since hardly any would accept the mutuality that would motivate such co-operation.

What we have instead are sectarian coalitions actively sought by those who should know better. Too often liberals and others on the Left have felt compelled to side with community leadership on public issues, even when this has compromised their own principles. Bowing to pressures of political correctness isn't going to advance a national debate on race and faith; all it does is grant the sheen of liberal respectability to illiberal positions. This has given birth to some bizarre alliances, and it's no wonder that the amenability of the Left to working partnerships with openly racist groups has been gleefully satirised by majoritarian thinkers. The problem is that the silent majority hasn't yet found a voice and that the Left hasn't been interested in hearing it. Both of these have to change if we are to dismantle the old order and with it the political arrangements that perpetuate divisions of majority and minority. A majoritarian future will never be beyond the pale until we retire state multiculturalism for good.

Notes

1. Francis Fukuyama, 'Identity, Immigration and Liberal Democracy', *Journal of Democracy*, 17.2, April 2006, pp. 5–20.

2. See Bhikhu Parekh and David Goodhart, 'Not black and white', *Prospect*, 110, May 2005.

3. See Bhikhu Parekh, *Rethinking Multiculturalism* (Basingstoke: Palgrave, 2000), pp. 270–4.

4. Alana Lentin, 'Multiculturalism or Anti-Racism?', *OpenDemocracy* (December 2004), http://www.opendemocracy.net/arts-multiculturalism/article_2073.jsp.

5. M. S. Gowalkar, *We, Or Our Nation Defined* (Nagpur: Bharat Publications, 1939).

6. Chetan Bhatt, 'Democracy and Hindu Nationalism', *Democratization*, 11.4, 2004, p. 149.

7. Ibid., p. 151.

8. The full report, *Living Apart Together: British Muslims and the Paradox of Multiculturalism* can be found at http://www.policyex change.org.uk/images/libimages/246.pdf.

9. What Mactaggart presumably wasn't aware of was that the violence on the opening night was alleged to have been perpetrated by members of the Sikh Federation, a group which formed when the International Sikh Youth Federation (ISYF) was proscribed under the Terrorism Act of 2000. The ISYF is a Sikh separatist group that has agitated for the creation of Khalistan, an independent Sikh state in India. It has been involved in assassinations, bombing and kidnappings against the Indian state.

10. Les Back, Michael Keith, Azra Khan, Kalbir Shukra and John Solomos, 'The Return of Assimilationism: Race, Multiculturalism and New Labour',
Sociological Research Online, 7.2, 2002, http://www.socresonline.org.uk/7/2/back.html.

11. Equal Opportunities Commission Report, September 2006.

12. Les Back et al., 'The Return of Assimilationism'.

13. Statistics cited in Edward Luce, *In Spite of the Gods: The Strange Rise of Modern India* (London: Little, Brown, 2006), p. 251.

14. Cited in Cristophe Jaffrelot (ed.), *The Sangh Parivar: A Reader* (New Delhi: Oxford University Press, 2005), pp. 4–12.

15. The Shankarcharya of Kanchi, whom the media simplistically referred to as the 'Hindu Pope', was accused of the murder of a temple official who was blackmailing him in exchange for silence over an affair with a female devotee.

16. Paul Gilroy, 'Joined-up Politics and Postcolonial Melancholia', *Theory, Culture & Society*, 18, 2001, p. 153.

Index